Roman Birmingham 6

*Overview and synthesis of 1934–2019 excavations
at Metchley Roman Fort, Birmingham*

Alex Jones

With contributions by:
Hilary Cool, Val Fryer and Jane Timby

Illustrations by:
Nigel Dodds

BAR BRITISH SERIES 696 | 2025

BAR
PUBLISHING

Published in 2025 by
BAR Publishing, Oxford, UK

BAR British Series 696

Roman Birmingham 6

ISBN 978 1 4073 6259 5   paperback
ISBN 978 1 4073 6260 1   e-format

DOI https://doi.org/10.30861/9781407362595

A catalogue record for this book is available from the British Library

COVER IMAGE: *Schematic reconstruction of Phase 1 fort and
Phase 2A annexes (Nigel Dodds).*

This book is available in printed format at http://www.barpublishing.com.

BAR
PUBLISHING

BAR titles are available from:

BAR Publishing
122 Banbury Rd, Oxford, OX2 7BP, UK
info@barpublishing.com
www.barpublishing.com

By the Same Author

Roman Birmingham 5: Metchley Roman Fort, Birmingham
Excavations in the fort interior and defences 2003–2004, 2010 and 2017–2019
Alex Jones with contributions by Marina Ciaraldi, C. Jane Evans, Jane Faiers,
Rowena Gale, James Greig, Kay Hartley, Samantha Hepburn, Emma Hopla,
Erica Macey-Bracken, Rosalind McKenna, Jane Timby, Roger Tomlin,
Roger White, Felicity Wild, David Williams and Steven Willis
BAR British Series **694** | 2025

Roman Birmingham 4: Excavations at Metchley Roman Fort 2004–2005
The western fort interior, defences and post-Roman activity
Alex Jones with contributions from Erica Macey-Bracken, Hilary Cool, James Greig,
Rob Ixer, Rosalind McKenna, Anthony Swiss, Jane Timby, Roger White,
Felicity Wild and David Williams
BAR British Series **552** | 2012

Roman Birmingham 3: Excavations at Metchley Roman Fort 1999–2001 and 2004–2005
Western settlement, the livestock complex and the western defences
Alex Jones
BAR British Series **534** | 2011

Excavations at Little Paxton Quarry, Cambridgeshire, 1992–1998
Prehistoric and Romano-British Settlement and Agriculture in the River Great Ouse Valley
Edited by Alex Jones
BAR British Series **545** | 2011

A Romano-British Livestock Complex in Birmingham
Excavations 2002–2004 and 2006–2007 at Longdales Road, King's Norton, Birmingham
Alex Jones, Bob Burrows, C. Jane Evans, Annette Hancocks and Josh Williams
BAR British Series **470** | 2008

Settlement, Burial and Industry in Roman Godmanchester
Excavations in the extra-mural area: The Parks 1998, London Road 1997–8,
and other investigations
Alex Jones
BAR British Series **346** | 2003

Of Related Interest

Ad Vallum: Papers on the Roman Army and Frontiers in Celebration of Dr Brian Dobson
Adam Parker
BAR British Series **631** | 2017

Roman Soldiers and the Roman Army
A study of military life from archaeological remains
Rikke D Giles
BAR British Series **562** | 2012

In memory of my late mother, A. M. I. Jones

Acknowledgements

The post-1996 fieldwork described in this volume was commissioned by University Hospital Birmingham NHS Trust and the University of Birmingham with the exception of fieldwork commissioned by West Midlands Combined Authority in advance of University Station redevelopment. The first draft of this report was prepared at Birmingham Archaeology.

The report was completed by the original author with funding from Historic England, which enabled updating of the summary, overview and synthesis sections, but not the finds and environmental contributions. The illustrations were prepared by Nigel Dodds. The texts were read and commented upon by Mike Hodder, who is thanked for his assistance.

Contents

List of Figures

List of Tables

Summary and Introduction

Summary

This report provides a synthesis and overview of excavations and other fieldwork from 1934 to 2019 at Metchley Roman fort, Birmingham (centred on NGR SP 045836, Figs 1.1 and 1.2). During that time more than 60 interventions have been completed at the Roman military complex, including excavations, trenching, and watching briefs. The fort is located to the southwest of the city centre, partly within the campus of the University of Birmingham, the Queen Elizabeth Hospital complex, and the University rail station.

An extensive programme of archaeological fieldwork has been undertaken at Metchley Roman fort, Birmingham, in advance of new hospital, university, and train station developments. The upstanding earthworks were first identified by antiquarians in the 18th and 19th centuries, but their Roman date was only confirmed in the 1930s. Large-scale excavations have been undertaken since that date, which have transformed our understanding of the complex. The earliest, under the direction of Dr Graham Webster in 1950–51, examined part of the northern annexe defences. Large areas of the fort interior were examined in 1967–9 under the direction of Trevor Rowley. The overall phasing used in this report is that devised from the 1930s and 1960s excavations. These excavations suggested that the fort was a Claudian foundation. A more recent review of the dating evidence from all excavations suggests that the first fort was a mid-Neronian foundation, which could place its first layout around the time of the Roman 'recovery' of the west midlands after the Boudiccan rebellion. Further excavations were undertaken from 1999 to 2010 in advance of major hospital and university developments. More small-scale fieldwork was undertaken from 2013 to 2019. In total, an area of approximately 2.7ha was excavated from 1963 to 2010, amounting to approximately 25% of the total area of the Roman military complex, making the site one of the most extensively investigated Roman military complexes in the midlands.

An important feature of the work has been the opportunities for public interpretation of the Roman military complex. This has taken the form of a number of interpretation panels, and the selective partial reconstruction of the fort ramparts, to provide an indication of the scale and extent of the forts.

A construction camp (Phase 1A, possibly mid-Neronian, Figs 1.3 and 1.4, Table 1.1) was probably the earliest Roman activity at Metchley. This was succeeded by a double-ditched fort (Phase 1B, mid-Neronian) measuring 240m square, enclosing 4.4ha. It contained an excavated facing pair of barrack-blocks, granaries, the *praetorium*, and a workshop. Two structural phases were distinguished by buildings laid out on very slightly differing alignments. A small settlement, including open-fronted shops and possible dwellings was laid out along a road to the west of the fort. Annexes (Phase 2A) were laid out on the northern, eastern, and southern sides of the fort during its later use. Following abandonment and systematic dismantling of the first fort, a military stores depot was laid out within the fort defences, which were modified but largely retained. Five periods of activity were recorded within the military stores depot (Phase 2B, later Neronian), comprising the clearance of the Phase 1B fort buildings, the layout of new timber-framed buildings, industrial activity, and the use of the fort interior and external areas to the west of the fort for livestock pens, followed by backfilling of the fort defences, in that order. After a period of abandonment, a smaller, second fort (Phase 3A, early Flavian), enclosing 2.6ha, was located within the interior of the first fort, whose inner ditches were re-cut to provide additional defence. The primary rampart of this second fort was of turf construction, later reinforced with timber bracing. Few buildings are recorded within the second fort interior – most comprising granaries which may have survived later disturbance because they were more deeply cut than other building types. Once again, the plateau to the west of the smaller fort was occupied, primarily by livestock pens, although evidence of industrial activity and a single timber-framed building was also recorded. Traces of small-scale Roman, presumably civilian activity have also been recorded to the east of the forts. Following the final military abandonment of the site in the later 1st century, the fort and annexe ditches were re-cut, to form pens for livestock herding. This activity may have come to an end by the late 2nd century.

During the early post-medieval period the site lay within a hunting park, and a hunting lodge was built within the fort interior. Later, the area was farmed. The Worcester and Birmingham Canal was cut through the southeastern angle of the fort in the late 18th century, followed by the adjoining railway in the mid-19th century. The earliest modern development at the complex took place in the 1930s for the University Medical School.

This report has been completed and updated with funding from Historic England.

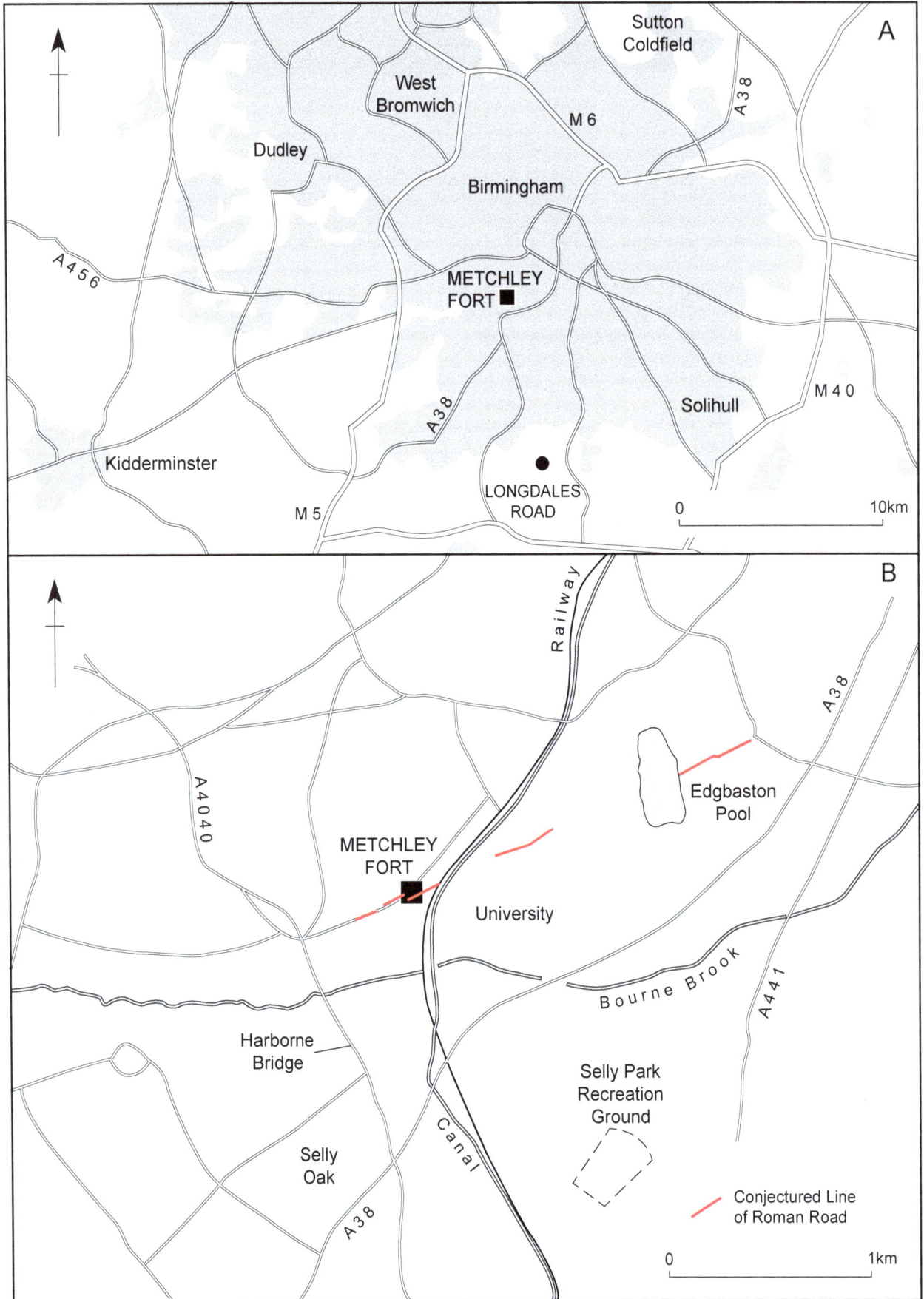

Figure 1.1. General location (A); detailed location of Metchley fort (B).

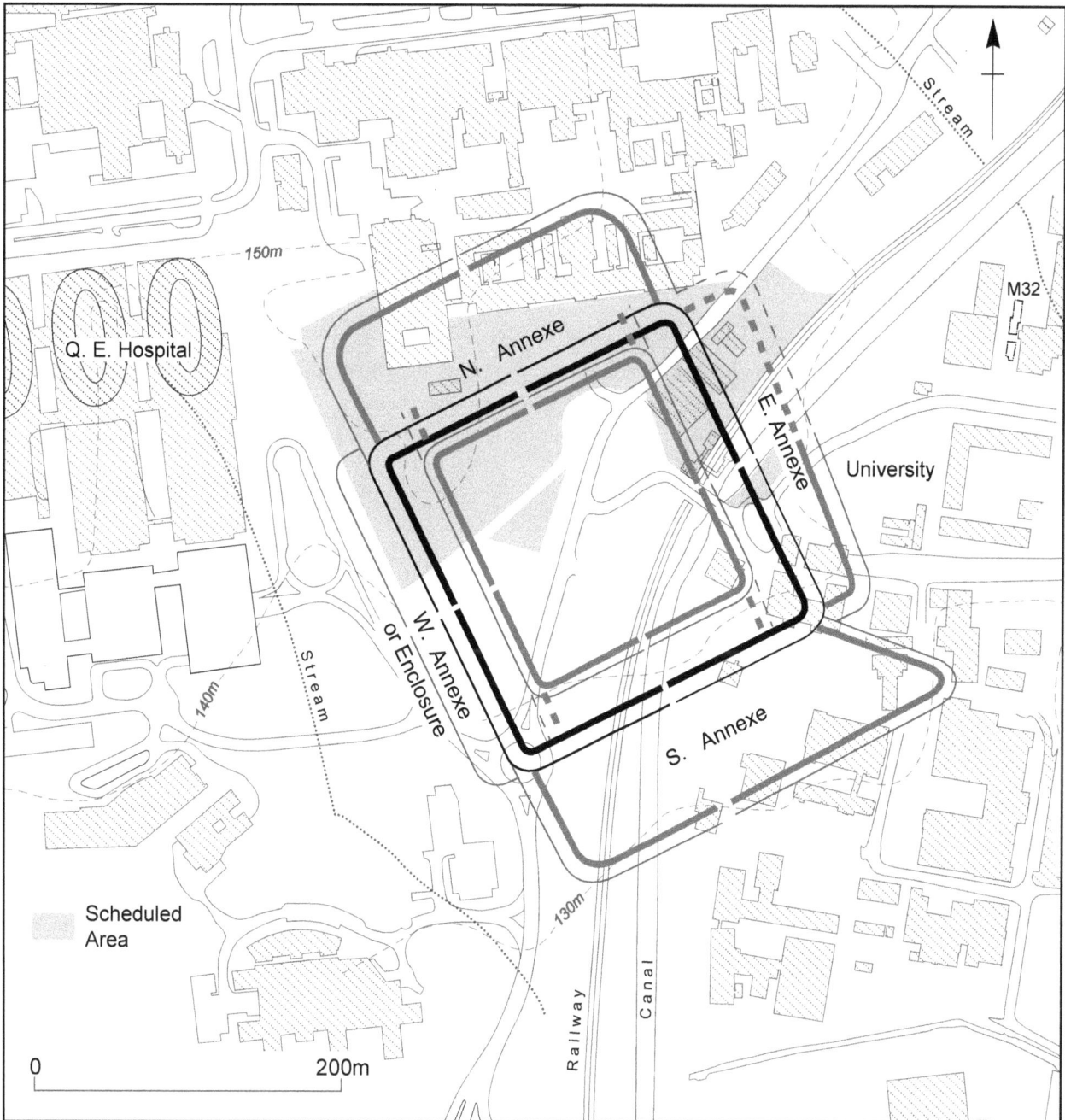

Figure 1.2. Metchley fort and its local setting.

Introduction

This report provides a synthesis and overview of excavations and other fieldwork from 1934 to 2019 at Metchley Roman fort, Birmingham (centred on NGR SP 045836, Figs 1.1 and 1.2). The fort is located to the southwest of the city centre, partly within the campus of the University of Birmingham, the Queen Elizabeth Hospital complex and the University rail station. This chapter presents a summary of the sequence of Roman military and civilian occupation at Metchley and the pre-Roman and Roman background. The following chapters provide a synthesis and overview of the stratigraphic, finds and environmental data from investigations within the fort interior, the defences and also areas outside the defences.

The detailed excavations have been reported in five volumes (Jones 2001, 2005, 2011, 2012 and 2025).

The sequence of Roman military activity at Metchley

The Roman fort complex at Metchley (Fig. 1.2), which comprises the earliest occupation of the site, was first identified from cartographic sources and antiquarian descriptions, and more recently by extensive trial-trenching and excavation. The fort defences, still surviving as above-ground earthworks in the 18th century, were mapped and described in detail at that time (Jones 2001, 10–12). The Roman date of the earthworks was only confirmed in the 1930s when limited slit-trenches were cut in advance of an earlier development (St Joseph and Shotton 1937).

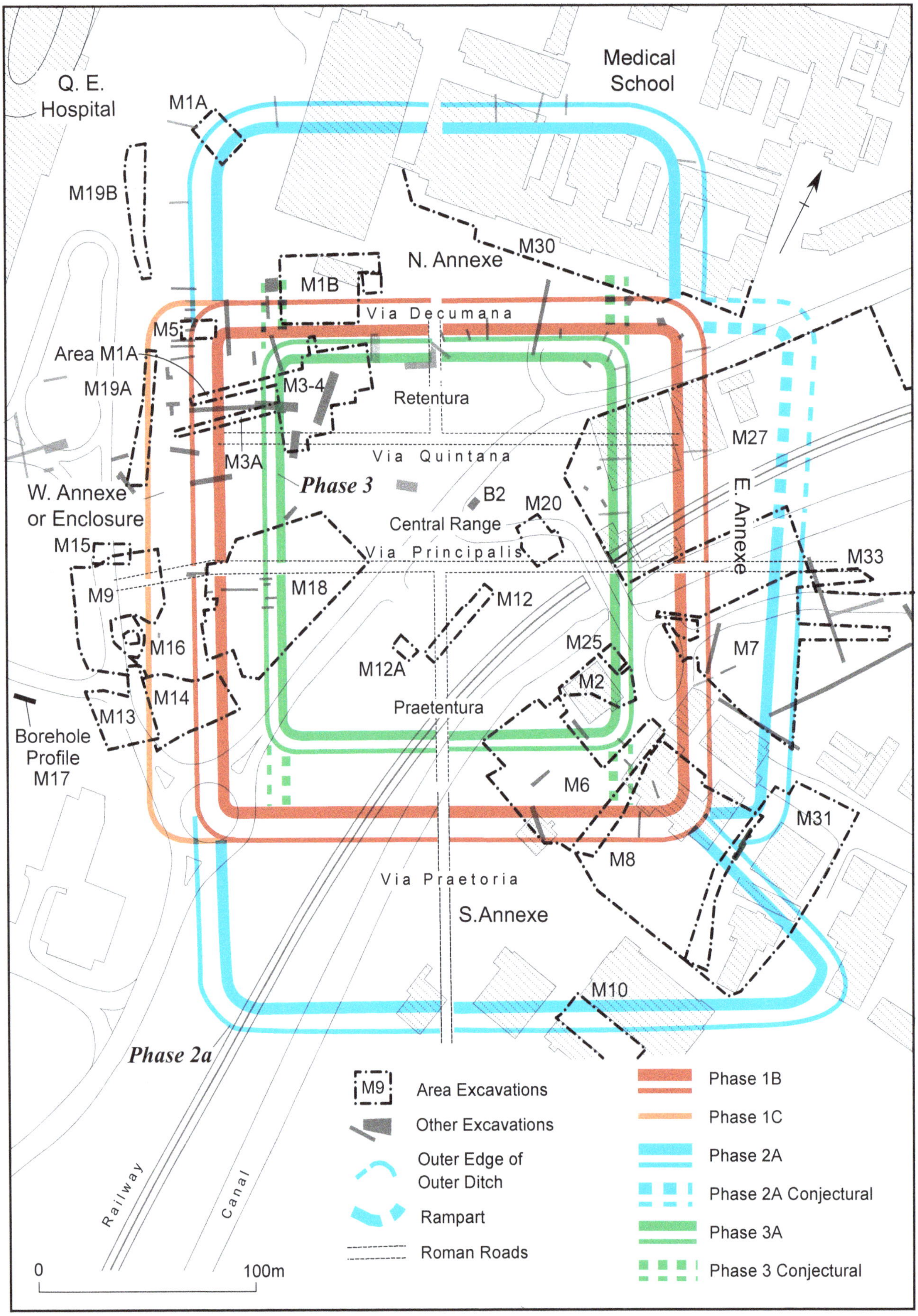
Q. E.
Hospital
Medical
School
M1A
M19B
N. Annexe
M30
M1B
Via Decumana
M5
Area M1A
M19A
M3-4
Retentura
M27
M3A
Via Quintana
W. Annexe
or Enclosure
Phase 3
B2
Central Range
M20
E. Annexe
M15
Via Principalis
M33
M9
M18
M12
M16
M12A
M25
M7
M2
M14
Borehole
Profile
M17
M13
Praetentura
M6
M31
M8
Via Praetoria
S.Annexe
M10
Phase 2a
M9
Area Excavations
Other Excavations
Outer Edge of
Outer Ditch
Rampart
Roman Roads
Phase 1B
Phase 1C
Phase 2A
Phase 2A Conjectural
Phase 3A
Phase 3 Conjectural
Railway
Canal
0
100m

Figure 1.3. Metchley fort, simplified extent, phasing, and main areas investigated to 2010.

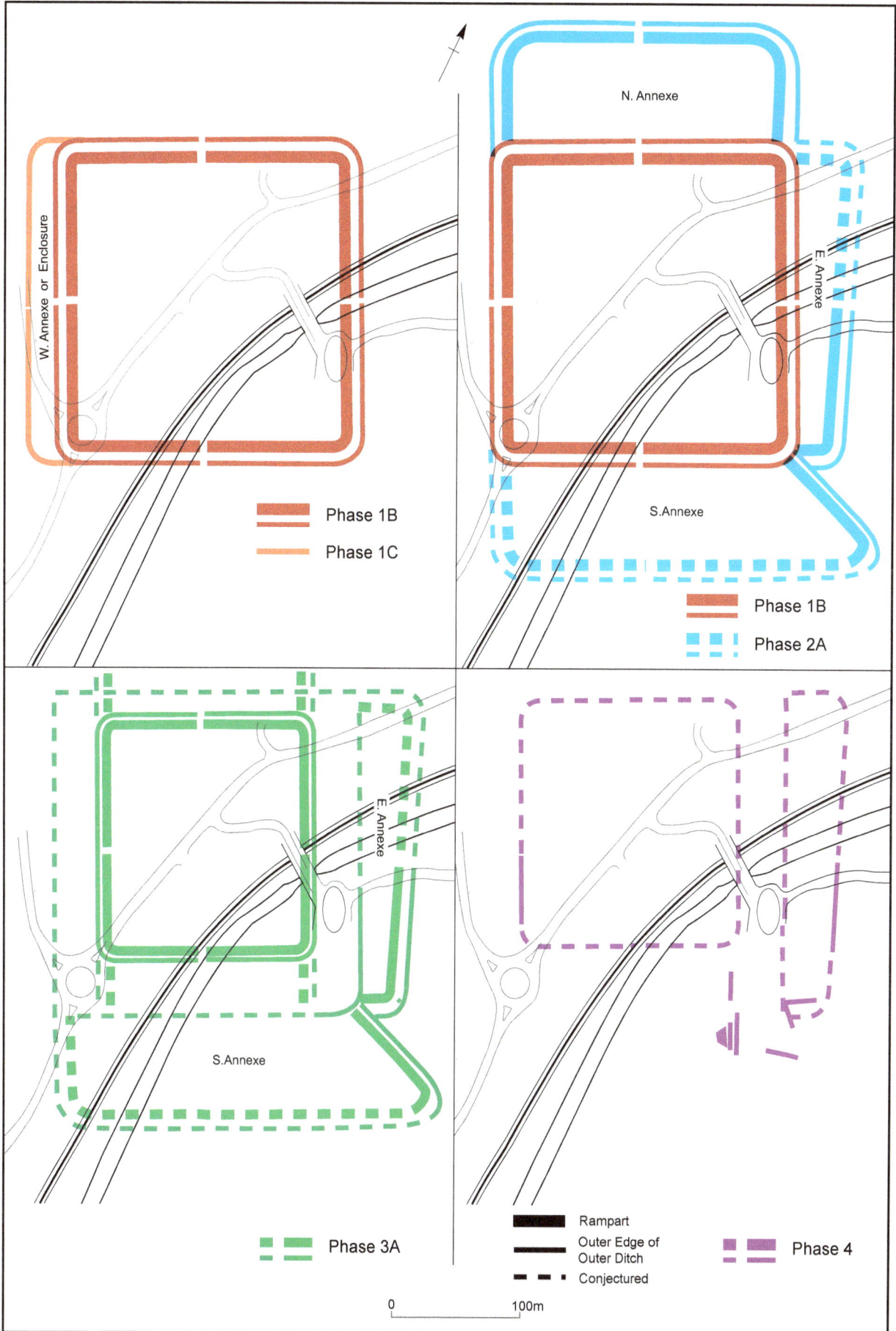

Figure 1.4. Metchley fort, simplified outline of phasing.

5

Table 1.1. Metchley Roman fort, summary of phasing.

Phase	Interior		Defences/external features	
1A Possible construction camp	–		Western *clavicula*?	
1 **First fort** 4.4 ha Mid-Neronian	**1D** Early building alignment	**1D/1E** Features which could belong to Phase 1D or Phase 1E, or to both	**1B** Double-ditched fort defences, rampart, square in plan; excavated *porta principalis dextra*, external *clavicula*	Western external settlement
	1E Later building alignment		**1C** Western annexe or enclosure	
2A **Annexes** Later Neronian	Possible rearrangement of internal buildings		Northern, eastern, and southern annexes	
2B **Military stores depot** Later Neronian	Periods: 1 Demolition Phase 1 buildings 2 New timber-framed buildings 3 Industrial activity 4 Livestock pens		New entrance arrangement for livestock sorting. Backfilling of Phase **1B** ditches at end of Phase **2B** (Period 5)	
3A **Second fort** **2.6 ha** Early Flavian	Granaries in *retentura* and central range; granary and cookhouse in *praetentura*		New rectangular circuit of defences, including excavated *porta principalis dextra*. Re-cutting of Phase **1B** defences to provide additional protection	
3A–4B **Activity to west of Phase 3A fort** ? Flavian+	-		Redefinition of Phase **3A** gatehouse, later arrangement associated with external palisade trenches forming livestock enclosures, industrial features, and timber-framed building west of fort	
4A **Re-cutting of Phase 3A fort ditches** Later Flavian to late 2nd century	-		Re-cutting of Phase **3A** defences	
4C **Post-military abandonment**	Three-sided ditched enclosure (Areas M3–M4). Palisade trench along eastern and southern sides of Phase 3A fort		Irregular partial blocking of Phase **3A** fort entrance, cultivation soil and stone surfaces to the west of Phase **3A** fort	
5 **Post-Roman**	Use of fort interior for livestock, 'entrance' inserted into Phase 3A *porta principalis dextra*. Re-use of fort roads, and cutting of ditches along their margins		Pollen evidence for ?Saxon/?medieval cultivation from Area M8	

Note: The main events are divided into phases, some of which are subdivided. Additionally, Phase 2B is subdivided into 5 periods.

The updated fort phasing is summarized in Table 1.1. The main events are defined as phases, some of which are sub-divided. Additionally, Phase 2B is sub-divided into five periods.

The earliest Roman military occupation may have taken the form of a construction camp (Phase 1A). The earliest fort, of mid-Neronian date (Phase 1B, Figs 1.3 and 1.4), was defended by double ditches and a rampart. Large-scale investigations directed by Trevor Rowley within the Phase 1B fort interior during 1967–9 (Jones 2001; Fig. 1.3, Areas M2, M3 and M4, M5) identified the well-preserved foundation trenches of timber-framed buildings, including barrack-blocks, a granary, a store building, and a workshop. This fort was contemporary with a small western settlement first identified in 2001 (Jones 2011). A narrow western annexe or enclosure, defined by a palisade trench (Phase 1C), probably contained a zone of pottery production (Jones 2011, 18–20).

Excavations in the 1960s, and latterly in 1998–9 and 2004, identified later Neronian (Phase 2A, Figs 1.3

and 1.4) annexes added to the northern, eastern, and southern sides of the Phase 1B fort (Jones 2005). Deliberate clearance of the Phase 1 fort buildings was followed as a single operation by the construction of temporary structures and fenced compounds associated with a military stores depot (Phase 2B, later Neronian; Jones 2001, 43–54), primarily concerned with livestock herding. Subsequently, after a period of abandonment, the site was reoccupied, and a smaller fort of early Flavian date (Phase 3A, Figs 1.3 and 1.4) was laid out within the interior of the Phase 1 fort. This second fort may have functioned as a supply depot, in particular for grain. To the west of the fort defences was a contemporary ditched livestock complex (Phase 3B–4B).

After the abandonment of the Phase 3A fort later in the 1st century, small-scale civilian occupation continued at Metchley through the 2nd century, and possibly beyond. This civilian occupation included the insertion of a livestock 'funnel' into the western Phase 3A–4A fort entrance, to facilitate the movement of livestock into the fort interior (Phase 4C). The surviving fort defences were utilized as a livestock enclosure in the post-Roman military or post-Roman periods (Phase 5), until piecemeal enclosure in the later 18th century. Lengths of the fort defences continued to be visible and mapped as upstanding earthworks into the 20th century.

Parts of the northern and eastern fort interior and adjoining defences have been designated a Scheduled Monument (NHLE 1020977 (https://historicengland.org.uk/listing/the-list/list-entry/1020977?section=official-list-entry).

Background

Iron Age

While the later Iron Age political geography of the region is difficult to reconstruct in detail (Booth 1996, 26; Hodder 2011, 48), Metchley was probably located at or adjoining the boundaries between three tribes; the Cornovii to the northwest, the Dobunni to the south and southwest, and the Corieltauvi to the northeast (Millett 1990, fig. 12). White (2007, fig. 12) and Jones and Mattingley (1990, fig. 4.24) place the tribal boundary between the Dobunni and Cornovii close to Metchley (Fig. 1.5), with the boundary of the Corieltauvi further to the east. Magilton (2006, 101) places the *civitas* boundaries at Coleshill, by analogy with other temple complexes located at *civitas* boundaries. Booth (2018, 36) identifies a division between Corieltauvian coinage in the north of Warwickshire and Dobunnic issues in the south of the county which may reflect tribal boundaries. Similarly, a distinction is drawn by Dalwood et al. (2018, 48) between the material culture within the north and west of Worcestershire and that within the south of the county.

Hillforts are a particularly notable aspect of the Iron Age landscape in the west midlands (Hurst 2011, 106, fig. 3.4; Hodder 2011, 45). They may have acted as ceremonial *foci* of the surrounding populations (Hingley 1996, 18; Bradley 2007, 252), or have been used as bases to farm nearby land (Darvill 2000, 139). Hillforts were built at different scales, the smaller sites being no larger than some ditched enclosures (Bradley 2007). Indeed, Wigley (2007, 178) has described smaller enclosures as constituting one end of a continuum which includes hillforts at its upper end. Unlike Droitwich, which was a centre of the salt trade in the later Iron Age (Hurst 2011, 117), and Alcester, assigned a local government function associated with the northern sept of the Dobunni (Booth 1996, 32), there is no evidence of Iron Age occupation at or near Metchley. This apparent lack of evidence could reflect disturbance by recent urban development and the lack of investigation. Recent excavations along the line of the M6 Toll have transformed our understanding of the Iron Age settlement pattern in the west midlands (Fitzpatrick 2008, 508) – suggesting a greater settlement density than is currently recorded (Hodder 2018, 158).

Roman military campaigns (Fig. 1.5)

Traditionally (e.g. Webster 1993), archaeological sequences within individual excavated forts have been assimilated within the historical accounts provided by Tacitus and other writers. The limitations of archaeological dating evidence and the imprecise and patchy information provided by the literary sources make the conflation of archaeological and literary evidence impossible (Esmonde Cleary 2011, 132; Mattingley 2006; White 2018, 23). Individual sites are not often mentioned, so that placing them within the overall pattern is a matter for interpretation (Burnham and Davies 2010, 33).

For the Roman army the West Midlands was 'an area of transition, to be moved through relatively swiftly in their push to crush the resistance led by Caratacus . . . and to occupy Britain up to the Mersey' (White 2018, 19), 'in part because of the apparent acquiescence of the tribes after being disarmed by Scapula'. During AD 45–47 the XIV and IX legions incorporated the territory of the Dobunni and Corieltauvi into the Roman Empire (Mattingley 2006, 98), a process completed by the end of the governorship of Aulus Plautius. In AD 47, during the early governorship of Ostorius Scapula, hostile tribes attacked allied forces within the Marches (Todd 2004, 50). Scapula drove off the raiders from Dobunnic territory, garrisoned from that date, if not earlier, along with Corieltauvian territory (Mattingley 2006, 101). The establishment of Metchley has been traditionally attributed to the Scapulan advance (Webster 1993, 71; Pengelly et al. 2001, 101), although recent reassessment of the small finds dating (Cool, Chapter 3 below) has suggested a mid-Neronian date for the earliest military occupation of Metchley. This dating could suggest that the first fort at Metchley was established around the time of, and in response to, the Boudiccan revolt.

Watling Street (Fig. 1.1) formed a key line of westwards advance (Mattingley 2006, 143), possibly by the XIV legion (Todd 2004, 53). Vexillation fortresses were provided at Mancetter, Kinvaston, Leighton, and also possibly Wall (Mattingley 2006, 143). These sites may be related to campaigns against the Ordovices in the late 50s. According to Todd (2004, 53), the gap between the Trent and Severn may have been 'closed' by means of forward control positions, including Wall and Kinvaston. This advance was continued to Leighton, near Wroxeter, and further westwards to Rhyn Park, which may be related, despite limited dating evidence, to the 'encirclement' of the Ordovices in the late AD 50s (Todd 2004, 53), together with further forts which extended from the lower Severn valley into the Usk and Wye valleys. On the west bank of the Severn a number of bases were also established in Cornovian territory, including Leintwardine (Mattingley 2006, 143). A legionary fortress was established at Wroxeter in the mid-AD 50s (Webster 2002), which continued to be garrisoned by the same legion until AD 66. A westward advance may have formed the military context for the earliest fort at The Lunt, which was located away from the strategic road network (Booth 1996, 28).

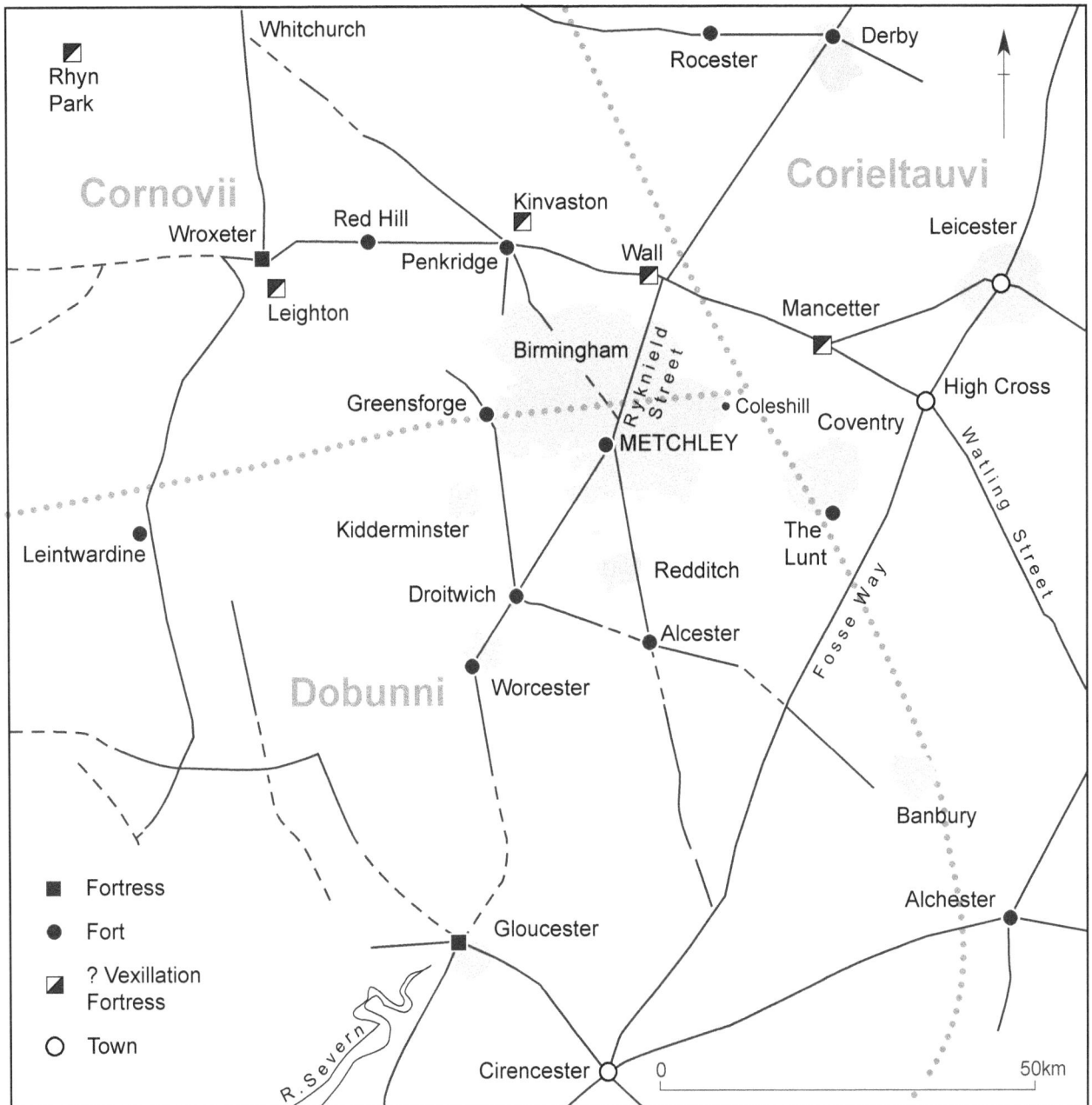

Figure 1.5. Metchley and the Roman road network, forts, and fortresses.

Between the invasion corridors later defined by Watling Street and Ermine Street/Akeman Street, an intermediate route has been recognized running northwest from Alchester, including Alcester and Droitwich (Mattingley 2006, 143), suggesting a further line of advance. This advance could have passed near to Metchley.

Following the fall of Colchester, London, and Verulamium to Boudicca, the governor, Suetonius Paulinus, defeated the rebels in a battle located variously near Mancetter, Warwickshire, or northwest of Towcester, Northamptonshire (Frere 1987a, 73) in AD 61. Such a revolt against Roman authority in the early empire was rare (Todd 2004, 55), although Todd suggests it was of Rome's own making. Following the recovery of the

province, Paulinus was stern in his response towards the rebels (Frere 1987a, 73). Reinforcements, including 2,000 legionaries, eight auxiliary infantry, and two auxiliary cavalry units were sent from the Rhine. Frere describes how the territory of the rebel tribes was thoroughly laid waste. New forts were built within the territory of the Iceni, and also elsewhere including The Lunt (Coventry) and probably Metchley also, with the primary aims of repression and punishment – including military government (Frere 1987a, 74).

Millett (1990, 55) observes that few sites can be dated to the post-Boudiccan phase of campaigning, and most forts of this date may be better interpreted as serving the supply network. This group may have included Metchley, particularly in Phase 2B (and possibly Phase 3A also). The

8

focus of campaigning in the later AD 60s by Vettius Bolanus lay within the territory of the Parisi as a base for operations to the north, in Brigantian territory (Todd 2004, 57). The withdrawal of *legio* XIV from Britain around AD 67 and a number of auxiliary units reduced the military manpower available, resulting in redeployment of the remaining units (Burnham and Davies 2010, 42). Vexillations from all three legions were sent to the continent to support rival imperial candidates during the civil war of AD 68–70 (Todd 2004, 57). Following the resumption of military campaigning in AD 71 there were significant changes in garrison, notably Gloucester, in the early AD 70s, as well as at Chester and Lincoln (Todd 2004, 57). Garrisons in the midlands were given up in the AD 70s, as the area was given over to civilian occupation (Booth 1996, 28). Mancetter and The Lunt were abandoned in the mid-70s (Booth 1996, 30). Exceptionally, at Wall and Alcester (Bleachfield Street), military occupation continued into the early 2nd century (Booth 1996, 32).

From the Flavian period onwards there was a policy of spreading garrisons thinly in occupied territory (Mattingley 2006, 135), to confront the pattern of dispersed resistance, leading to the establishment of more numerous but smaller bases (Hopewell and Hodgson 2012, 43), which may explain the location of the later Alcester fort, and also the Phase 3A fort at Metchley. Iulius Frontinus, who became governor in AD 73/74, undertook the final conquest of Wales, including the territories of the Silures, Ordovices, and Demetae (Mattingley 2006, 116). This campaigning could provide a broader context for the removal of the Phase 3A fort garrison from Metchley, dated by the limited pottery evidence to the early Flavian period (see Chapter 3 below).

Aims

The aims of the excavations were to:

1) provide details of the fort defences, including environmental evidence;

2) contribute towards an appreciation of the layouts of internal buildings and other structures, and of subsequent changes to these layouts;
3) contribute towards an understanding of the overall chronology of the complex;
4) contribute towards an understanding of the pattern of military supply;
5) locate and map external features, including annexes, roads and settlements;
6) contribute towards an understanding of the overall pattern of military deployment in the west midlands.

Methodology

Excavation was undertaken on a piecemeal basis, as individual areas became available in advance of development (Fig. 1.3). Large areas were excavated in the 1960s, 1998–2001, and 2004–5. The areas excavated from 1997 were stripped of topsoil and overburden by a 360° excavator working under continuous archaeological supervision. The machined subsoil surface was hand-cleaned as necessary to define features, or possible features, of archaeological interest. Additional machining was selectively undertaken with a mini-digger to remove post-medieval features and deposits, following their testing by hand-excavation. Roman features were tested by hand-excavation only.

The first draft of this report was prepared at Birmingham Archaeology. The report was completed by the original author with funding from Historic England, which enabled updating of the stratigraphic and discussion sections. The finds and environmental contributions prepared in 2003–10 have not been updated.

Throughout this report it is assumed for simplicity that the fort was aligned north–south, although the drawings are labelled with compass north.

Summary of Excavation Results, 1934–2019

Introduction

The phasing has evolved as an iterative process during the staged analysis and reporting of the fieldwork (Figs 1.3 and 1.4), to reflect the incremental complexity of the excavation results. Changes have involved both retrospective subdivision of single phases and some re-phasing, so that some feature groups described in this chapter were originally reported in a different phase.

This phasing relies heavily on the recorded stratigraphy and the identification of changes in activity, since the pottery, in particular the coarse wares, are often heavily abraded and not chronologically diagnostic. Some of the phases (e.g. defences and fort interiors) will have overlapped.

Phasing (Figs 1.3, 1.4)

The revised and updated scheme of phasing is as follows:

Phase 0: Pre-Roman activity

Phase 1: First military activity and first fort (mid-Neronian), subdivided:

> Phase 1A, possible construction camp (and external possible *clavicula*)
> Phase 1B, first fort defences
> Phase 1C, western annexe or enclosure
> Phase 1D, first fort early building alignment
> Phase 1E, first fort later building alignment
> Phase 1D–1E, features attributable to either Phase 1D or 1E, or to both, including the western external settlement

This phasing has distinguished the defences (1B) from the contemporary internal activity (Phase 1D, Phase 1E, and Phase 1D–1E), for clarity. Distinction of the Phase 1D and 1E structures depends on identification of their different alignments, or the recorded stratigraphy.

The sub-phases cannot be distinguished from the pottery dating evidence.

For clarity, both the fort and annexe defences are simplified in the drawings. The thick grey line represents the rampart and the narrow grey line defines the outer limit of the ditch or ditches. Conjectured defences are shown with a dashed line.

Phase 2: External annexes and military stores depot (later Neronian), subdivided:

> Phase 2A, northern, eastern and southern annexes

Phase 2B, military stores depot (subdivided into five periods)

Phase 3: Second fort (early Flavian), subdivided:

> Phase 3A, defences and internal buildings
> Phase 3B–4B, rearrangement of *porta principalis dextra*, external livestock enclosures, and other features

Phase 4: Re-cutting of Phase 3A fort defences and rearrangement of entrance (later Flavian–late 2nd century), subdivided:

> Phase 4A, re-cutting of second (Phase 3A) fort ditches
> Phase 4C, irregular partial 'blocking' of Phase 4A fort entrance

Additionally, the livestock enclosures and other features (Phase 3B–4B, Jones 2012) to the west of the Phase 3A fort may have continued in use during this phase. Phase 4C belongs in a Roman civilian or even post-Roman context.

Phase 5: Post-Roman activity

This phase relates to medieval/post-medieval activity, which has been distinguished from Phase 4C, which could belong in a pre-medieval context. Phase 5 or possible Phase 5 features are not described in this report.

Arrangement of results

Within each phase, a summary of the main features is followed by description of the defences (in clockwise order, beginning with the western side), and finally, the internal features. Description of the internal features begins with the *retentura*, followed by the central range, concluding with the *praetentura*.

For brevity, this chapter emphasizes the interpretable military buildings and other structures. Full details of other features may be found in the published reports (St Joseph and Shotton 1937; Webster 1954; Jones 2001; 2005; 2011; 2012; and 2025, chapters 2–6).

A selection of simplified ditch sections is illustrated.

For simplicity it is assumed that the fort is aligned north–south, although the drawings are labelled with compass north.

Phase 0: Pre-Roman activity (not illustrated)

With the exception of a group of burnt mounds (Jones 1988) located to the west of the fort, no features, or possible features, of prehistoric date have been recognized during the investigations. A total of six flint artefacts, including an arrowhead and two blades, were reported by Sheratt (2001, 85–6) from Areas M2–M5 (Fig. 1.3), including material of early Neolithic date. Globular jar fragments of possible Iron Age date were found in Areas M7–M8 (Hancocks 2005, 65). A sherd of scored ware was recorded in Area M9 (Evans et al. 2011, 65), together with grog-tempered wares typical of transitional, Late Iron Age–early Roman assemblages (Evans et al. 2011, 71). A few native or pre-Roman wares were recorded in the Area M18 excavation, which continue to be found in sites within the region up to the end of the 1st century, and beyond (Timby 2012, 86). Excepting the burnt mounds, pre-Roman occupation of the site is unlikely. Local Iron Age settlement sites in the region are often artefact-poor, for example at Langley Mill (M6 Toll, Powell and Ritchie 2008, only 14 sherds found).

Phase 1: First military activity and first fort (mid-Neronian)

Description and interpretation of Phase 1A, possible construction camp (Fig. 2.1; Areas M7, M9, M14, and M18), and possible clavicula *(Area M9)*

The earliest military activity at the site is attributed to a construction camp (Fig. 2.1), comprising a few scattered features pre-dating the Phase 1B defences (see below) which fortuitously protected them from later disturbance.

Along the later Phase 1B fort western defences, fragments of two roughly north–south aligned Phase 1A ditches (Area M14; Jones 2011, 11, fig. 2.2) were slightly misaligned with the overlying Phase 1B rampart. To the north, an L-shaped building, Structure 18.1 (Jones 2012, 11 and 17, fig. 2.3) and a number of associated post-holes and a pit were sealed beneath the Phase 1B rampart. The building measured a maximum of 7.5m north–south, and 2.5m east–west. It could represent a lean-to shed (e.g. Elginhaugh, Hanson 2007, 189 and fig. 7.31). The positioning of this building near to the Phase 1B *porta principalis dextra* suggests that it could have formed a temporary shelter – perhaps guarding the western entrance of the construction camp – assuming that the Phase 1A and Phase 1B entrances were roughly coincident.

Part of a second timber-framed building, Structure 7.1 (Area M7), was sealed by the eastern Phase 1B rampart, with which it was slightly misaligned. The western wall of the building, and the western ends of two internal walls, defined by beam-slots, were excavated (Jones 2005, 30, figs 8 and 14).

A group of features outside the later Phase 1B *porta principalis dextra* (Fig. 2.1) may be the only evidence of this phase to be located outside the later Phase 1B fort (Area M9, Fig. 1.3). The earliest of these features was a palisade trench (Jones 2011, 37–42, fig. 3.2), cut by the southern terminals of three re-cut, north–south aligned ditches, associated with a rampart. Other contemporary features to the west of the fort included a southwest–northeast possible cart-rut (Jones 2011, 43 and fig. 3.2), and a trackway bounded by two ditches, 7m apart (Jones 2011, 43 and fig. 3.2).

The ditches outside the later western Phase 1B fort defences could have formed a *clavicula*, providing additional defence against attack (e.g. Elginhaugh, Hanson 2007), an interpretation supported by the apparent lack of evidence for their continuation away from the entrance. Such outworks could have been laid out during initial fort construction (e.g. Castledykes, Lanarkshire) or as part of more extensive defensive outworks (Wilson 1984, fig. 5).

No Phase 1A features could be identified within the interior of the later Phase 1B fort, possibly because of later truncation.

Description of Phase 1B, first fort defences including porta principalis dextra *(Figs 2.2, 2.3)*

The Phase 1B fort measured 210m square (from the rampart tail), an area of 4.4ha, or 240m square (from the outside of the outermost ditch), an area of 5.76 ha. The fort gates were probably positioned centrally along the four sides. The *praetentura* occupied the southern half of the fort interior, and the central range and *retentura*, the remainder. Measured between the *via principalis* and *via quintana*, the central range was 52m in width. The *retentura*, between the *via quintana* and the northern rampart tail, measured 42m in width. The *via quintana* has not been located by excavation, so that its positioning is illustrative only.

The fort was defended by double ditches, the innermost re-cut in Phase 3A (see below), and a turf rampart. The size of the Phase 1B fort ditches varied according to the degree of localized modern disturbance (Fig. 2.3.S.1–S.3, Table 2.1).

Only one Phase 1B fort entrance, the *porta principalis dextra* (Area M18, Jones 2012), has been excavated. It measured 9m between the ditch terminals. The associated gatehouse, Structure 18.2 (Jones 2012, 17–18, table 2.1, fig. 2.3; Fig. 2.4) measured 10.5m north–south and 3.5m east–west. The building was defined by a total of seven post-pits, three along its western (outer) side and four at a separation of 3.5m along its eastern side. It contained a northern guard chamber measuring approximately 3m square; no trace of a southern guard chamber could be located.

The primary western rampart was of turf construction (Table 2.1). Subsequently, a timber revetment was inserted to the rear of the rampart (Area M18, Jones 2012, 18, fig. 2.3; Area M3A, Jones 2001, 18), to the north but not to the south of the entrance along this side of the defences, which suggests that it was a localized response to waterlogged ground conditions.

Figure 2.1. Phase 1A construction camp, features adjoining western and eastern defences of later fort.

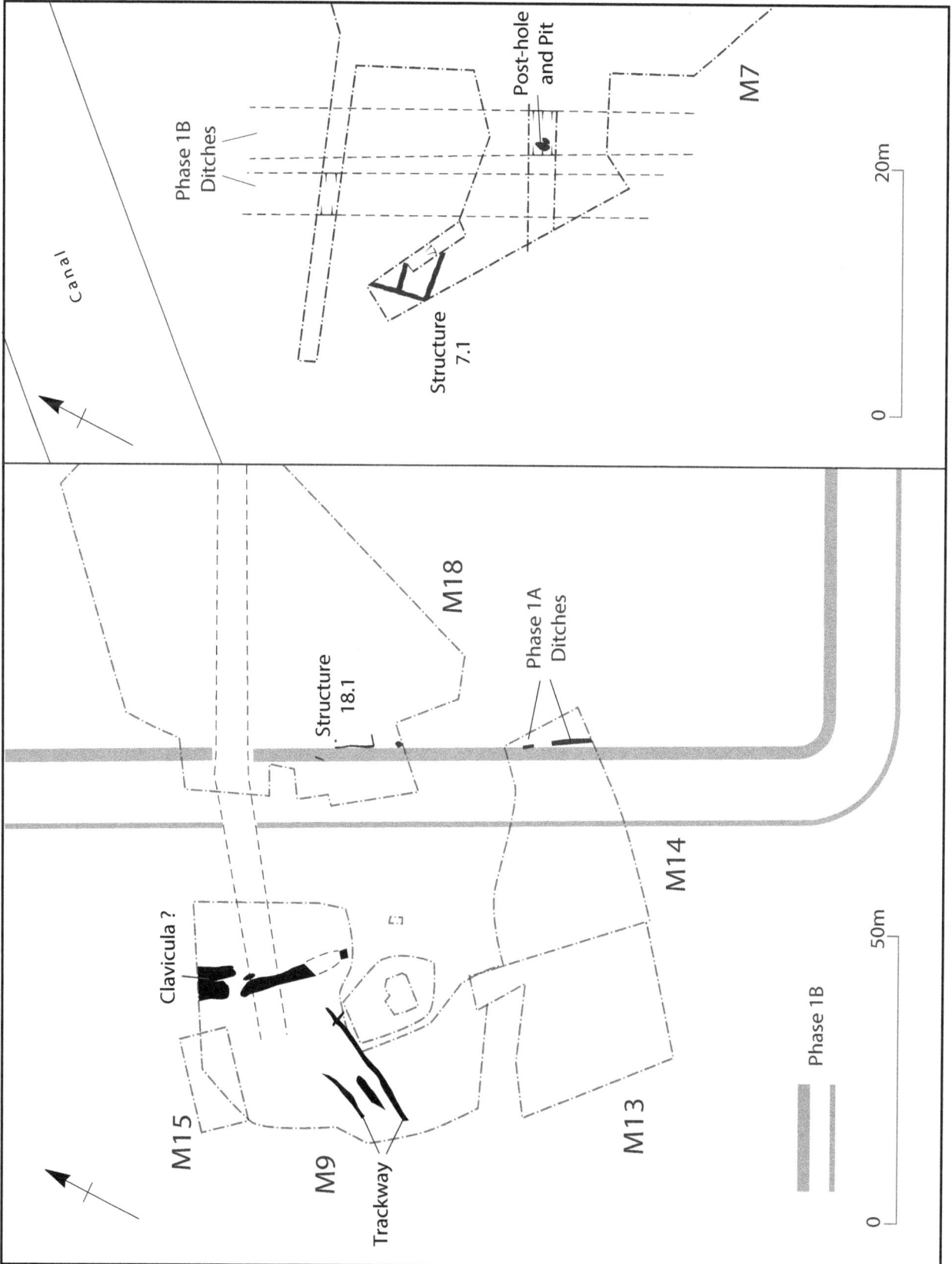

Phase 1B Ditches

Post-hole and Pit

M7

Canal

Structure 7.1

20m

0

M18

Structure 18.1

Phase 1A Ditches

M14

Clavicula ?

M15

M9

Trackway

M13

Phase 1B

50m

0

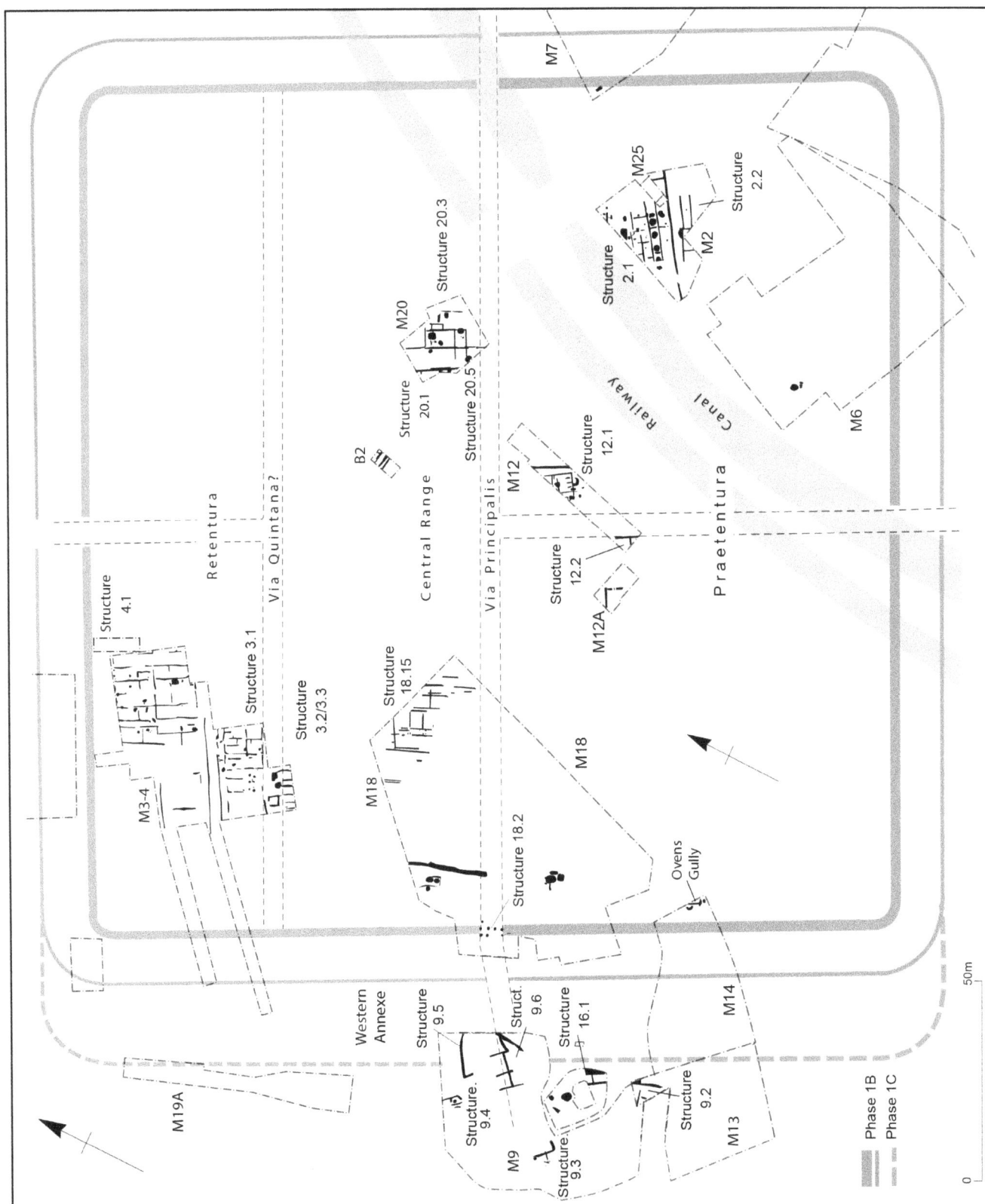

Figure 2.2. Phase 1 excavated features, simplified plan. The position of the *via quintana* is illustrative.

PHASE 1

Area M3B
S2

N

S

D3

D1A

Area M5B
S1

E

W

D2

D3

2m

0

Area M8
S3

SE

NW

F250.04

F252.04

F251.04

PHASE 1C

Area M19A
S5

E

W

[5003]

2m

Area M14
S4

NE

SW

F495.04

0

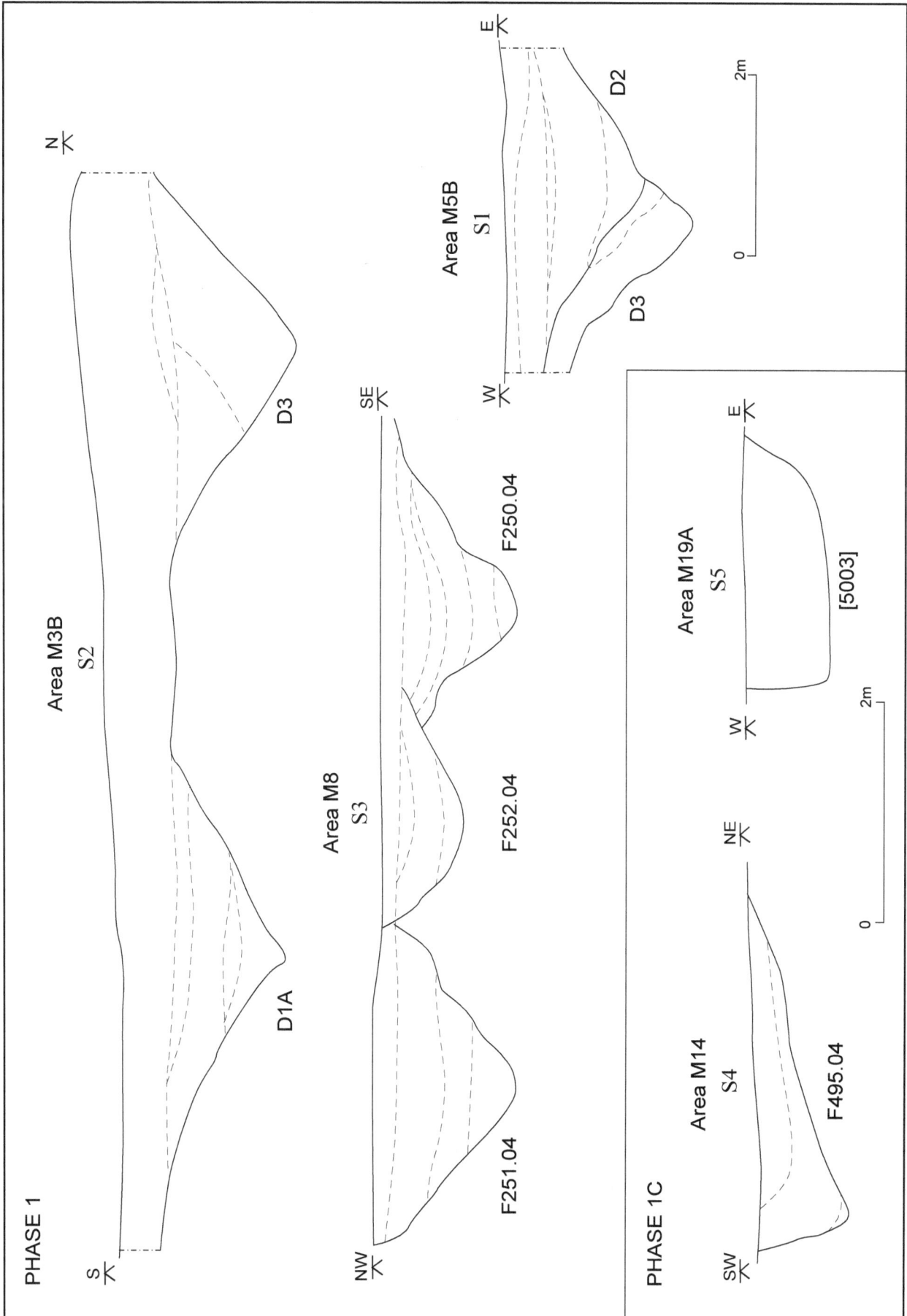

Figure 2.3. Phase 1 defences and Phase 1C annexe or enclosure ditches, simplified profiles. Profiles located on Figs 2.4 and 2.5.

Table 2.1. Phase 1B defences, details.

Area	Fig.	Outer ditch	Berm	Inner ditch	Berm	Rampart
Western defences (Fig. 2.3.S.1)						
M14	2.2 RB3	5m × 1.5m	2.1m	4m × 1.3m	1m	Turf, 5m × 0.2m
M18	2.3 RB4	–	2–2.5m	3.5–5.2m × 1.3–1.8m	–	Rear timber revetment N of entrance
M3A	6 RB1	3m × 1.5m	2.4m	4m × 1.8m	2m	Sand, buried turf lines, 5m × 0.4m
M5	D3, 2.3.S.1	1.7m × 1.2m (truncated by N annexe ditch)	3m; third 'ditch' at NW angle	Re-cut in Phase 3A	–	–
Northern defences (Fig. 2.3.S.2)						
M3B	Fig. 2.3.S.2	4.2m × 1.7m	2.3m	Re-cut in Phase 3A		–
Eastern defences						
St J and S 1937		3.2m × 1.5m		3.2m × 1.5m		
M7	8 RB2	–	1.7m (ditches re-cut)	1.38m deep (truncated by Phase 3A re-cut)	–	Turf, 5m × 0.1m
M8	9–10 RB2	Re-cut in Phase 3A	4m (ditches re-cut)	4m x 1.7m		–
Southern defences (Fig. 2.3.S.3)						
M8	Fig. 2.3.S.3	3.2–4.2m × 1.5m	4m	3.2m × 1.5m	–	–
M6	10 RB1	3.5m W		4m × 1.5m		

Note: Later ditch re-cuts shown where identified.
RB1 Jones (2001); RB2 Jones (2005); RB3 Jones (2011); RB4 Jones (2012).
St J and S 1937 = St Joseph and Shotton (1937).
For section locations see Fig. 2.4 (Fig. 2.3.S.1–S.2), Fig. 2.5 (Fig. 2.3.S.3).

Additional defensive obstacles were provided between the Phase 1B ditches along the southern side of the fort (Jones 2001, 18, 20 and fig. 6) and the western defences (Jones 2005, 96). The northwestern and southern defences were strengthened by the addition of a layer of clay between the two ditches, providing an additional obstacle to attackers (Area M5, Jones 2001, 20; Area M6, Jones 2001, 22).

Possible traces of corner-towers (not illustrated) were located at the northwestern (Jones 2001, 20 and fig. 7) and southeastern corners of the fort (Jones 2005, 15 and fig. 9). Each was only represented by the rearward pair of post-pits, positioned approximately 3m apart.

Interpretation of Phase 1B fort defences (Fig. 2.3)

Measuring 3m and 4m in width, the western ditches lay in the middle of the size range suggested by Jones (1975, 106; 2.4–6m in width; 1.2–2.7m in depth) for double-ditched systems. At 3m, the berm between the ditches on the western and southern sides is of average dimensions (Johnson 1983, 55), although at Metchley this space may have been designed to accommodate a palisade or other obstacle. The Metchley rampart lay at the lower end of the range of 5.5–7m suggested by Jones (1975, 70) for turf revetted ramparts, slightly smaller than the reconstructed rampart at The Lunt, which measured 6m in width (Hobley 1975, 19–23).

With reference to the gatehouse typology published by Bidwell et al. (1988, fig. 1.1 and 4), the Metchley structure is similar to type IIa, a double portal gateway with flanking towers, except that there is only a single flanking tower at Metchley. Additionally, the gate must have been located flush with the rear of the structure (e.g. Pen Llystyn, Hogg 1968, fig. 20). Single portal gates are recorded at Caerhun (west) and Castell Collen (northwest, primary and secondary structures) (Burnham and Davies 2010, 74).

The lack of a southern guard chamber at Metchley is particularly unusual, since the *portae principales* would have provided one of the main access and exit points to the fort. The central post-pit for the gate (*spina*) was both broader and more deeply cut than the other post-pits forming the gate structure, which suggests it was intended to support the rampart walkway and not merely to act as a gate-post. The lack of a southern guard chamber could reflect the hurried construction of the fort.

Description and interpretation of Phase 1C, western annexe or enclosure (Figs 2.2 and 2.4-2.5)

The re-cut palisade trench forming the outer side of a western annexe or enclosure was excavated (Area M14, Jones 2011, 18, fig. 2.2) and tested by salvage recording (Area M19A, Jones 2011, 93, fig. 5.1). It lay 19m to the west of the outer Phase 1B fort ditch (measured centre-to-centre) enclosing approximately 0.4ha internally.

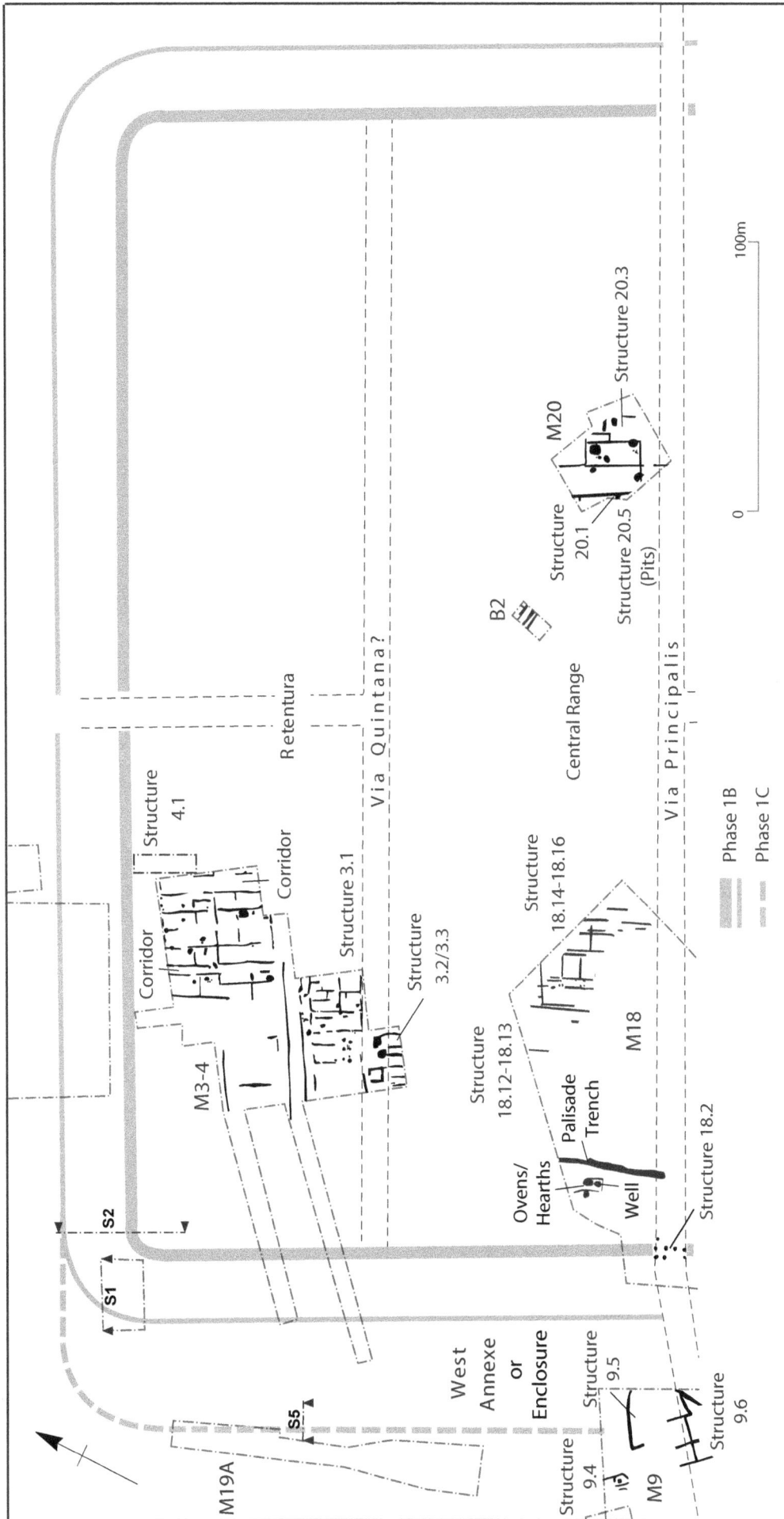

Figure 2.4. Phase 1D, Phase 1E, Phase 1D/1E excavated features, simplified plan, *retentura*, and central range. The position of the *via quintana* is illustrative.

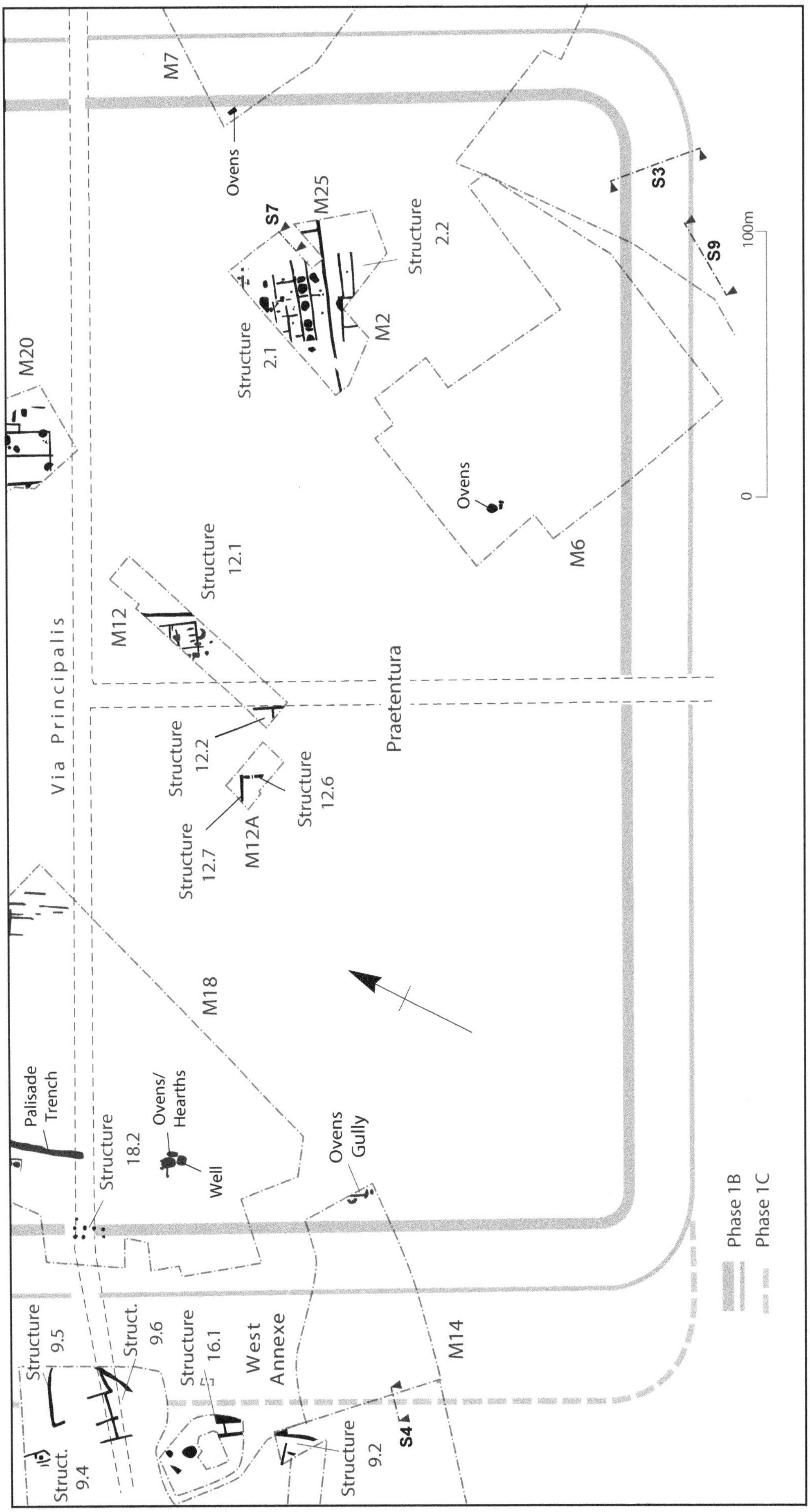

Figure 2.5. Phase 1D, Phase 1E, Phase 1D/1E excavated features, simplified plan, *praetentura*.

Measuring a maximum of just 1.1m in width and 0.4m in depth in Area M14, the palisade trench was clearly not defensive in function. It was dug with a gently sloping inner edge and a more steeply sloping outer face (Fig. 2.3.S.3–S.4). No associated structural features were recorded within its interior. The same feature was not recognized adjoining the *porta principalis dextra* (in Area M9), possibly because it was interrupted by a broad entry gap at this entrance. It was not possible to test the projected points of intersection of this annexe or enclosure with the Phase 1B fort circuit. The western annexe or enclosure may have defined an area given over to pottery production, mortaria in particular (see below).

Description of Phase 1D, early first fort building alignment and other contemporary features (Figs 2.4, 2.5)

Phase 1D is defined to include fragmentary timber-framed buildings cut on a slightly different alignment (varying by seven degrees) to the later Phase 1E buildings, and through recognition of stratigraphic relationships. Phase 1D buildings and other features are recognised in the central range and *praetentura* (Areas M18 and M20, Fig. 1.3) only.

Part of a pair of adjoining Phase 1D timber-framed buildings were located within the left (western) side of the central range (Area M18). The western of the pair, Structure 18.12, was represented by its eastern wall and a possible adjoining veranda beam-slot (Jones 2012, fig. 2.6). The western wall of the eastern building of the pair, Structure 18.14, was located 8m to the east of Structure 18.12, both following a common orientation. Within the interior of Structure 18.14 a number of north–south aligned internal beam-slots and post-holes were recorded, but the internal layout of the building could not be reconstructed.

A further possible Phase 1D building, Structure 20.5 (Fig. 2.4; Jones 2025, chapter. 3, fig. 3.2), was recorded in the right (eastern) side of the central range (Area M20, Fig. 1.3). It was represented by pebble-surfaced roads and three (or possibly five) pits in total, positioned 3.5m apart, cut or overlain by Phase 1E timber-framed buildings.

Evidence of Phase 1D industrial activity was also recorded in the right (eastern) side of the *praetentura* (Area M12/ M12A, Jones 2025, chapter. 2, fig. 2.4).

Interpretation of Phase 1D, early building alignment (Figs 2.4, 2.5)

The functions of Structures 18.12 and 18.14 cannot be interpreted from a single wall. The significance of these structures is the evidence they provide for an early layout. The similarity in location if not in alignment of Structure 18.14 with Phase 1E Structure 18.15 (see below) could suggest that the earlier building was also a *praetorium*, although it is unwise to place too much reliance on retro-projecting building interpretations.

The pebble surfaces were probably the earliest Phase 1D features in Area M20, pre-dating the layout of Phase 1E Structure 20.5. The centreline of surface 4186 was approximately 66m to the west of the eastern fort defences, one third of the distance (east–west) across the fort interior. Within the typical central-range fort plan (e.g. Johnson 1983, fig. 19), this road separates the central third which usually contained the *principia*, and the eastern third, which may have contained other buildings, including granaries. Surface 4168 may represent the first definition of this road.

Structure 20.5, comprising three (or possibly five) pits, may have formed part of an ambulatory around the central courtyard of a building, mostly located outside the area excavated.

Description of Phase 1E, later building alignment (Figs 2.4, 2.5)

The Phase 1E buildings were arranged *per scamna* (east–west).

This phase could only be defined in Area M18 (central range) and Area M12 (*praetentura*).

Central range

Structure 18.15 (Area M18, Jones 2012, 19–23, fig. 2.6 for the numbering of the individual rooms) adjoined the northern *via principalis* frontage on the left side of the central range. It probably represented a rebuild of Phase 1D Structure 18.14 (see above), which was coincident, although laid out on an alignment varying by seven degrees. The Structure 18.14 beam-slots and post-holes were cut by the Phase 1E building. Parts of the western, northern, and eastern external walls of Structure 18.15 were recorded; the southern part of the building, adjoining the *via principalis*, had been scoured-out by later disturbances. The excavated part of the building measured 17m east–west and a minimum of 18m north–south. A total of seven rooms or corridors were identified within the original layout, arranged in five rows across the width of the building. Rooms R1 and R7 comprised corridors measuring respectively 3m and 1.5m internally in width, adjoining the western and eastern sides of the building, respectively. To the east of R1 was a further corridor, R2, measuring 1–1.3m in width. Further to the east were three rooms, R3–R5, each measuring 4.2m (east–west). R4 and R5 were originally undivided. Another room, R6, also 4.2m in width, lay to the east of rooms R3–R6 and to the west of corridor R7 in the east of the building. The eastern part of the building was later rearranged (Jones 2012, 23).

To the west of Structure 18.15 was the east wall of a contemporary building, Structure 18.13. The outer walls of Structures 18.13 and 18.15 were cut 8m apart, maintaining the separation and positioning between Structures 18.12 and 18.14, their Phase 1D predecessors.

Praetentura

Part of the eastern side of a single Phase 1E timber-framed building, Structure 12.2 (Jones 2025, ch. 2, figs 2.2, 2.3), was recorded in the left *praetentura*, adjoining the western frontage of the *via praetoria*. The excavated remains of this building comprised part of its eastern side and part of an internal wall.

The southern end of a rectangular building, Structure 12.1 was recorded in the right (eastern) *praetentura*, adjoining the eastern *via praetoria* frontage (Jones 2025, chapter. 2, figs 2.2, 2.3). The southern side of this building, and the southern ends of its eastern and western sides, were excavated; the northern end of the building lay outside the excavated area. An unusual feature was the continuation of the southern and western walls beyond the southwestern corner of the building, possibly forming verandas. The southern half of the southern end of the building was subdivided by three equidistant partitions, each 1.3m in length, into four 'compartments', measuring an average of 0.8m in width. This arrangement suggests stalling for animals, possibly pack animals. Further to the east was a north–south ditch, misaligned with the building.

Interpretation of Phase 1E, later building alignment (Figs 2.4, 2.5)

Central range

The location of Structure 18.15 in the left (western) side of the central range, to the west of the presumed location of the *principia*, supports its interpretation as the *praetorium*. In Britain, *praetoriae* were generally located to the left of the *principia* (Marvell and Owen-John 1997, 182). The *praetorium* may have occupied the whole of one side of the central range, unless this space was shared with another building, often a granary (Johnson 1983, 139), as at Metchley (Structures 3.2, 3.3).

This interpretation cannot be proved because only part of the building was excavated. More generally, because *praetoriae* functioned as the private dwelling of the commanding officer (Marvell and Owen-John 1997, 177), they were more varied in layout than other building types within the fort interior (Johnson 1983, 133; Hanson 2007, 48; Burnham and Davies 2010, 77).

Assuming that Structure 18.15 was a *praetorium*, the later structural changes in the east of the building interior may evidence a change in commanding officer, or rearrangement to suit his changing needs.

It is difficult to estimate the full size of the Metchley example from the limited ground plan provided by excavation. If the building extended southwards to the *via principalis* frontage, it could have measured a maximum of 26m north–south. This building is smaller than some excavated examples (Jones 2012, fig. 2.8). The north wall

of this building extended approximately midway between the *via praetoria* and the suggested location of the *via quintana* (Jones 2012, fig. 2.8).

Some excavated *praetoriae* comprised two distinct structural units, one the domestic arrangement, the second a compound containing a range of sheds and outbuildings (Johnson 1983, 137; Pen Llystyn, Hogg 1968, 130–32 and fig. 19). It is possible that Structure 18.13 formed the eastern wall of such a compound, although this is a purely speculative interpretation on the present evidence.

Structure 18.15 was a notably long-lived building. It continued in occupation during the earlier use of the military stores depot, being only cleared preparatory to the layout of livestock compounds within the fort interior (Period 3 of Phase 2B, see below).

Praetentura

Structure 12.1 was located in the right *praetentura*, to the rear of the *via praetoria* frontage. The arrangement of the southern end of this building could perhaps suggest divisions for the stabling of horses. Davison (1989, 160) suggests a width allowance of 1.16m per horse, and a length allowance of 2m, although smaller pack animals would require less space. More usually, horses are arranged along the long axis of a military stables (e.g. Johnson 1983, figs 134, 136; Davison 1989, 151, building type O). Rows of small compartments are sometimes interpreted as space for fodder, grooms, and equipment, although, again, these compartments are more usually arranged along the long axis of the building (Davison 1989, 152, building type R).

Description of Phase 1D/1E buildings, attributable to either Phase 1D or 1E, or both (Figs 2.4, 2.5)

Part of a facing pair of east–west aligned barrack-blocks were the only Phase 1D/1E buildings excavated in the left *retentura* (Areas M3–M4, Jones 2001, Structures 3.1 and Structure 4.1, 25–32, fig. 11). A granary (Structure 3.2) and an associated loading-platform (Structure 3.3) were recorded in the left side of the central range. Two buildings were recorded in the right side of the central range (Structures 20.1 and 20.3). Parts of two buildings, a *fabrica* (Structure 2.1) and an adjoining building (Structure 2.2), were recorded in the right *praetentura*.

Retentura

Structure 4.1, the northern barrack-block of the pair, measured 21m in width, and was recorded for a length of approximately 50m; its eastern and western ends lay outside the area excavated. The excavated part of the building originally contained a total of 20 rooms, arranged in three structural units (eastern, central, and western), divided by two north–south aligned corridors which extended across the width of the building. A veranda ran along the southern side of the central and western structural units.

The eastern unit mostly lay outside the area excavated. It was separated from the central unit by a corridor. The central unit was originally subdivided into 16 rooms, arranged in four rows across the width of the building, each containing four rooms. A midrib divided the central unit into two equal halves, the original arrangement of the rooms within one half forming a mirror image of the arrangement within the other. The western corridor, dividing the central and western units, may originally have been just 1.2m in width. The southern part of the corridor, to the south of the midrib, was probably subsequently enlarged, and was misaligned with the original build. The purpose of this rebuild could have been to enlarge the central unit by the addition of a further pair of rooms to the south of the midrib. The western structural unit was also divided along its length by a continuation of the midrib, although few other details of its internal arrangement could be discerned. A total of four rooms were recorded in the eastern excavated part of the western structural unit. Fragments of other internal walls could be discerned, but not their overall arrangement. Traces of rebuilding could also be identified.

Structure 3.1, the southern barrack-block of the pair, was separated from Structure 4.1 by a gap measuring 3m in width. It measured 12m in width, and was recorded for a length of 24m. Once again, the eastern and western limits of the building lay outside the area excavated. Two structural units were recorded, separated by a corridor which ran across the width of the building. A veranda extended along the northern side of the building. The eastern unit comprised two pairs of rooms of unequal size subdivided by partitions, and a further room to the west, also subdivided. The western unit comprised the remainder of the building, subdivided by north–south aligned beam-slots into a minimum of three rooms of unequal size. Other features, including post-holes and stake-holes, were also recorded within the interior of this unit.

Central range

In the left side of the central range was part of the northern end of a granary (Structure 3.2), represented by five parallel, equidistant, north–south aligned beam-slots (Jones 2001, 28 and fig. 11). It adjoined a square loading platform (Structure 3.3). Three parallel beam-slots recorded in Trench B2 (Fig. 1.3) could have represented part of a further granary, although only a small part of this building lay within the area trenched. These features did not follow the fort alignment.

Parts of two buildings were recorded adjoining the northern *via principalis* frontage in the right side of the central range (Area M20, Jones 2025, ch. 3). The westernmost, Structure 20.1, was represented by its eastern wall, and by fragments of two internal walls. To the east of the building was a passageway 5m wide. To the east of the passageway was a second building, represented by a primary build, Structure 20.3a, and a rebuild, Structure 20.3b. A difference of 3° was noted in the alignments of the Structure 20.3a and

20.3b beam-slots. The primary build, Structure 20.3a, was represented by a beam-slot, L-shaped in plan, defining an internal room measuring a minimum of 5m across. The rebuild, Structure 20.3b, was cut into a backfilled Phase 1D pit. The western wall of the rebuild was formed by a southward continuation of the western wall of the primary build. This wall was extended to the south, partly severing the *via principalis*. The northern terminal of the western side of the rebuild abutted the southwestern corner of Structure 20.3a, with which it was slightly misaligned. A minimum of five rooms were recorded within the Structure 20.3b interior, which was irregular in plan, as a result of rearrangement.

Praetentura

Structure 2.1 (Jones 2001, fig. 14, 32–4) in the right *praetentura* was aligned east–west, and measured a maximum of 7m in width and 15m in length. The eastern and western ends of the building lay outside the area excavated. The building was divided along its length by two east–west beam-slots, which together with north–south aligned beam-slots defined a minimum of nine rooms. Towards the south of the building were a total of five pits, positioned carefully between the internal dividing walls. Although no industrial residues were recorded at excavation (in 1967), this building may be interpreted as a *fabrica*, because the pits were integral to its internal arrangement.

To the south of the building an east–west aligned drainage gully separated the *fabrica* from Structure 2.2 to the south. This building measured a minimum of 3m in width, and was recorded for a maximum length of 16m. Only the central part of the northern side of this building, which contained a minimum of three internal rooms, was excavated. Its northern wall was offset, like Structure 2.1 to the north. The two offsets were approximately flush, suggesting an association between the two buildings.

In the left *praetentura* (Area M12a) the earliest features were two post-holes, an oven, and a pit. They were succeeded by two buildings (Structures 12.6 and 12.7), each represented by an external and an internal beam-slot only.

Interpretation of Phase 1D/1E buildings (Figs 2.4, 2.5)

Retentura

Structure 4.1 may be interpreted as a double barrack-block, formed by two barrack-blocks constructed back-to-back, without an intervening passageway. The dividing wall would have been formed by the midrib. In Britain double barrack-blocks have been identified at Colchester, South Shields, Elginhaugh, and Llanfor (Burnham and Davies 2010, fig. 7.83), although all these examples are distinguished from the Metchley building by the presence of a double midrib. Double barrack-blocks without the double midrib have been identified on the continent at Heidenheim, Kunzing, Valkenburg Castellum 2–3 (Glasbergen 1972), and Neuss. A notable feature of the internal beam-slots is the absence of evidence for 'crossovers'; the east–west aligned walls terminated short of the north–south walls. This arrangement was adopted for stability, to ensure that the beam-slot ends did not break down (Davison 1989, 217 and figs 4, 5).

The eastern unit may be interpreted as comprising structurally or functionally distinct 'end rooms' or 'end buildings', forming a *fabrica*, although it is also possible that the decurions were housed at both ends of the barrack-block (Breeze and Dobson 1974, 13). Because the Metchley building was a double barrack-block, a total of four *turmae* could have been accommodated in the building, with two decurions housed at either end of the building. An alternative interpretation of the building is considered in Chapter 5.

The central unit comprised eight *contubernia*. Each *contubernium* was divided into two rooms, the *arma* towards the front (north) used for equipment storage, and the *papilio* to the rear (south) for sleeping. This part of the building would have provided accommodation for two cavalry *turmae*. Each pair of rooms would have housed eight men, making the total assumed *turma* strength of 32 men. The Structure 3.1 and 4.1 *contubernia* shared two unusual characteristics, the larger size of the *arma* (Structure 3.1, 61%; Structure 4.1, 55%), and the comparatively large area of each *contubernium* (Structure 3.1, 31.5 m²; Structure 4.1, 30 m²). In contrast, in the double barrack-blocks at Heidenheim, Kunzing, Valkenberg, and Neuss the *arma* was either smaller than or the same size as the *papilio*. The Metchley *contubernia* were larger than the *contubernia* at Valkenburg Castellum 2–3 (23 m²), but they were smaller than the *contubernia* at Heidenheim (33.6 m²). The recorded similarity in overall size and the size differences between the *arma* and *papilio* suggests that the two facing barrack-blocks were intended to house units of similar composition. Alternatively, they could have housed two 'halves' of a single unit, as suggested by Maxfield (1986, 62–3) based on the apparently alternating layouts of barrack-blocks at Valkenberg Castellum 1. An alternative interpretation of this building is considered in Chapter 5 below.

It may be assumed that the narrow western corridor originally extended across the whole width of the Metchley building. This corridor was maintained in the northern half of the building, but in the southern half of the building the corridor was later removed, and replaced by a fifth *contubernium*, possibly a special *contubernium*, carved out of the eastern end of the officer's quarters (western unit).

Measuring 21m in width, Structure 4.1 at Metchley is most closely paralleled in size and internal arrangement by double barrack-block 2/3 at Valkenburg Castellum 2–3. Although not fully excavated, the Valkenburg barrack-block contained six *contubernia* in the men's quarters, possibly flanked on the inside of the fort by a range of end rooms, forming the *fabrica* for each century (Glasbergen 1972), similar to the end rooms identified at Hod Hill (Richmond 1968, 80), which may be represented at Metchley by the incompletely excavated eastern unit.

Although only part of Structure 3.1 was excavated, its location, in the left side of the *retentura*, and its layout suggest it can be confidently interpreted as a barrack-block, probably conforming to Type A (Davison 1989, fig. a). Barrack-blocks were usually L-shaped in plan, the wider part of the building housing the officers' quarters, possibly including the western unit, located adjoining the western *intervallum*. The remainder of the building was divided into paired *contubernia*, forming the men's quarters. The excavated part of the central unit comprised three pairs of *contubernia*.

The individual *contubernia* were only of average breadth (3.7m compared with a range of 3.3–4.4m, Davison 1989, 97). At 31.5 m² the internal floor area of the *contubernia* lay just beyond the range of 14–29 m² suggested by Davison (1989, 13) for auxiliary barracks. The size ratio between the *armae* and *papiliones* (based on R3–R4, see Jones 2001, fig. 11) is 61% to 39%, whilst it is more usual for the size ratio between the two rooms to be in reverse proportions, or the same. Two *armae* and one *papilio* were subdivided with partitions, which may mark a later rebuild, possibly indicating a change of use of the building. Another adaptation was the insertion of a corridor along the eastern side of Room R5, truncating an earlier hearth. This corridor could have divided the officers' quarters from the remainder of the building. Rooms 6–8 in the western unit may have formed the officers' quarters, to the east of the inserted corridor. The excavated part of the western unit measured 240 m² in area, which may be considered exceptionally large for officers' quarters. Davison (1989, 97) suggests a size range of 64–170 m² for Claudio–Neronian officers' quarters. It is possible therefore that Rooms R5–R6 may have formed special *contubernia*.

Central range

Structure 3.2 may be confidently interpreted as a granary, located close to a gate within the central range of the fort to facilitate loading/unloading (Johnson 1983, 152).

Structure 20.1 and the main elements of Structure 20.3a/b were slightly misaligned (by 3°), suggesting rebuilding, as in Areas M3–M4 (Structure 4.1 and rebuild). On the basis of similarity in alignment with Area M18, Structure 20.1 would be the later of the two buildings in Area M20. Only part of the eastern wall of Structure 20.1 was located within the area excavated. The overall arrangement or function of this building clearly cannot be confidently interpreted from part of a single wall. The location of this wall is however significant. It is sited approximately 66m to the west of the eastern rampart tail, equivalent to one third of the overall width (east–west) of the central range. It was usual to locate the *principia* within the central third of the central range (Johnson 1983, fig. 19). In the absence of evidence to the contrary, the eastern wall of Structure 20.1 may be interpreted as the eastern wall of the *principia*. The *principia* generally comprised a central courtyard, surrounded by colonnaded ambulatories and small rooms (e.g. Johnson 1983, fig. 98).

The function of Structure 20.3a cannot be interpreted from its extreme southwestern angle, although its location within the central range may suggest that it formed part of a *fabrica* (e.g. Carlisle, Zant 2009). The remainder of the excavated part of the building belongs to a later rebuild, Structure 20.3b. The main element of the rebuild was a rectangular room. The western sides of the original structure and its rebuild were slightly misaligned. Unusually, the southern wall of the room was continued to the south, partly severing the *via principalis*.

Praetentura

Structure 2.1 (Fig. 2.5) may be interpreted as a *fabrica*, as suggested by the deliberate placement of industrial pits within its interior.

Phase 1D/1E intervallum

A total of six ovens and a gully were recorded in the small area of the western *intervallum* tested by Area M14 (Jones 2011, 16 and fig. 2.2). Further to the north (Area M18, Jones 2012, 27–31, fig. 2.3) were recorded an oven, a well and a further oven/hearth (Jones 2012, fig. 2.3) within the central range. Within the *retentura*, further industrial features, consisting of two pits filled with large rounded pebbles and a three-sided palisade trench, were recorded (Jones 2012, fig. 2.3).

The ovens/hearths located in the central range *intervallum* may be interpreted as the bases of breadmaking ovens, cut into the rampart tail. Given the association suggested between adjoining barrack-blocks and adjoining *intervallum* ovens (e.g. Elginhaugh, Hanson 2007, 183ff.; Pen Llystyn, Hogg 1968, figs 18, 20), is it possible to suggest that the excavated ovens in the central range were associated with the use of the *praetorium*? Although centralized cookhouses are recorded in Roman military contexts, the securely identified cookhouse buildings are few in number (Johnson 1983). A Phase 3A cookhouse has been identified at Metchley (Structure 2.4 (Jones 2001, fig. 18).

Three bowl-shaped ovens, backfilled with burnt clay, were recorded along the eastern *intervallum* (Area M7, Jones 2005, 30). Along the southern *intervallum* the bases of four heavily truncated hearths or ovens were found (Area M6, Jones 2001, fig. 16 and 34). The northern *intervallum* space was not investigated.

Description and interpretation of Phase 1D–1E external features, the western and possible eastern civilian settlements (Figs 1.3, 2.5)

A small-scale civilian settlement briefly occupied the natural plateau outside the *porta principalis dextra* (Fig. 1.3; Jones 2011, 45–9, phase B). This settlement post-dated the abandonment of the latest Phase 1A *clavicula*, whose later use may have been contemporary with the Phase 1B fort defences. It is possible that this settlement did not represent the earliest external occupation at Metchley, merely the relocation of an earlier settlement, perhaps located on the eastern side of the fort, adjoining the *porta principalis sinistra*, cleared to make way for the layout of the Phase 2A eastern annexe (see below).

The western settlement was represented by a small-scale, low-density, irregular layout, mainly along the Phase 1A gravel trackway, which remained in use. The Phase 1B roadside ditches had probably silted-up and gone out of use during the early use of the settlement. Pebble surfaces, forming hardstandings, were laid out on both sides of the trackway along the steep west-facing slope adjoining the fort defences. Later, the trackway and associated yard surfaces were encroached upon by buildings.

A notable feature of the settlement was the lack of a coherent plan, suggesting a piecemeal layout, although the natural slope may have made surveying difficult. The buildings were mostly misaligned with each other (with the exception of Structures 9.3 and 9.6), with the fort defences, and with the short lengths of the two boundary ditches recorded. Another important feature of the excavated part of the settlement was its notably small size: a maximum of six buildings were located, including one building (Structure 9.4), which may be a temporary shelter. The layout of buildings with their long axes along the trackway frontage (e.g. Structures 9.5 and 9.6) suggests a lack of pressure for space, and contrasts with the usual Roman 'end-on' arrangement. Some classes of features, such as pits and post-holes, were almost entirely absent. One of the notable features excavated was a midden, containing a quantity of pottery (Jones 2011, 48).

Open-fronted timber-framed buildings, Structures 9.5 and 9.6, interpreted as shops or booths, were recorded to the north and south of the trackway (Jones 2011, fig. 3.4 and 45–9), occupying a steep natural slope which may have been unsuitable for habitation. Structure 9.5, to the north of the trackway measured 10m east–west by 3m north–south. Structure 9.6 to the south of the trackway measured 9.5m east–west and 5m north–south. Its interior was divided into at least four rooms, the northernmost being open on their northern side. Further structures (Structures 9.2 and 16.1), were located to the rear of the trackway frontage. Some of the structures provided evidence for rebuilding.

Trial-trenching (Area M27, Jones 2025, fig. 6.2) has identified scattered features to the east of the fort. These include a possible north–south road, a palisade trench and post-holes which probably belong to a civilian settlement, but are undated within the Roman period. Further trenching within the University campus (Area M32, Fig. 1.2) has identified the metalled surface of a road, probably a spur road linking the fort with Ryknield Street, on an alignment first identified as a field boundary (red lines on Fig. 1.1B).

Phase 2: Annexes and military stores depot

Phase 2A annexes (Figs 2.3, 2.6, 2.7, later Neronian)

The ditched annexes along the northern, eastern, and southern sides of the Phase 1B fort are important components of the military complex (Figs 2.3.S.1, 2.6, and 2.7.S.6).

Description and interpretation of northern annexe

The northern annexe extended along the whole length of the Phase 1B fort's northern side, enclosing an area comprising 210m east–west × 75m north–south, measured from the outside of the fort defences, an area of 1.57ha. It occupied the highest ground within the complex overall. It was defended by two ditches, cut 5m apart (measured centre-to-centre). The inner ditch measured 3.6m wide × 1.5m in depth, and the outer 3.3m wide × 1.2m deep (St Joseph and Shotton 1937, 72). No associated rampart was recorded.

Excavation (Area M5, Jones 2001, fig. 7 and 42), at the junction between the southwestern corner of the annexe and the northwestern corner of the Phase 1 fort, established that the annexe ditch was cut into the fills of the outer fort ditch (Fig. 2.3.S.1), forming a continuous defensive circuit around the fort and northern annexe. The Phase 1B outer fort ditch was deliberately backfilled with gravel capped with a layer of turf packing at the intersection, to retain the ditch profile. By the time the northern annexe ditch had been cut across the outer fort ditch it had accumulated up to 0.7m of silt (Jones 2001, 42) – possibly no more than a season's silting, and unlikely to represent an intervening abandonment. St Joseph and Shotton (1937, 73) noted that the first fort ditch developed a W-shaped profile in the area forming the junction between the fort and the southeastern corner of this annexe, representing their intersection, although the significance of this profile was not appreciated at the time of excavation.

The northwestern corner tower of the northern annexe was excavated by Webster (1954, 1). It measured 3.05m square. No other annexe corners have been excavated at Metchley.

An area of 1,300 m² in the southwest of the annexe interior was excavated by Pretty in 1963, but no internal features were identified (Jones 2001, 42; Area 1B, Fig. 1.3). No large-scale excavation has taken place subsequently within the northern annexe interior. An extensive watching brief in Area M30 to the south of the University Medical School (Jones 2025, chapter. 6, fig. 6.1) identified a length of the northward continuation of the *via decumana*, represented by two flanking ditches, although the metalled road surface itself did not survive. An earlier watching brief (Duncan 2008) produced negative results.

Description and interpretation of eastern annexe

The eastern annexe ditch was misaligned with the eastern side of the Phase 1B fort (Fig. 1.3; Jones 2005, fig. 8), although its precise alignment is difficult to establish because of several re-cuts. It has been assumed that this annexe (like other annexes at Metchley) extended for the full length of the fort's eastern side, although this is unproven. Assuming the annexe extended over the full length of this side of the fort, it would have enclosed 0.58ha.

The eastern defences of this annexe comprised a single ditch interrupted by a broad entrance causeway and a rampart (Jones 2005, 18). The ditch was cut to a V- or W-shaped profile, the latter suggesting re-cutting (Fig. 2.7.S.1, F240.03). The full profile of the primary annexe ditch could not be recovered because of later intensive re-cutting. Two post-pits, positioned at a separation of 6m (measured centre-to-centre), framed the entranceway. The contemporary turf rampart survived to a width of 7m and a height of 0.4m (Jones 2005, 25). A number of features, including gullies, ovens, and areas of pebble surfacing, were recorded in the small excavated part of the annexe interior (Jones 2005, 29). These are the only features to be excavated within an annexe interior at Metchley. Outside the eastern annexe ditch were two palisade trenches, probably retaining fences, the outermost slightly misaligned with the annexe ditch (Jones 2005, fig. 8; 2025, ch. 6, M33, Trench D, fig. 6.2).

Description and interpretation of southern annexe

The western and southern sides of this annexe were first recognized from Ordnance Survey mapping (Jones 2001, fig. 5A). Its excavated eastern side was cut at a tangent to the southeastern corner of the Phase 1B fort (Jones 2005, fig. 9). As so defined, this annexe enclosed a total of 1.23ha. The eastern side of the southern annexe was represented by a series of heavily truncated, flat-based palisade trenches aligned northwest–southeast (F302–F304, Jones 2005, 25 and fig. 9). These measured a maximum of 0.3m in depth and 3.5m in width. A watching brief within the University campus (Area M31, Jones 2025, fig. 6.3) also identified the truncated remains of the eastern ditch of the southern annexe. The relationship between the primary Phase 2A eastern and southern annexe ditches could not be established because of re-cutting (see below) and modern disturbance; the relationship between the annexe and fort ditches could not be established for the same reason. Further to the west the southern annexe defences were formed by a single, heavily truncated ditch (Area M10, Jones 2005, 25 and fig. 14), dug to a V-shaped profile. No internal features could be identified within the small excavated part of the southern annexe interior, which was very heavily truncated by modern disturbance.

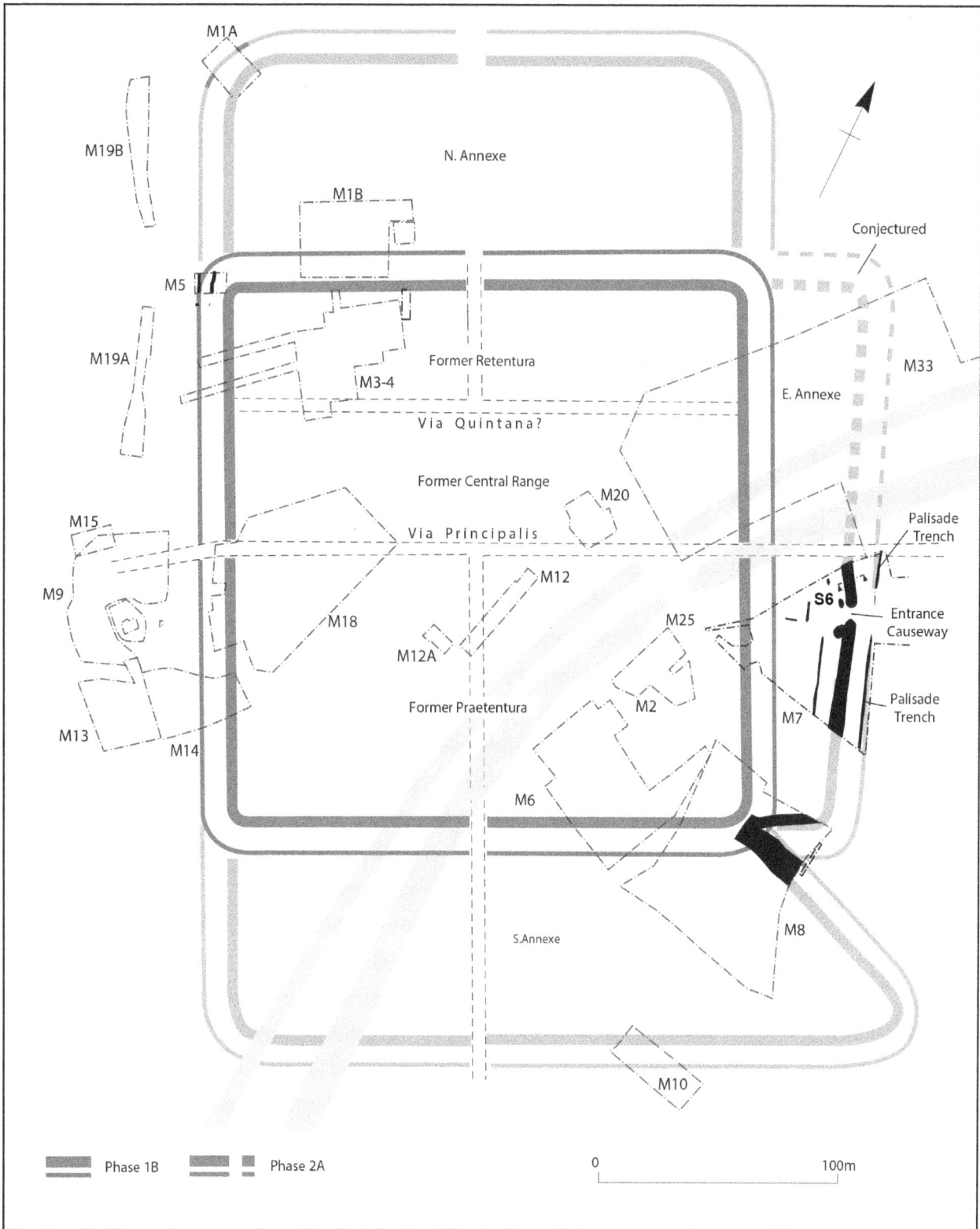

Figure 2.6. Phase 2A northern, eastern, and southern annexes.

Phase 2B military stores depot (later Neronian) (Fig. 2.8)

Five periods associated with the military stores depot have been recognized:

Period 1	Deposition of charcoal-rich destruction deposit
Period 2	Temporary timber-framed buildings
Period 3	Industrial activity
Period 4	Livestock pens within, and to the west of the first fort
Period 5	Clearance of military stores depot interior and backfilling of Phase 1B defences before the first military abandonment of the site

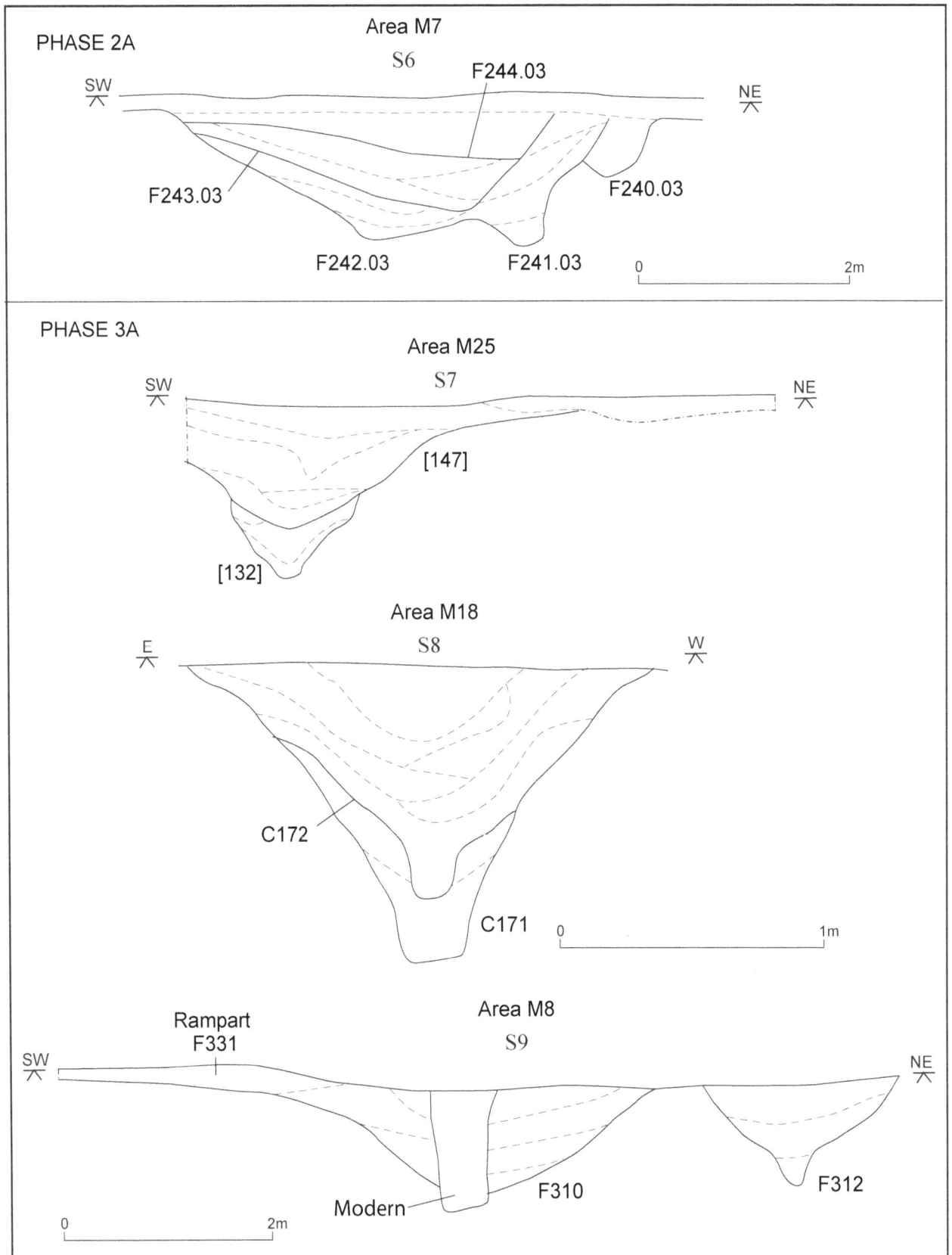

Figure 2.7. Phase 2A eastern annexe and Phase 3A/4A, simplified profiles. Profiles located on Figs 2.6 and 2.13 (S.6); Fig. 2.12 (S.7, S.8); Fig. 2.13 (S.9).

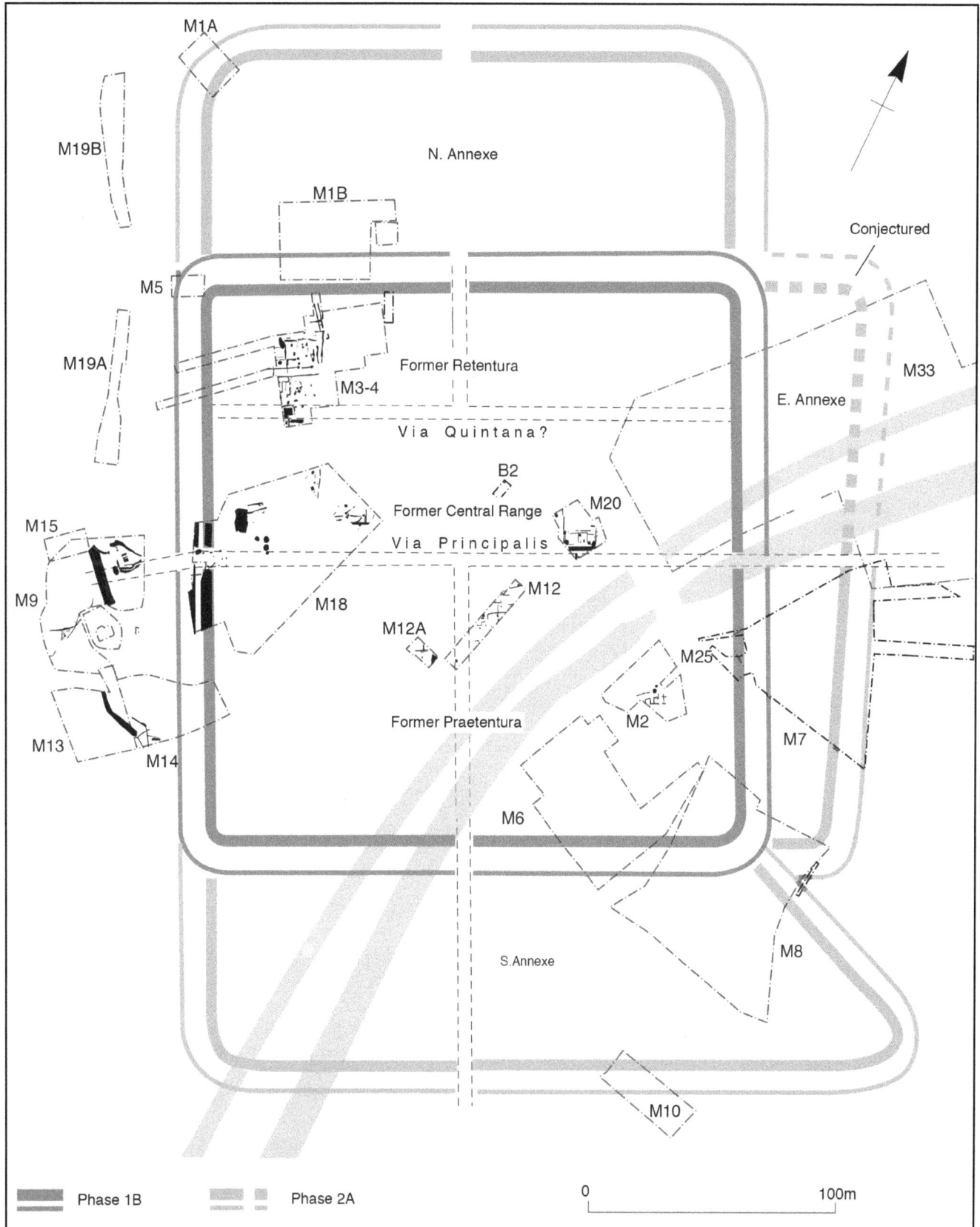

Figure 2.8. Phase 2B, simplified plan of features within and outside military stores depot (also showing Phase 2A annexes).

For simplicity, the military stores depot is described according to the tripartite internal divisions within a garrison fort, although the layout of the military stores depot deviated from the standard military fort layout.

Description and interpretation of Period 1: destruction deposit

The earliest Phase 2B event was the deposition of a charcoal-rich destruction deposit, presumably associated with clearance of the remaining Phase 1D/1E structures. In Area M12 the destruction deposit contained large quantities of charcoal (Gale 2025), indicating the burning of at least one building, whether deliberate or accidental.

Description of Period 2: timber-framed buildings

Summary

The Phase 2B timber-framed buildings were often formed by partial re-excavation along the line of the Phase 1D/1E beam-slots, confirming that these earlier building lines were still visible when the military stores depot was first established, and that demolition of the first fort buildings formed part of the same operation as the layout of the Period 2 buildings, both being undertaken under military control (Jones 2001, 115–17). Later rebuilding is represented by different building alignments, too fragmentary to be interpretable.

Former *retentura* (Fig. 2.9)

Three partly excavated timber-framed buildings were recorded in the former left *retentura* (Areas M3–M4, Fig. 1.3). The northernmost building of this group, Structure 3.6, was represented by two parallel north–south aligned beam-slots (Jones 2001, fig. 17 and 46). Although the plan or use of the building cannot be interpreted, it represented encroachment onto the northern *via sagularis* (the road running inside the fort defences).

To the southwest was Structure 3.5 (Jones 2001, 44–6 and fig. 17), which was irregular in plan. The stepped eastern side of the building, and the eastern ends of its northern and southern sides, were revealed by excavation; the western end of the building lay outside the area excavated. A minimum of five rooms were recorded within its interior. An unusual feature of the building layout was the continuation of two east–west aligned internal divisions for a maximum distance of 12m beyond the eastern wall of the building, possibly defining an eastern 'annexe'.

The southernmost structure was an irregular, incompletely excavated small building or shelter formed by a red clay floor and a misaligned, curving beam-slot, Structure 3.4 (Areas M3–M4, Jones 2001, 44 and fig. 17). The L-shaped clay floor may have constituted the primary build and the misaligned beam-slot a rebuild. The beam-slot was interrupted by an entry-gap. Beam-

slots aligned north–south and east–west containing a number of stake-holes cut along their length were recorded to the south.

Former central range (Fig. 2.10)

Parts of three Phase 2B buildings, Structures 18.9–18.11 (Jones 2012, 40–44, fig. 2.17) were recorded in the left side of the former central range (Area M18, Fig. 1.3). Structure 18.10, in the northwest of the feature group, comprised part of its eastern wall, and a fragment of a joining internal wall. Structure 18.9, to the east, was formed by an interrupted north–south aligned palisade trench. The palisade terminals were flush with a post-hole group to the west which may have been associated. The main Phase 2B structure in this group was the northeastern angle of a building, Structure 18.11 (Jones 2012, fig. 2.17). As excavated, the northern side of the building measured 13m in length, and its eastern side was 2.8m in length. Entry-gaps were recorded along the northern side of the building, and at its northeastern corner. Two adjoining beam-slots were recorded within its interior. The siting of Phase 2B Structures 18.10 and 18.11 appeared to respect the location of at least part of Phase 1E Structure 18.15, the *praetorium*, which continued in use during the early occupation of the military stores depot.

Fragmentary remains of a later episode of Phase 2B building were also represented by a number of scattered beam-slots cut following different alignments within the left side of the former central range (Area M18, Jones 2012, fig. 2.17). These beam-slots following discrepant alignments suggest the continued building of temporary structures after the fort alignment was abandoned.

Parts of three Phase 2B timber-framed buildings were recorded in the right (eastern) side of the former central range (Area M20). The westernmost, Structure 20.2 (Jones 2025, chapter. 3, fig. 3.6), was represented by its eastern wall, which was cut in three, slightly misaligned sections, incorporating at least one entry-gap. It may have adjoined Structure 20.1, the *principia*, which could have remained in use (Fig. 2.4). The largest excavated Phase 2B building, Structure 20.4, was located to the east. The stepped northern side, and the northern ends of the eastern and western sides of the building were recorded. Its southern side lay outside the area excavated. The building was divided into three rooms of unequal size. The southern side of a third building, Structure 20.6, to the north of Structure 20.4, was represented by two offset beam-slots aligned east–west, but modern truncation had scoured-out all other traces of this building.

Former *praetentura* (Fig. 2.11)

Parts of two Phase 2B buildings, Structures 12.4 and 12.3a,b were recorded in the right side of the former *praetentura* (Area M12/M12a, Jones 2025, chapter. 2), adjoining the *via praetoria*. Structure 12.4 comprised red silt-clay-sand floor surfaces measuring 6m × 4.5m, and

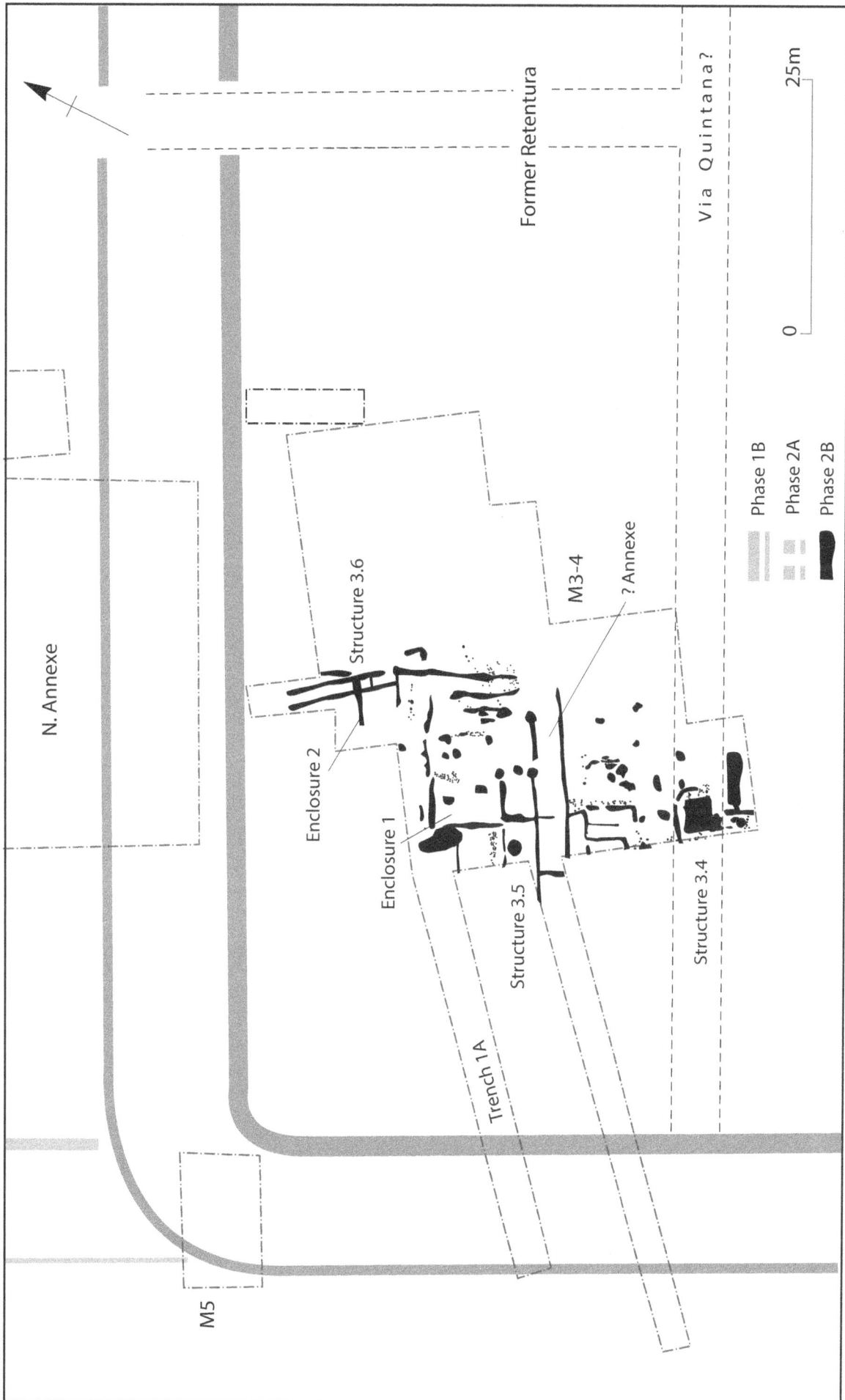

Figure 2.9. Phase 2B, left side of former *retentura*.

N. Annexe

M5

Trench 1A

Structure 3.5

Structure 3.4

Enclosure 1

Enclosure 2

Structure 3.6

M3-4

? Annexe

Former Retentura

Via Quintana?

0 — 25m

Phase 1B

Phase 2A

Phase 2B

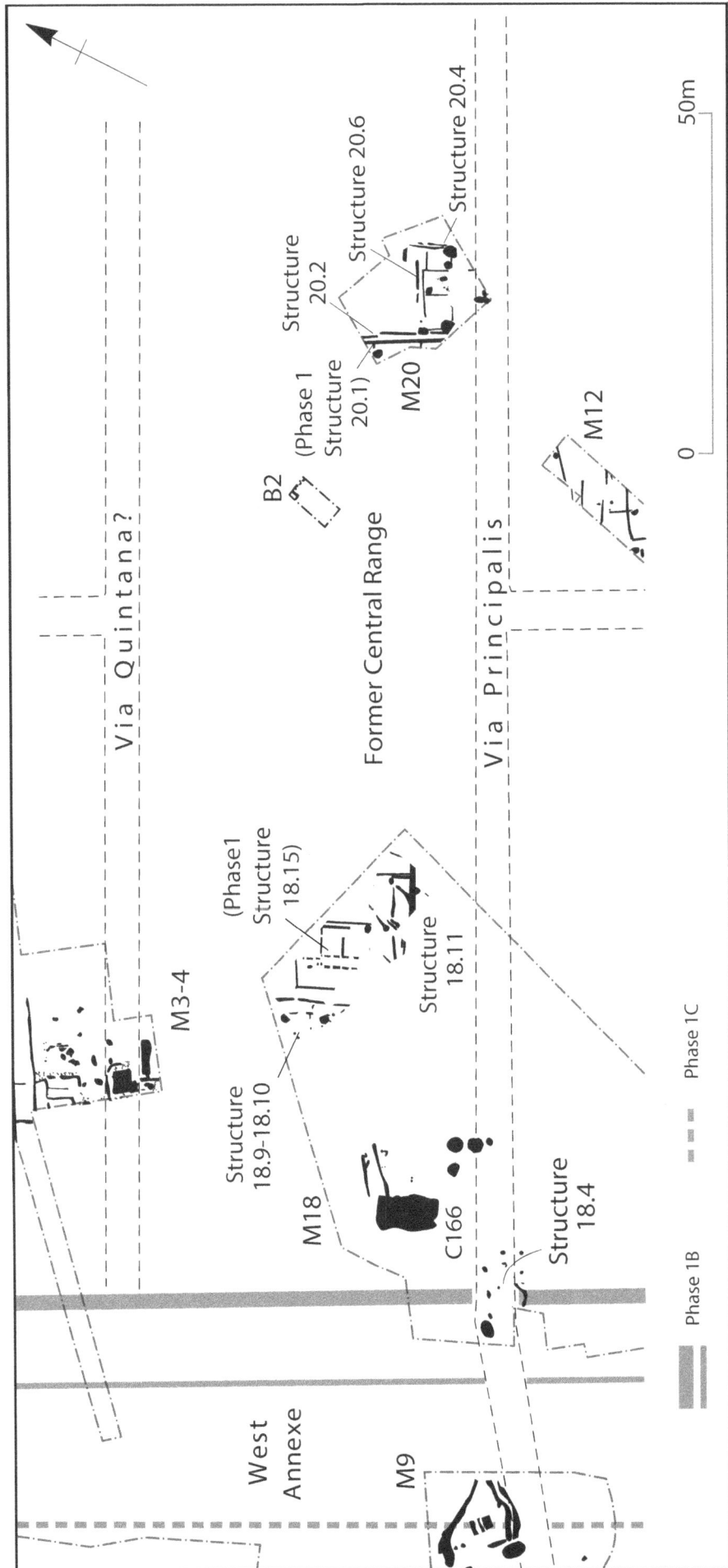

Figure 2.10. Phase 2B, former central range and external features.

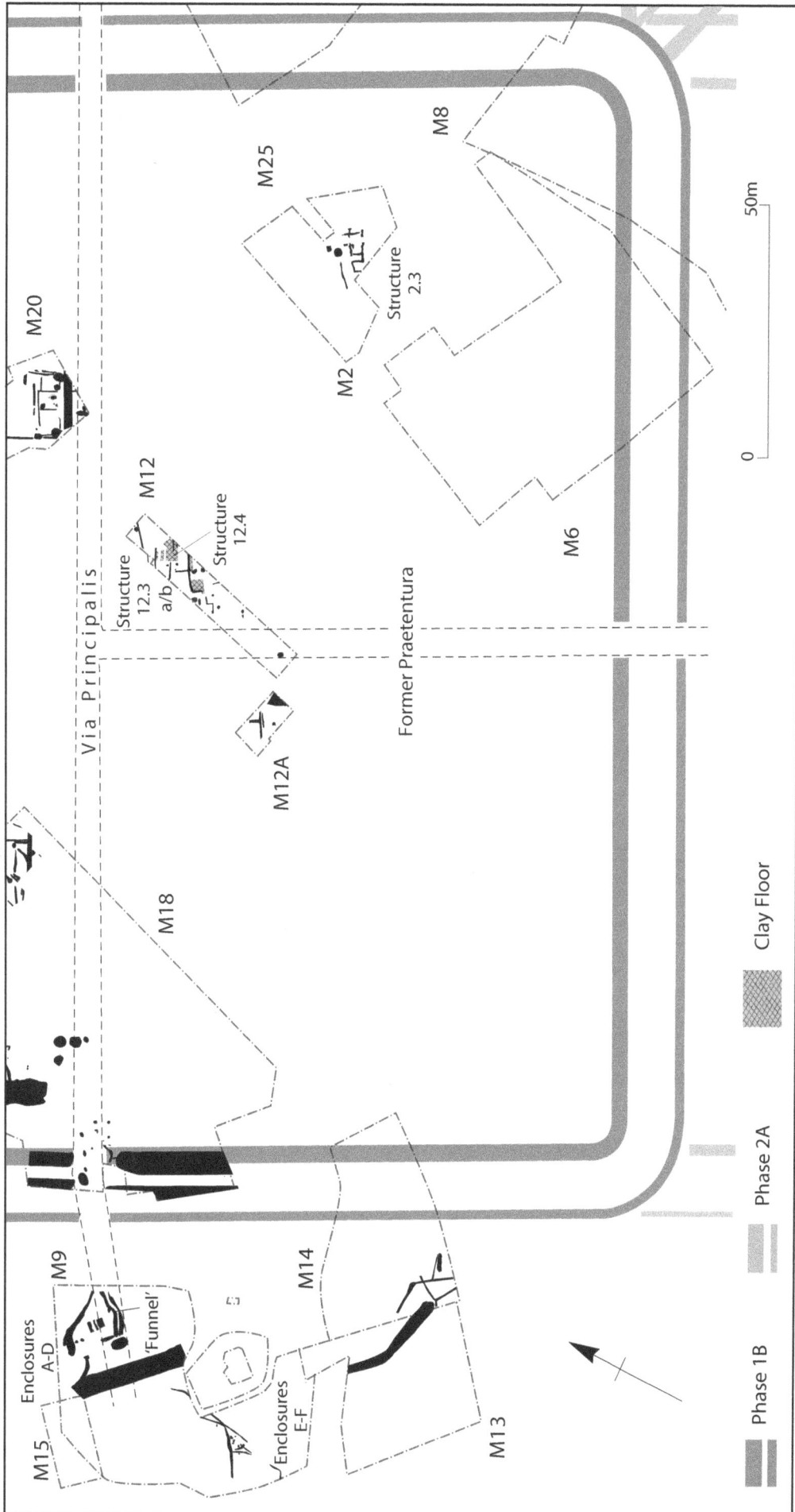

Figure 2.11. Phase 2B, former *praetentura* and external features.

2.5m square. Structure 12.3a,b was the main Phase 2B building recorded here, although its full ground-plan could not be recovered within the area excavated. Its beam-slots cut the clay floor surfaces of Structure 12.4. The western and eastern units measured 3.6m and 15m respectively in length, and the eastern unit measured 11m in width. The two units were separated by a corridor measuring 1m in width. The northern wall of the building was formed by two slightly misaligned beam-slots, their projected point of intersection outside the area excavated. A corridor measuring a minimum of 1.2m wide ran along the northern side of the building. Three rooms were identified within the excavated part of the structure.

Part of an irregular, roughly rectangular Phase 2B building was recorded adjoining the eastern defences in the right side of the former *praetentura* (Area M2). Structure 2.3 (Jones 2001, 48–9 and fig. 18) was defined by irregular beam-slots formed by partial re-excavation along the line of the Phase 1D/1E Structure 2.1 beam-slots. Structure 2.3 measured 4.5m in width, and was recorded for a length of 8m; the eastern and western ends of the building were outside the areas excavated. The building was divided centrally along its axis. Its northern half was mostly undivided, and may have formed a corridor or veranda. Its southern half was divided into a minimum of four rooms.

No Phase 2B features were recorded in Area M6 (Fig. 1.3).

Interpretation of Period 2: timber-framed buildings

Former *retentura*

It is difficult to find military parallels for Structure 3.4. It may have formed a wicker granary, similar to an example from Godmanchester (Green 1975, fig. 7), with a clay floor, and a roof of wicker set in clay, reconstructed a number of times, as is suggested at Metchley by the numerous stake-holes. The beam-slots could have belonged to a rebuild. A second Phase 2B clay-floored building (Structure 12.4) in the former *praetentura* was interpreted as a barn or stable, because of the associated plant remains. It represented encroachment along the suggested line of the *via quintana*, which may have gone out of use.

Structure 3.5 was formed by the partial re-excavation of Phase 1E beam-slots, as at The Lunt (Hobley 1975, 15). This building may be interpreted as a store, its interior subdivided in a cellular pattern, as at Wall (Round 1983, fig. 5), where the excavator interpreted the internal walls as supports for a raised floor. Alternatively, the excavated part of the building could have formed the officers' quarters of a barrack-block, in which case the partial re-use of the earlier wall lines belonging to barracks might be expected (Jones 2001, 51).

Former central range

With the exception of a curvilinear beam-slot, Phase 2B Structures 18.9–18.11 are located outside the footprint of

Phase 1E Structure 18.15. This arrangement suggests that the excavated part of the footprint of the Phase 1E building survived demolition at the end of Phase 1. Although the fragmentary ground-plans of these Phase 2B buildings do not permit their function to be determined, it is possible that they formed a compound associated with the *praetorium*. The recovery of a quantity of high-status Samian pottery (Wild 2012) originally derived from Structure 18.15 from within the backfills of the western *intervallum* pit group C166 (see below) suggests that clearance of the Phase 1E *praetorium* post-dated the disuse of Phase 2B pit C166. By implication, therefore, the pit was contemporary with the later use of the *praetorium*. A less likely alternative is that the Samian found in pit C166 represented material originally disposed of elsewhere at the end of Phase 1E, and used to level up the pit in Phase 2B.

It is more difficult to ascribe a function to the excavated Phase 2B buildings in Area M20. It is notable, again, that elements of all three Area M20 buildings (and Structure 20.2 in particular) appear to respect at least part of their Phase 1D/1E predecessors (as in the *retentura*), although their functions could have been different. One possibility is that Structure 20.4 was the northern end of a barrack-block. If this interpretation was correct, Rooms R1 and R2 could have been *contubernia*, and Room R3 the veranda. This interpretation could fit the offset recorded between the suggested *contubernia* and the veranda – the latter possibly a subsequent addition, as well as the continuation of the possible outer wall of the veranda, B19, also presumably a later addition, which extended beyond the northern side of the building. Structure 20.6 is not interpretable.

The Period 2 building layouts in the former central range suggest that the Phase 1 *praetorium* and *principia* were retained during part of this phase, in contrast to the evidence from the former *retentura* and former *praetentura*, where total clearance of the first fort buildings may be suggested.

Former *praetentura*

Structure 12.4 comprised areas of clay flooring, overlying the Phase 2B destruction deposit. It was not possible to establish the full ground-plan of this structure because of intense later disturbance. The charred plant remains associated with the clay floor suggest that this building was a barn or stable (Ciaraldi 2025).

The layout of Structure 12.3a,b was irregular. The stepped arrangement of the southern (and presumably also the northern) side of this building was similar in plan to the eastern side of contemporary Structure 3.5 (Jones 2001, 51), interpreted as a store building. In the absence of sufficient internal dividing walls to support a raised floor, the same interpretation cannot be suggested for Structure 12.3a,b.

Structure 2.3 was also formed by partial re-excavation along Phase 1D/1E beam-slots. Interpretation of this building is difficult, not least because excavation provided only a partial ground-plan. It is possible that the building was a stable, despite the absence of a drain, which is not always present (Johnson 1983, 178; Frere and Wilkes 1989, 123). Stables were usually long rectangular buildings with space for one or two rows of horses, typically with a passage on one side of the building, possibly represented by the northern half of Structure 2.3. The remainder of the building may have been subdivided into small 'rooms' (e.g. Davison 1989, type R building). An alternative interpretation of the Metchley building could suggest that it accommodated drivers, grooms or store-keepers, living two men per room, although this interpretation of a Strageath building has been questioned (Davison 1989, 160).

Description of Period 3: industrial activity

Former *retentura* (Fig. 2.9)

The third period of Phase 2B activity in the former left *retentura* (Areas M3–M4, Jones 2001, fig. 17 and 46–7) included pits, hearths, and ovens. The arrangement of these features appeared to respect Structure 3.5 (see above), although a single oven was recorded within the interior of the building.

Two groups of industrial features were recorded; to the northeast and southwest of Period 2 Structure 3.5. The northwestern group comprised a total of 11 hearths or ovens which were mostly circular in plan, including ovens backfilled with crushed stone. Most of the hearths were backfilled with red clay. Two were associated with stake-holes which may have defined part of a fence or post-rest. The group of industrial features to the southeast of Structure 3.5 included 13 ovens or hearths. Most were circular in plan, and backfilled with red clay. Other industrial features, constructed wholly above contemporary ground level, were represented by spreads of burnt clay, interpreted as the remains of the collapsed domes of these features.

Former central range (Fig. 2.10)

To the north of the *porta principalis dextra* the timber supports in the rear of the Phase 1B rampart were removed (Jones 2012, fig. 2.3). The rampart was encroached upon by industrial features, although it continued to be maintained along with part of the Phase 1B gatehouse, Structure 18.2, until Period 4.

The largest single Phase 2B feature was a massive rectangular pit, C166 (Jones 2012, 36–9, fig. 2.15), measuring a maximum of 9m north–south × 5.5m east–west. This feature was cut following the fort's north–south alignment. Its western edge truncated the tail of the Phase 1B rampart, and its eastern edge cut the western ditch of the Phase 1B *via sagularis* (the road running around the outside the fort defences, not illustrated). The pit base was irregular, measuring between 0.5m and 0.9m in depth. It contained one post-hole and two stake-holes. Three post-holes cut outside the pit could have been associated. The sequence of pit backfills was complex, including silts flecked with charcoal.

Following the abandonment and backfilling of the pit, three smaller intercutting pits were dug towards its centre. Further ovens were cut along the eastern edge of C166. Other features, including ovens, were cut to the east of pit C166, across the line of the projected Phase 1 *via sagularis*, indicating its disuse. Further to the south was a complex of three large, re-cut pits (Jones 2012, fig. 2.16). An adjoining pit was cut into the northern edge of the projected alignment of the *via principalis*. The precise function of this pit cluster is not clear.

Other Phase 2B industrial features were recorded within the left (western) side of the former central range (Jones 2012, fig. 2.17). Two pits were dug in the area of earlier Phase 2B abandoned Structures 18.9 and 18.10. Three post-holes adjoining a pit could have been associated, perhaps forming a windbreak or shelter. Further to the east, an elongated oven was cut into one of the entry-gaps of Phase 2B Structure 18.11, indicating its abandonment. A further oven was cut within the interior of the building, and a second hearth was cut immediately outside the building. Further evidence of industrial activity towards the centre of the former central range was provided by the spreads of burnt clay recorded in Trench B2 (Jones 2005, 102). These are interpreted as the remains of hearths or ovens built above ground level.

Phase 2B industrial activity was also recorded in the right (eastern) side of the former central range (Area M20). Here, industrial features were cut into the beam-slots of disused earlier Phase 2B Structures 20.2 and 20.4 (Jones 2025, chapter. 3, fig. 3.6). Other pits were cut into the internal divisions of Structure 20.4, confirming their disuse. Other industrial features including pits and possibly associated post-holes and stake-holes were cut within the interiors of the disused buildings, presumably after their abandonment. Two pits located within the interior of disused Structure 20.4 were 'enclosed' by a ring of stake-holes. Further to the south were a group of ovens, characterized by burnt red clay and charcoal backfills, with adjoining stake-holes.

Former *praetentura* (Fig. 2.11)

A pit and two ovens were recorded in the right (eastern) former *praetentura* (Area M2, Jones 2001, 49 and fig. 18). They may have been cut within the interior of disused Phase 2B Structure 2.3 (see above). There was no evidence of Phase 2B industrial activity in the right (eastern) former *praetentura* within Areas M12/M12a and M2.

Interpretation of Period 3: industrial activity

The largest single Phase 2B feature in the former central range was pit C166. The location of this feature, together with the dismantling of the Phase 1B rearward rampart post-pit supports, indicates that the Phase 1 rampart was partly reduced in width during Phase 2B. Lengths of the Phase 1 *via sagularis* will also have gone out of use in this phase.

The function of Phase 2B pit C166 is enigmatic. There was no evidence for the *in situ* burning of its sides. The large quantities of cobbles found within the pit probably relate to an episode of site clearance. The finds from the pit backfills, including ironworking residues, are likely to relate to its secondary use for rubbish disposal and site clearance. The metalworking debris included fragments of hearth bottom, slag, burnt clay, and hammerscale, deriving from smithing, which may have originated from ironworking elsewhere in the Phase 2B military stores depot (Fig. 2.6; e.g. Jones 2001), mixed with general detritus.

The bowl-shaped hearths in the former *retentura* could have been used for primary smithing, which involves heating iron blooms to 900° degrees C (Dool 1986, 174; Bestwick and Cleland 1974, 175). The burnt clay backfills could have originally represented lining material. Other circular bowl-shaped furnaces from Derby similar in morphology to the Metchley examples were interpreted as being used for the secondary forging of iron tools and weapons (Dool 1986, 174–5). The stone-lined pits at Metchley could have been used as smelting furnaces by analogy with similar features found at Manchester (Bestwick and Cleland 1974, 151). A third type of metalworking feature found at Metchley comprises spreads of burnt clay, interpreted as the collapsed remains of domed or shaft furnaces built wholly above ground level, which may have been used for iron smelting, by analogy with excavated parallels from Manchester (Bestwick and Cleland 1974, 145). The stake-holes recorded around a number of features could represent the supports of a turf or clay dome (e.g. Derby, Wheeler 1986, 170), with branches providing support to the domed frames as in pottery kilns (Bestwick and Cleland 1974, 150). Other stake-holes may mark the positions of portable anvil bases or portable bellows, often mounted on a wooden frame with two or more legs (e.g. Derby, Wheeler 1986, 168, 175; Manchester, Jones and Grealey 1974, 67, 148–50).

Description of Period 4: livestock enclosures

Period 4 activity was recorded in the former *retentura* and to the west of the military stores depot.

Within fort interior (Figs 2.9, 2.10)

Parts of two enclosures, Enclosures 1 and 2, defined by wattle fences, and associated features were recorded in the former left *retentura*. These wattle fences were related to Structure 3.5 (see above) which may have remained in use.

The main feature of this period was a four-sided enclosure, Enclosure 1 (Fig. 2.9; Jones 2001, 47, fig. 17), which measured 16m east–west × 18m north–south. It was slightly misaligned with the earlier Phase 2B buildings, although the enclosure was irregular in plan. It included an interrupted 'inner wall' on its northern and eastern sides. Other north–south aligned internal divisions within the enclosure interior, defined by stake-holes, probably formed individual livestock 'pens'. The southeastern angle of a further enclosure, Enclosure 2, was also recorded, cutting Phase 2B Structure 3.6 (see above).

Although no detailed records survive for Area 1A (Fig. 1.3; Jones 2001, pl. XIV), the archive photographs show several scatters of small stake-holes. These may be interpreted as further irregular fence-slots, possibly associated with Period 4.

The Phase 1B *porta principalis dextra* (Area M18, Fig. 1.3) was altered in Period 4 by the insertion of an irregular temporary building, Structure 18.4 (Fig. 2.11; Jones 2012, fig. 2.13). The northern side of the structure was formed by three post-holes or post-pits, positioned at an average separation of 3.5m (measured centre-to-centre), extending up to the northern side of the Phase 1B gatehouse, Structure 18.2 (Fig. 2.4; Jones 2012, figs 2.12, 2.13). The southern side of Structure 18.4 was formed by two pairs of post-holes and a further post-hole, cut inside the line of the gatehouse portal. Two Phase 2B post-holes were cut into the post-pit forming the *spina* of the Phase 1B portal, which continued to be maintained. The implications of this arrangement are twofold. Firstly, its main purpose will have been to 'funnel' livestock from the ditched livestock compounds to the west of the fort. Secondly, it represents a diminution or cessation of other traffic into this gate. The arrangement provides a nexus between the livestock enclosures recorded within the interior of the fort and the similar features located to the west of the defences.

Livestock complex to west of fort (Areas M9, M13, M14, Figs 1.3, 2.11)

Parts of an extensive ditched livestock complex located to the west of the fort, adjoining a natural water supply, have been excavated (Areas M14 and M9, Fig. 1.3, Jones 2011, fig. 2.3). In Area M9 the enclosures were cut into the abandoned remains of the western external settlement.

A funnel-shaped arrangement, formed by a pair of curvilinear palisade trenches, was located adjoining the *porta principalis dextra* to facilitate the driving of livestock into the fort interior. The northernmost trench measured 15m in length, and its southern counterpart measured 10m in length (Jones 2011, 49–53 and fig. 3.7). Both were re-cut. The outer (western) funnel entrance measured 9m in width, narrowing to a width of 1m at its eastern end, which formed a livestock 'crush' (whose eastern limit lay outside the area excavated), positioned flush with the *porta principalis dextra*. An internal gully and three post-holes may have formed part of a gate structure controlling access into the outer end of the 'funnel' (Jones 2011, fig. 3.7). This 'funnel' arrangement forms a nexus between the livestock enclosures to the west of the fort and the similar features recorded within the fort interior. The arrangement of the enclosure C ditches in particular suggests they were part of the same layout as the livestock 'funnel', although other enclosures could also have formed part of this arrangement.

The main feature in Areas M13 and M14 was the southwestern corner of a ditched enclosure (Jones 2011, 20 and fig. 2.7) represented by a primary ditch, and two re-cuts. Its alignment suggests that it may have joined the southwestern corner of the fort. The ditch profiles were relatively unweathered, suggesting rapid backfilling. An entry-gap was further defined by three successive layouts of fence-slots cut across it, used for livestock 'sorting'.

The ditched enclosures (A–D) in Area M9 comprised a primary ditch and three re-cuts, dug approximately parallel to the fort's western defences (Jones 2011, 49–53 and fig. 3.7), adjoining the *porta principalis dextra*. None of the enclosure ditch profiles suggests a defensive function – particularly those cut to flat-based profiles. The enclosure D ditches were interrupted by an entrance-gap measuring 8.5m in width. To the west were two successive livestock pens, possibly hexagonal in plan, enclosures E and F, defined by shallow palisade trenches cut in straight sections, with changes in angle. The entrance to enclosure F was further defined by an arrangement of fence-slots and post-holes used for livestock 'sorting', forming part of the Period 4 military stores depot.

Interpretation of Period 4: livestock enclosures

Phase 2B Structure 18.4 may have formed a livestock 'funnel', which adjoined the western side of the Phase 1B gatehouse, Structure 18.2, used to 'drive' livestock into the fort interior. The eastern end of the Phase 2B arrangement related to the earlier gatehouse, which continued in use. Structure 18.4 is likely to have functioned as an integral part of the livestock 'funnel' located 20m to the west (Fig. 2.14; Area M9, Jones 2011, fig. 3.7). The closest parallel for the 'funnel' is a similar arrangement at Elginhaugh (Hanson 2007, 652), where ditches crossing an annexe were intended to 'funnel' movement along a road and through a gateway into the outer part of the annexe. At Elginhaugh, this activity marks the reuse of the site for livestock requisition by the military, after the abandonment of the garrison fort. At Metchley the 'funnel' is interpreted as part of Period 4 in the use of the military stores depot.

Outside the fort defences this phase is also represented by the abandonment of the small-scale western settlement, and its replacement with several enclosures set within a stockyard, located on the western side of the fort to take advantage of the water supply provided by an adjoining stream (Fig. 1.3). The main livestock features here were a series of roughly north–south aligned ditches, defining four successive enclosures (A–D), mostly cut to flat-based or irregular profiles, suggesting that defence was not their primary function. These ditches could have defined one side of livestock enclosures which adjoined the western side of the fort. Two further enclosures (E and F) may have represented subdivisions (e.g. Orton Hall Farm, Peterborough, Mackreth 1996), within their interior.

Description and interpretation of Period 5: clearance of military stores depot interior and backfilling of Phase 1B defences

In the former left *retentura* and former right *praetentura*, the remains of Period 4 were sealed by a layer of dark brown soil, flecked with charcoal, and containing fragments of burnt clay and daub, recorded beneath the western Phase 3A rampart (Jones 2001, 47, 49).

The Phase 1B fort ditches were partly backfilled in Period 5, prior to the first Roman military abandonment of the site. The Period 5 backfills comprised sand-silts which accumulated after the ditch ceased to be kept clean, overlain by a destruction deposit including burnt clay and daub, sealed by sand. The burnt clay may have derived from Period 3 activity, although the ditches (and *porta principalis dextra*) continued to be maintained during Period 4.

Phase 3: Second fort (early Flavian)

Phase 3A

Description of Phase 3A fort defences (Figs 2.7, 2.12)

The Phase 3A fort measured 165m (north–south) × 150m (east–west), an area of 2.47ha. It was defended by a single ditch (Table 2.2) and a turf rampart, partly re-built with a timber revetment. The full profile of the Phase 3A ditch (Fig. 2.7.S.7, 2.7.S.8) was not recorded because of re-cutting (Phase 4A, see below). The innermost Phase 1B ditch was also re-cut in Phase 3A, to provide additional defence along the northern (Jones 2001, 60) and eastern (Jones 2005, 30) defences. One fort entrance, the *porta principalis dextra* was fully investigated (Jones 2012, 48–51); part of a second, the *porta decumana* was excavated by Webster (1954) and Rowley (Jones 2001).

Along the western defences to the south of the *porta principalis dextra* the primary rampart was of turf construction, measuring a maximum of 5.8m in width and 0.4m in height (Jones 2012, figs 2.19, 2.20). The secondary build of the western rampart involved the insertion of a frontal timber revetment, formed by post-pits 2.1m apart (Jones 2001, 56, fig. 19).

The *porta principalis dextra* measured 10m in width. A gatehouse, Structure 18.16 (Jones 2012, fig. 2.19), measuring 7m by 4.2m internally was recorded to the north of the *via principalis*, but no corresponding guard chamber could be located to the south of this road. A fragment of a north–south beam-slot, P113 (not illustrated), to the south of the *via principalis* was positioned flush with the western side of Structure 18.16, but on its own it is not sufficient evidence to deduce the existence of a southern guard chamber (Jones 2012, fig. 2.22.S.74).

Two post-pits, dug at a separation of 2.85m apart to the rear of the western rampart defences, defined the rearward

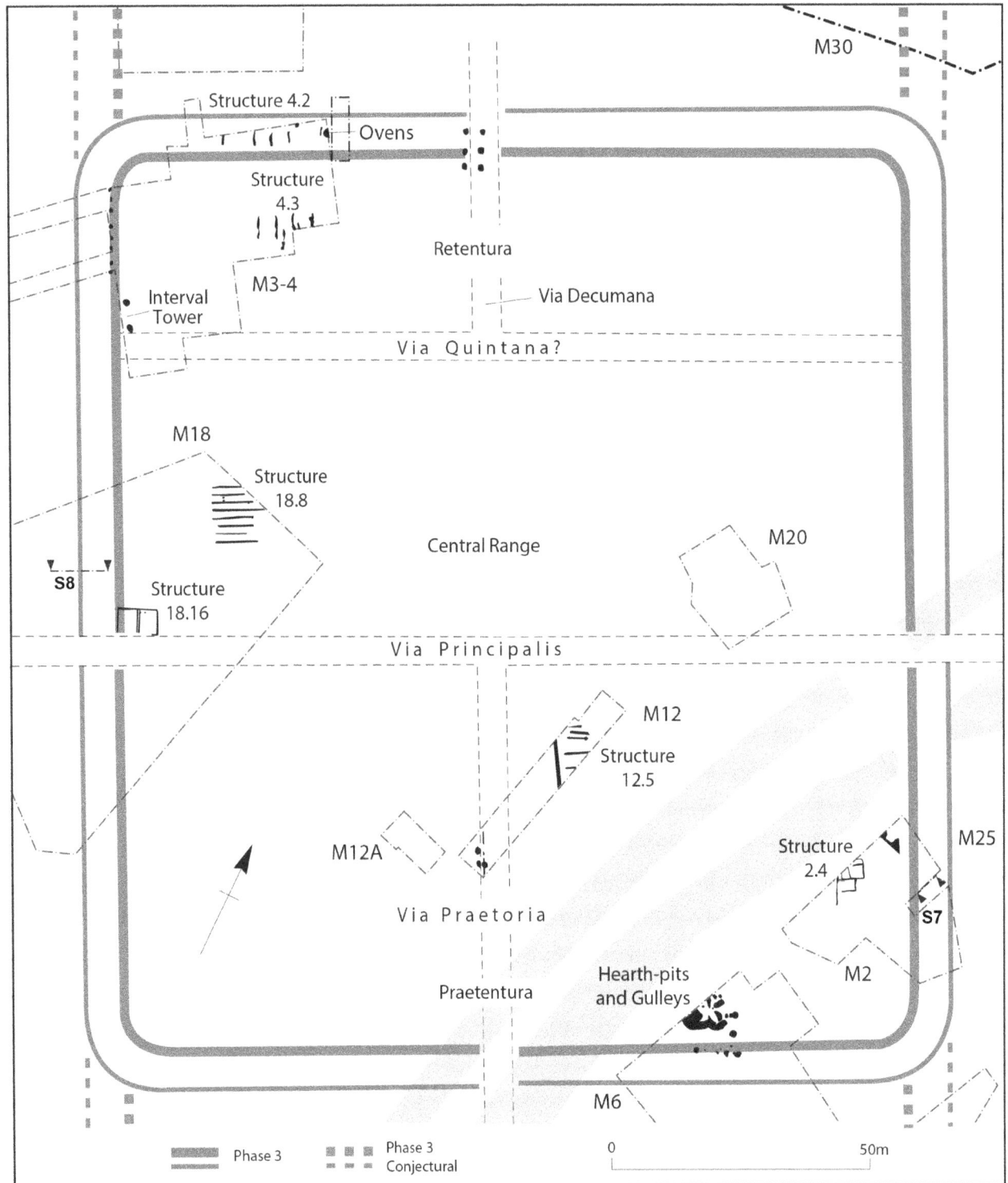

Figure 2.12. Phase 3A, simplified plan of defences and internal buildings.

Table 2.2. Phase 3A defences, details.

Area	Fig.	Ditch	Rampart
M18	Fig. 2.7.S.8, C171	2.4m × 0.6m	Turf: 5.8m × 0.4m: inserted post-holes
M3–M4	19 (Jones 2001)	3.8m × 1.2m	Decayed turf: 5.5m × 0.4m
St J and S 1937	–	3–3.6m × 1.35–1.5m	Turf: courses 0.15m thick
M2/M25	Fig. 2.7.S.7, [132]	4m × 1.2m	Turf 3.3 × 0.1; timber revetment
M6	10 and 16 (Jones 2005)	4.25m × 1.5m	–

For section locations, see Fig. 2.12.

uprights of a square interval tower (Jones 2001, 59, fig. 19) – the only such Phase 3A feature to be identified at Metchley.

Adjoining the northwestern corner of the defences and along the northern defences, the turf rampart was anchored by a group of closely set tapering stakes, driven into the subsoil, surviving as organic stains (Jones 2001, 56, fig. 20, Area M3C; 60).

The northern turf rampart measured a maximum of 5.5m in width and 0.45m in depth. An arrangement of five parallel north–south aligned beam-slots, Structure 4.2 (Jones 2001, 60, fig. 19), was recorded for a length of 20m. The beam-slots each measured approximately 3m in length. The beam-slots were positioned symmetrically; the innermost three were dug at a separation of 3m, and the outermost were dug at a distance of 6m from the outer pair of the innermost group. This structure provided a rearward support to the northern rampart.

Webster (1954) and Rowley (Jones 2001, 60, fig. 21) examined part of the *porta decumana* (Jones 2012, fig. 2.23). Its excavated western half contained a rectangular arrangement of six post-pits comprising two rows 3m apart (measured centre-to-centre), each containing three post-pits. The excavated post-pits defined a western guard chamber.

St Joseph and Shotton (1937, 75) recorded courses of laid turf each 0.15m thick along part of the eastern rampart, which comprised an earthen bank with a frontal turf revetment along other parts of its eastern side. Towards the southern end of this side the rampart measured a maximum of 3.3m in width and 0.1m in height (Area M2). The primary turf rampart was cut back for the insertion of a box rampart. This comprised post-pits measuring an average of 0.4m in diameter, braced in a triangular arrangement, alternating between examples facing inwards and outwards (Jones 2001, 62 and fig. 18), also recorded along part of the southern defences (Jones 2001, fig. 16).

No trace of the southern fort turf rampart could be recorded because of modern truncation.

Interpretation of Phase 3A fort defences

Structure 18.16 may be interpreted as the northern gatehouse of the *porta principalis dextra*, even in the absence of clear evidence for a corresponding southern guard chamber. Accordingly, like the Phase 1B *porta principalis dextra*, this Phase 3A entrance may have been designed from the outset to provide limited accommodation. Excavation provided no details of the contemporary gate-structure, presumably because of later Roman and modern disturbances. The western guard chamber of the *porta decumana* (Webster 1954; Jones 2012, fig. 2.23) comprised six post-pits arranged in two rows of three post-pits. It may correspond with a single-portalled 12-post type with flanking towers (as at Fendoch, Bidwell et al. 1988, fig. 2.21).

The Phase 3A ditch (Fig. 2.7.S7, S.8) lay towards the lower end of the size range of 3.7–4.9m in width and 1.2–2.7m in depth (Jones 1975, 106), for single-ditched systems, although the Phase 3A defences were reinforced by re-cutting of the innermost Phase 1B ditch. Measuring 5.5m wide, the Metchley rampart was also at the lower end of the size range for turf-revetted ramparts of 5.5–7.6m. The eastern box rampart was also slightly narrower than the average for ramparts of this type (Jones 1975, 70).

The use of timber stakes for rampart foundation is unusual, although paralleled at Valkenburg (Glasbergen 1972). It is better known in a civilian defensive context, notably at Alcester, Warwickshire (Mahany 1994, pl. 11, fig. 106).

Structure 4.2 is paralleled by a similar structure at Valkenburg (Jones 1975, fig. 4), suggesting that the timbers of the Metchley structure may have been jointed at 45° to the timber rampart tail supports. At Wall, Staffordshire (Lyon and Gould 1960, 12), a disturbance in the subsoil to the rear of the rampart was interpreted as evidence of a similar structure.

Description of Phase 3A fort internal features (Fig. 2.12)

With one exception (Structure 2.4) the Phase 3A buildings comprised granaries that may have been more deeply founded than other contemporary building types, which may not have survived later truncation. The Phase 3A fort may also have fulfilled a specialist function in grain supply.

Retentura

One rectangular granary, Structure 4.3 (Jones 2001, 66 and fig. 19), was recorded in the left *retentura*. It measured approximately 8m east–west × 3.5m north–south. It was defined by four, or possibly five, north–south aligned beam-slots, four dug 3.5m apart. Other contemporary features in the left *retentura* comprised ovens cut into the tail of the northern rampart (Jones 2001, 67 and fig. 19). These often adjoin barrack-blocks (e.g. Elginhaugh, Hanson 2007, fig. 12.3), although none belonging to this phase were found at Metchley.

Central range

A second granary, Structure 18.8 (Area M18; Jones 2012, 51–3, figs 2.19 and 2.24), was the only Phase 3A structure located within the left side of the central range. It adjoined the northern *via principalis* frontage. It comprised eight parallel, east–west aligned beam-slots, positioned at a separation of 1.5m. The building measured a maximum of 10m east–west and 11m north–south.

Praetentura

Part of a third Phase 3A granary, Structure 12.5 (Jones 2025, chapter. 2, fig. 2.7) was recorded adjoining the eastern *via praetoria* frontage in the right (eastern) side of the *praetentura*. It comprised five parallel, irregularly spaced beam-slots aligned east–west. As excavated, the building measured a maximum of 8.5m north–south × 5.5m east–west, but its full extent could not be recorded. The beam-slots were positioned at an irregular separation of 1.1–3m (measured centre-to-centre). It may be interpreted as a granary despite the irregular positioning of the beam-slots. The close spacing of beam-slots in the northern excavated part of the building could represent a later strengthening. The northernmost beam-slot (Jones 2025, chapter. 2, fig. 2.7) was backfilled with charcoal, perhaps suggesting burning of the beam *in situ*, either accidentally or as part of the clearance process.

To the west of the building was a north–south aligned ditch, with which it was slightly misaligned. The *via praetoria* was also resurfaced in this phase, and ditches were cut on both sides of the resurfaced road. Other contemporary features comprised pits, dug along the western *via praetoria* frontage (Jones 2025, chapter. 2).

A second building was recorded in the right side of the *praetentura* (Area M2, Fig. 1.3), Structure 2.4 (Jones 2001, 67–8 and fig. 18), aligned north–south. It adjoined the eastern rampart. As excavated, the building measured 8m north–south × 5m east–west. The northern side of the building lay outside the area excavated. The interior of the building was divided into five rooms. Possible corridors were recorded along the northern and western sides. One room contained a hearth built on a foundation of cobbles, and a second hearth immediately adjoined the eastern wall of the building. A third hearth cut an internal beam-slot. This building is interpreted as a cookhouse.

The southern *intervallum* in the right (eastern) *praetentura* (Area M6, Jones 2001, fig. 68–70) contained the truncated remains of a number of sub-oval hearth-pits and gullies.

Interpretation of Phase 3A fort internal features (Fig. 2.12)

Three of the four Phase 3A buildings were arranged *per strigas* (north–south), with only Structure 4.3 being aligned *per scamna*. Of the only four Phase 3A buildings identified by excavation within the entire Phase 3A fort, three comprise granaries (Structures 4.3, 18.8, 12.5), the other a possible cookhouse (Structure 2.4).

Usually, granaries were located in the central range, adjoining the *principia* (Johnson 1983, 142), close to a gate, to simplify the loading/unloading of grain, for example Structures 3.2 (Phase 1D/1E) and Phase 3A Structure 18.8 at Metchley. Often granaries are located on the opposite side of the central range to the *praetorium* (Burnham and Davies 2010, 80), which could suggest that the Phase 3A

praetorium at Metchley was located on the right (eastern) side of the central range (an area where Phase 3A features did not survive later truncation).

Although no direct correlation can be made between the size of the Phase 3A Metchley granaries and the overall strength of the garrison, it is notable that all the granaries of this late phase are small (Jones 2012, fig. 2.24). Johnson (1983) notes that timber-framed granaries measured an average of 20–30m in length × 6–10m in width, although smaller examples do occur. Five granaries at Usk each measured 21m × 7.5m (Manning 1981, 140–161).

Description and interpretation of Phase 3A annexes (Figs 1.3, 2.12 and 2.13)

The Phase 2A eastern annexe ditch was re-cut in Phase 3A (Fig. 2.7.S.6, F241.03; Jones 2005, 30 and figs 17, 18), slightly to the west of the earlier ditch. The Phase 3A re-cut ditch along the eastern side of the eastern annexe appeared to be slightly curvilinear in plan, although its alignment was obscured by later re-cutting. A few ovens within the annexe interior were probably contemporary with this re-cut (Jones 2005, 38).

During this phase, double-ditched annexes were probably redug to the south and north of the fort. The eastern side of the Phase 3A southern annexe was defended by double ditches (Fig. 2.7.S.9; Jones 2005, 32) and a turf rampart (F331). The eastern side of the northern annexe was defined by double ditches (not excavated, Area M30, Jones 2025, fig. 6.1). Neither of these double ditches could be stratigraphically related to the fort defences, but their alignment formed a continuation of the line of the eastern Phase 3A fort defences. It is not known how far these annexes extended beyond the Phase 3A defensive perimeter.

Phase 3B–4B (Flavian +, Figs 2.13, 2.14)

During this phase, the fort interior and an area to the west were used for livestock. The area immediately outside the *porta principalis dextra* (Area M18) provided the only evidence for unenclosed external activity associated with the Phase 3A fort, which may also have continued into Phase 4A (see below). Areas outside the other Phase 3A fort gates have not been investigated.

Description of the rearrangement of the former porta principalis dextra

Phase 3A gatehouse Structure 18.16 was replaced by successive Phase 3B–4B rearrangements within the *porta principalis dextra*. The first rebuild (Jones 2012, fig. 2.26), measured approximately 5m square (Structure 18.6). Its northern side, defined by post-pits and cut into the south wall of abandoned Phase 3A Structure 18.16, was flush with the southern terminal of Phase 3A ditch P123. The remainder of Structure 18.6 was formed by post-holes. Traces of a possible rebuild were also recorded.

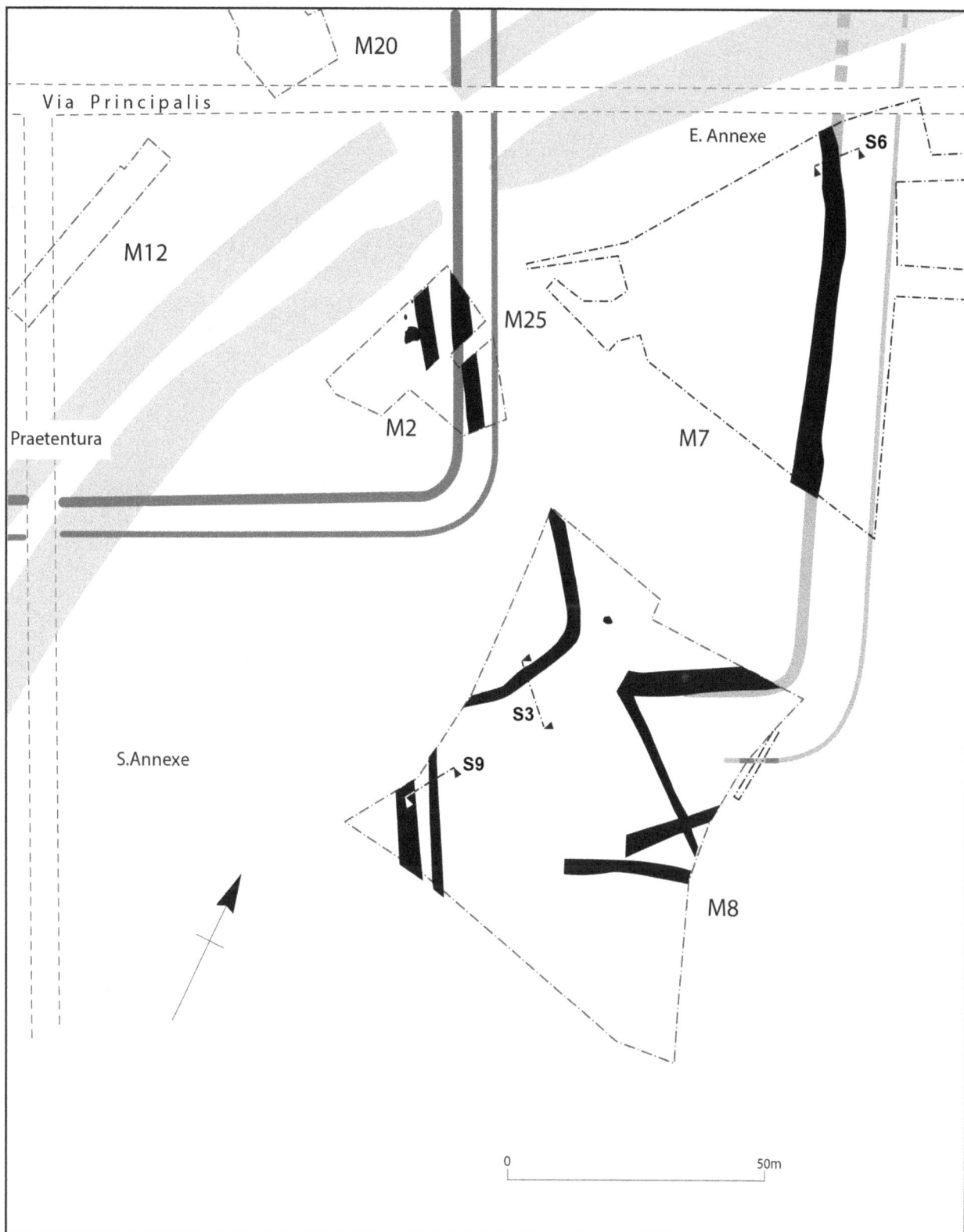

Figure 2.13. Phase 3A eastern annexe and Phase 3B–4B, external activity: southeast of complex.

The rebuilt Structure 18.6 was in turn replaced by a larger, L-shaped building, Structure 18.5 (Jones 2012, fig. 2.26) cut across the entranceway. This building was defined by shallow, irregular palisade trenches which may have retained wattle fences. It measured 9.7m × 6m. Its western side probably abutted the terminal of the Phase 3A western ditch P123. The northern and eastern sides of this building may have been open, although a fragment of the eastern side of the building was recorded adjoining its southeastern corner. This building formed an integral part of an arrangement of palisade trenches recorded to both the north and the south of the Phase 3A fort entrance, associated to the west of the entrance with a series of enclosures (see below).

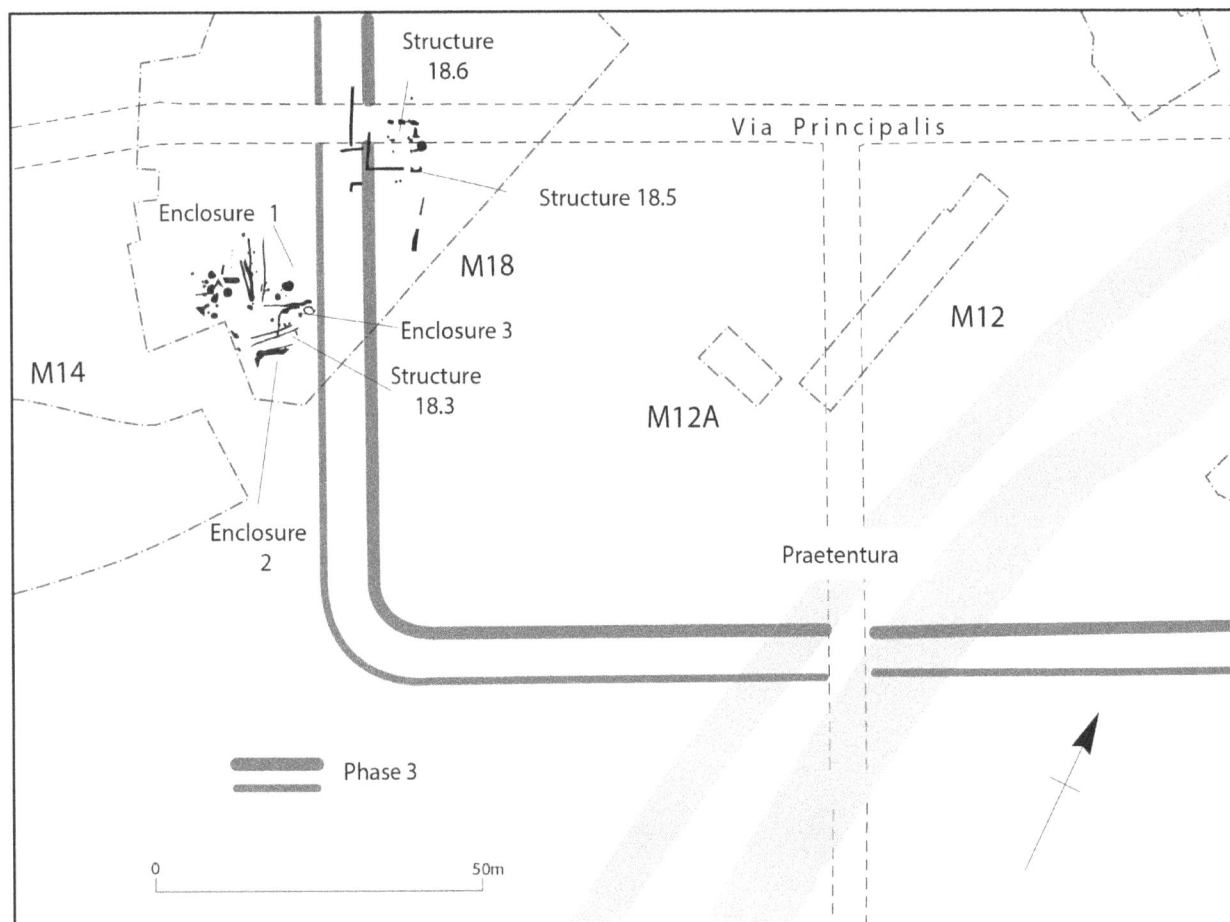

Figure 2.14. Phase 3B–4B, external activity: southwest of complex.

Interpretation of Phase 3B–4B entrance features

During this phase there were two successive rearrangements of the Phase 3A *porta principalis dextra*. In the first, undertaken within a military context, the Phase 3A northern gatehouse went out of use, and was replaced by a smaller, perhaps temporary building, Structure 18.6. Although full details of the arrangement were irrecoverable because of later disturbance, in part it resembles the arrangement of post-pits at the *porta decumana* excavated by Webster (1954; Jones 2012, fig. 2.23). The drainage gully located by Webster at this entrance could be reinterpreted as part of a similar arrangement to Structure 18.5, although only one side of this structure was excavated by Webster.

The later Phase 3B–4B re-arrangement, Structure 18.5 will not have been defensive in function, although it was positioned to 'control' the entrance-way, together with the ditches and rampart which will have been retained. In association with the external livestock enclosure palisade trenches (see below), it functioned as a 'stock-control system'.

Description of external features

A number of hearths and ovens were recorded to the west of the Phase 3A fort defences (Jones 2012, fig. 2.28), including examples associated with oval firing chambers.

This feature group was backfilled with charcoal and fragments of burnt clay.

The most coherent remains outside the Phase 3A fort comprised three livestock enclosures (Enclosures 1–3, Jones 2012, fig. 2.28), laid out following the north–south fort alignment. They were defined by palisade trenches and fence-lines, cut through the Phase 3B–4B industrial features and into the subsoil. Enclosure 1, to the southwest of the fort entrance-way was rectangular in plan, measuring a maximum of 20m north–south × 8m east–west. Its eastern side was cut into the western edge of the partly backfilled western fort ditch. Parts of its eastern, southern, and western sides were defined. A narrow entrance was recorded at its southeastern corner, and a further entrance may be inferred at its northeastern corner, adjoining an L-shaped palisade trench. To the west of the enclosure was a north–south aligned palisade trench which defined the western side of a droveway.

Fragments of two further enclosures, Enclosures 2–3, were also recorded. The extreme northwestern corners of Enclosures 2 and 3 were recorded. The Enclosure 3 palisade trench was cut into the backfilled southern Enclosure 1 palisade trench. The Enclosure 3 palisade trenches incorporated an entry-gap, 0.75m wide.

Other palisade trenches following different alignments, along with other external features, probably form part of a later sub-phase of activity. These features may have been contemporary with the layout of a timber-framed building, Structure 18.3 (Jones 2012, fig. 2.28) to the west of the Phase 3A fort defences. This structure was notably misaligned with the western fort defences, and also with Enclosures 1–3. It may have been one of the later features of this phase outside the Phase 3A fort perimeter. The Structure 18.3 beam-slots were cut into the abandoned Enclosure 3 palisade trench. The beam-slots forming this structure were irregular in plan and profile, suggesting hurried construction, or that it was a temporary structure only. It was defined by three parallel, roughly east–west aligned beam-slots. The excavated part of the building measured 9m east–west × 5m north–south. This latest episode of activity included a number of industrial features cutting the palisaded enclosures. Also recorded were a number of stone surfaces forming temporary areas of hardstanding (Jones 2012, fig. 2.28), comprising the latest activity outside the western fort perimeter (not illustrated).

Interpretation of external features

The external features identified in Area M18 provide the only evidence for undefended activity outside the Phase 3A fort perimeter. External activity will have been constrained by the continued use of the eastern annexe.

Some of the earliest features may be pits used for an industrial function, perhaps ironworking. A number of these pits were cut by the Enclosure 1–3 palisade trenches. The L-shaped palisade trench arrangement in the entrance-way, also probably forming part of Enclosure 1, suggests that the Phase 3A entrance-way remained in use. The siting of entry-gaps at the southeastern and possibly the northeastern corners of Enclosure 1 supports its interpretation as a livestock enclosure.

Subsequent activity is represented by palisade trenches following different alignments, presumably after abandonment of the 'planned' layout. Equally, Structure 18.3, which was laid out at a slight tangent to the fort alignment, represents later Phase 3B–4B activity for the same reason. The function of this building is unknown.

By analogy with the evidence from Elginhaugh (Hanson 2007, 650), this external activity could represent the occasional use of the site for the military supply of livestock, perhaps on a seasonal basis. It need not be interpreted purely as evidence of Roman civilian occupation, in particular because many of the external features (although not all) continued to respect the military alignment and western fort entrance.

Some industrial features were cut into backfilled palisade trenches, including some which did not follow the predominant fort alignment. The latest episode of activity was represented by the layout of extensive pebble and cobble surfaces, overlying the abandoned remains of livestock enclosures and other features. These are interpreted as hardstandings.

Phase 4: Later military/post-military activity (later Flavian–end of 2nd century) (Fig. 2.15)

Description and interpretation of Phase 4A features

This phase is represented by the re-cutting of the Phase 3A fort ditch, and by external features. No contemporary internal features could be recorded.

The Phase 4A ditch re-cuts on either side of the *porta principalis dextra* were separated by an entry-gap measuring 10m in width. To the south of the entrance the re-cut measured a maximum of 2.9m in width and 1.5m in depth, mostly V-shaped in profile (Jones 2012, figs 2.19–2.21). To the north of the entrance (where modern truncation was more severe), the re-cut was dug to a maximum width of 1.9m and a depth of 0.9m. In the northernmost excavated segment (Jones 2012, fig. 2.21.S.68), the ditch base was backfilled with alternating deposits comprising rampart material and deposits of clay-sand.

A Phase 4A re-cut was recorded along the eastern Phase 3A defences (Area M25, Jones 2025, chapter. 4, fig. 4.3.S.4). It was dug to a V-shaped profile, and measured a maximum of 3.4m in width and 0.9m in depth.

During Phase 4A the eastern annexe ditch was repeatedly re-cut (Jones 2005, 39–42 and fig. 18). Although no entry-gap was recorded, a bridge structure may have been built. The third and fourth re-cuts were distinguished from the earlier re-cuts by their distinctive flat-based profile, with gently sloping sides (Fig. 2.7.S.6, F243.01, F244.01) – clearly not a defensive feature. Later, a dump of coarse gravel may have provided a causeway across the eastern annexe ditch.

Also recorded in Area M8 (Jones 2005, fig. 18) were a number of short lengths of ditches following different alignments, cut with Punic profiles (Fig. 2.15). These features may be interpreted as practice ditches.

Description and interpretation of Phase 4C features (Fig. 2.15)

This phase represents the earliest post-Roman military activity at the complex, dating to the later Roman or post-Roman periods.

A three-sided ditched enclosure, Enclosure 3 (Jones 2001, 67 and fig. 19), was recorded in the northwestern corner of the Phase 3A fort interior. It measured 22m north–south and 27m east–west. Its curvilinear northwestern angle respected the line of the Phase 3A rampart. The enclosure ditch was cut to a U-shaped profile, measuring an average of 0.7m in width and 0.2m in depth. No ditch was recorded along the southern side of the enclosure, which could have been open or marked by a fence, leaving no trace at excavation. No associated features could be identified. A zone of possible later civilian occupation was also recorded in Area M5 (Jones 2001, 70–71), then interpreted to later Phase 3.

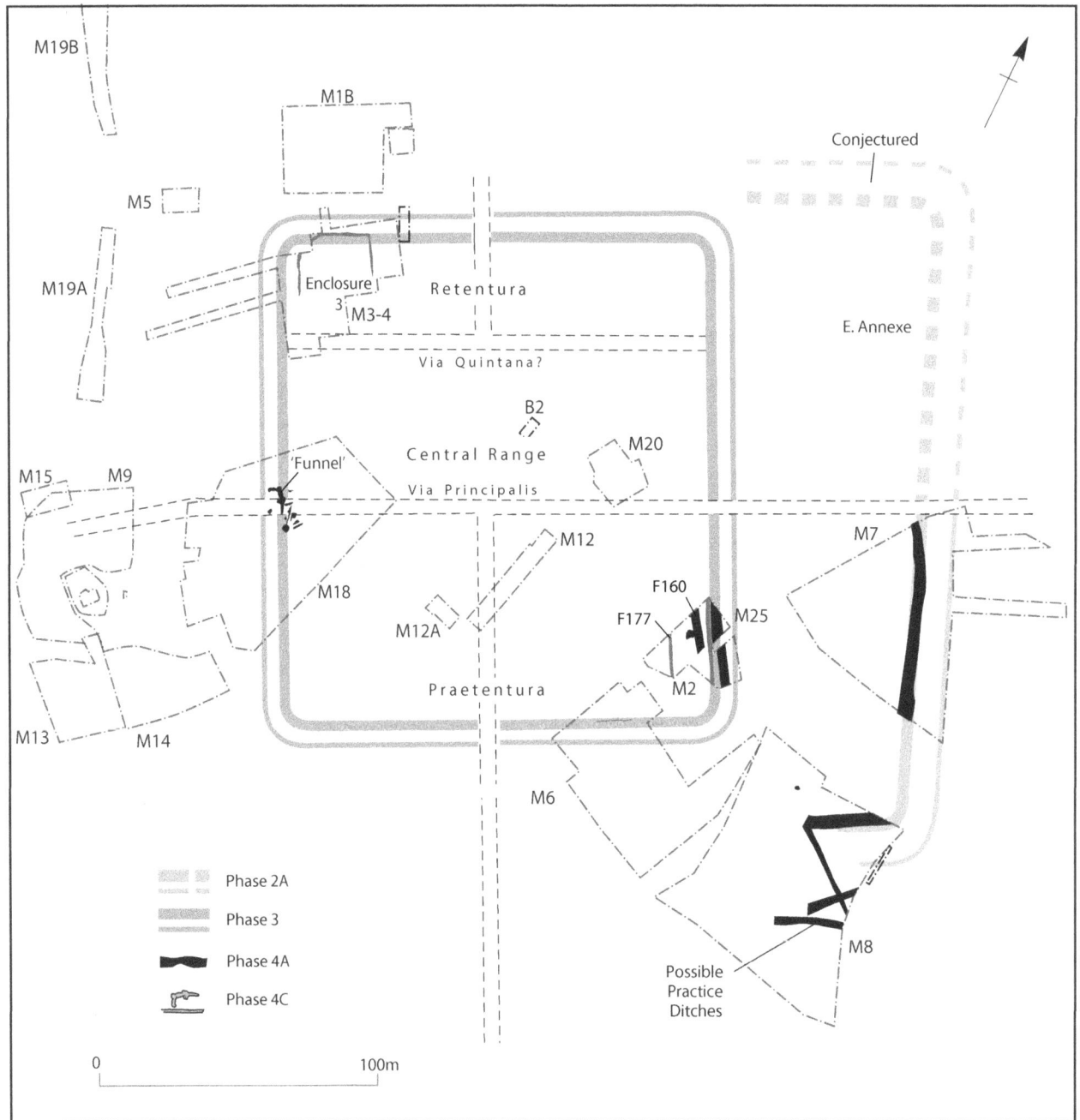

Figure 2.15. Phases 4A and 4C, main features.

The former *porta principalis dextra* was partially blocked (Jones 2012, fig. 2.30) by two ditches and other features, together approximately forming an L-shape in plan. The purpose of this 'blocking' was to funnel livestock into the fort interior between the fort ditch terminals.

Two roughly parallel, north–south aligned ditches were recorded in the right (eastern) *praetentura* of the Phase 3A fort (F160, F177: Jones 2001, 68 and fig. 18; Area M2, Fig. 2.15). The ditches were irregular in plan, and also slightly misaligned with the Phase 3A eastern defences. The eastern ditch of the pair (Jones 2001, fig. 18) was cut along the berm between the Phase 3A fort ditch and the rampart. It measured a maximum of 1.25m in width and had a number of post-holes cut along its length. This ditch was also recorded in Area

M25 (Jones 2025, fig. 4.4). The second ditch, cut approximately 13.5m to the west (measured centre-to-centre), measured a maximum of 1m in width. It was sealed by a charcoal-rich destruction deposit measuring up to 0.35m in depth.

During Phase 4C a north–south palisade trench (Trench A2, Jones 2005, 104 and figs 29, 31) was dug to the east of the innermost Phase 1B ditch towards the northern end of the western defences. This palisade trench was flat-based in profile, measuring a maximum of 1.8m in width and 0.5m in depth.

An alternative phasing of the final Phase 4A eastern annexe re-cut ditch (Fig. 2.7, S.6, F244.01, Jones 2005, figs 8 and 11, F244) could place it in Phase 4C.

3

Finds

This chapter was prepared in 2010, and has not been updated, nor does it include reference to finds from excavations from 2013 to 2019.

Small finds
Hilary Cool

Introduction

This overview is based on inspection of all the specialist reports relating to excavations between 1963 and 2010. The only items that the author has personally inspected are the fragments of vessel glass from Area M9 (Cool 2011, 58–9) and Area M18 (Macey-Bracken with Cool 2012). It will be appreciated that working with paper records created by different individuals, sometimes using different reporting conventions, is not necessarily straightforward.

At the outset it may be noted that bone does not survive well on this site, so we lack an important element of the small finds assemblage. The only worked bone items recorded came from the excavations across the western defences of the first fort (Area M1A, Sharpe and Henig 2001, 106–8; Jones 2001, 47–8; 2025, ch. 5). This material consisted of three items whose stratigraphic positions were somewhat ambiguous. What may be noted from the published illustrations is that none of the items is typologically typically Roman. It was suggested that one, a fragment of a large openwork disc retaining the image of a bird, was possibly a bone *phalera* (Sharpe and Henig 2001, 106, no 1). It has to be said that it does not particularly resemble the *comparanda* in copper alloy cited. If the identification was correct, then a late 2nd to 3rd-century date would be implied which is somewhat later than all of the rest of the material culture. In what follows, these bone items have been ignored because it seems unlikely they are Roman.

The absence of worked bone has some implications for what we can learn about the nature of the occupation on the site. Bone was an important raw material in the Roman period, especially for items such as hairpins, needles, and gaming counters. For the early to mid-Roman period, bone hairpins are one of the most useful pointers to the presence of females on a site. Though Roman military sites were never an exclusively male environment, females are to be more expected on civilian sites. Given the proposed civilian occupation on the site in the later 1st to 2nd centuries, a period when hairpins were common, the non-survival of bone means that we are denied a useful piece of evidence.

Metalwork does survive on the site, though it would appear that frequently it was not in very good condition. There is evidence from the reports that X-radiography was used for at least some iron items, but there are hints that it may not have been used routinely for all of them. *Styli*, for example, are easily recognized from an X-radiograph image, but the description of the only item identified as one from Metchley (Bevan 2011, 57, cat no. 2 from a Phase A context = Phase 1) would imply that an X-radiograph image was not being used. The combination of the poor quality of preservation and lack of routine X-radiography also means that less can be learnt from the items than could be hoped for. Though iron nails are regularly mentioned in the reports, for example, there is no way of producing a useful quantified overview of those from different parts of the site, as the numbers of complete examples and the number of fragments with heads have not been noted. This is the sort of information that only emerges when X-radiography is used routinely.

All of these factors mean that, although a considerable number of areas have been dug over the years, they have produced a relatively small assemblage of recognizable small finds. Those that can be assigned to the various functional categories are summarized by area in Table 3.1, and by the date of the context and area in Table 3.2. These tables exclude unidentifiable fragments of metal and items such as rings, fragments of wire, etc. and nails. The grouping into area has used the various parts of the fort as a broad organizing principle. It will be appreciated that, given the superimposition of forts of various sizes over the years, some excavation areas may be within, for example, the *praetentura* during one phase but lie beyond its defences in another. The convention has been adopted in the hope that the reader will find it a useful mental aid that obviates the need to consult a plan every time a trench is mentioned. The *retentura* consists of Areas M1A, M1B, and M3–M4. The central range includes Area M20 and part of Area M18. The *praetentura* comprises Areas M2, M6, M12, M12a, M25 and part of Area M18. The eastern annexe is Area M7 and the western external settlement is Areas M9 and M14. None of the other excavated areas produced small finds. The date bands in Table 3.2 are the ones assigned to the contexts in the updated phasing (see Chapter 2 above). Dating will be considered further in the chronology section below.

As can be seen from Table 3.1, most of the usable information relates to the excavations in the *retentura*, so the potential for using the small finds to define intra-area differences is limited. Table 3.2, which shows the distribution by dated context, also shows that a third of the items came from unphased contexts. This also limits what can be said about changing patterns of use through time.

Table 3.1. Small finds, by area and functional category.

Function	Retentura	Central range	Praetentura	Annexe	External	Total
Personal	16	–	3	3	6	28
Household	9	2	–	5	1	17
Recreation	–	–	1	1	2	4
Weighing	–	–	1	–	1	2
Writing	–	–	–	–	1	1
Tools	21	–	3	2	5	31
Fittings	5	1	1	–	1	8
Military	11	1	1	–	1	15
Religion	1	–	–	–	–	1
Total	**63**	**4**	**11**	**11**	**18**	**107**

Table 3.2. Small finds, by area and date of context.

Part of fort	Mid-Neronian	Later Neronian	Early Flavian–late C2	Unphased	Total
Retentura	8	24	2	29	63
Central range	–	–	2	2	4
Praetentura	2	–	7	2	11
External	15	–	1	2	18
Annexes	–	6	5	–	11
Total	**25**	**30**	**17**	**39**	**107**

Table 3.3. Small finds, vessel glass by area.

Part of fort	Area	Fragment count	PMB blue/green	Strong colours blown	Blue/green bottle	Blue/green other
Retentura	M3	5	–	–	X	X
Central range/ *Praetentura*	M18, M20/ M18, M12, M2/M25	6	–	–	–	X
Praetentura	M12	19	X	X	X	X
Praetentura	M12A	4	–	–	(X)	(X)
Praetentura	M2	2	X	–	–	X
Praetentura	M25	1	–	X	–	–
External	M9	11	–	X	X	X
External	M12	4	–	X	–	–
Annexe	M7	1	–	–	X	–
Total		**53**				

'X' indicates presence of various categories; (X) indicates a rim fragment noted as either a bottle or a jug.

The vessel glass survives well, but only that from the excavations reported by Shepherd (2001, 89), Cool (2011, 58–9), and Macey-Bracken with Cool (2012) has been inspected by recognized glass specialists. This will always be a problem on sites with a Claudio-Neronian military presence, as the glass to be expected at that point covers a wide range of manufacturing methods and colours which are useful diagnostic indicators. Non-specialists will be unlikely to recognize the full range of the material. Within the confines of Metchley, Area M12 (Macey-Bracken 2025) produced one of the larger assemblages, and this was one of the areas not inspected by a specialist. Table 3.3 lists the vessel glass by excavation area and fragment count. Presence (X) and Absence (–) data are listed for certain key categories, and the importance of these will be discussed further in the chronology section below. In the case of the vessel glass, it is the *praetentura* and the external area to the west of the fort that have produced the bulk of the material.

As will be clear, the amount of information that can be extracted from this material is limited both by problems of preservation and by reporting conventions; but useful information can be extracted about the nature of the occupations and the chronology of the site, and these are discussed below.

Chronology

At the outset it will be useful to summarize the coinage from the site following the same conventions for grouping the excavation areas as in Tables 3.1–3.3, and this is done in Table 3.4.

This type of coin list is typical of forts occupied in the Claudio-Neronian period, but as there were problems with the coin supply at that time, a coin list such as this is not always as helpful in refining the periods of occupation as could be hoped for. Regular coinage of small denominations was in short supply up to the currency reforms that took place under Nero in AD 64. There was no base metal coinage issued during the period AD 54–64, and the lack of small change was dealt with by the production of copies of the last coinage of Claudius and sometimes by the countermarking of coins that showed they had been revalidated (Brickstock and Casey 2002, 86). Two Claudian *sestertii* from Phase 3A contexts in Area M3, for example, had been countermarked PROB (Reece 2001, 72 nos 7–8), indicating a revalidation under Nero (Brickstock and Casey 2002, 86). To what extent the coins can be taken to indicate occupation prior to the Neronian period is thus an open question.

The two categories of finds under consideration here that have most to contribute to questions of chronology are the brooches and the vessel glass, as both are undergoing considerable typological change during the period. The assemblages of both from Metchley show features that are not necessarily typical of Claudian to early Neronian military assemblages, as might be expected if occupation did indeed start in the AD 47–48 period.

Table 3.5 summarizes the bow and disc brooches from Metchley together with those from other military sites with origins in the Claudio-Neronian period in the west midlands. The legionary fortresses at Usk (Neronian) and Chester (Flavian) have been included for comparison. The brooches have been gathered into broad date bands. The

period up to AD 75 comprises mainly the one-piece brooches such as the Colchester and the Nauheim derivatives. The mid- to late 1st-century category comprises mainly early hinged brooches such as the Aucissa and the Hod Hill family and the early plate brooches. The mid-1st to 2nd-century category is predominantly composed of the two-piece Colchester Derivative family. The late 1st to mid-2nd-century category consist mainly of the trumpet, fantail, and headstud families that first appear in the very early Flavian period. Obviously, individual brooches can sometimes have long lives, but looking at assemblages in this way helps to provide a more reliable picture that is not unduly influenced by the individual biographies of particular brooches. Rocester is included here, as it provides a useful example of the sort of assemblage that can be expected from a site that starts in the later 1st century in this region. Table 3.5 provides the references for the sites used.

Inspection of the table reveals a curious feature about the Metchley assemblage. This is the scarcity of the typical brooches of the mid-1st century such as the one-piece brooches, the Aucissa and the Hod Hill brooches, normally a dominant feature of Claudian to early Neronian forts. There is a fragment of one Hod Hill brooch from Area M1A (Jones 2025, chapter. 5) across the western fort defences (Mackreth 2001, 77, no. 8). Not included in the table is an iron brooch that is noted, with no further details; as coming from external settlement in Area M9 (Bevan 2011, 57, no. 1). The dimensions given would favour a bow brooch rather than a penannular one. Iron one-piece brooches are not uncommon, so it is possible that this brooch would supply an example for the other missing early category, but even so the profile of the Metchley assemblage, with its strong focus on Colchester Derivative brooches, is not typical of a Claudian fort; it would be more appropriate coming from a Neronian fort, and not necessarily one that started in the earliest years of Nero. This does not appear merely to be a reflection of the relatively small size of the assemblage. The Derby site that provided the data for Table 3.5 is Strutt's Park, the fort thought to date to the AD 50s on the opposite side of the river to the later fort at Littlechester (Dool 1986). The small excavation only produced three brooches but, as can be seen, the early forms are well represented. A similar situation can be seen at the Neronian fort at Dodderhill near Droitwich (McAvoy 2006). Again, there are only five brooches, but the early forms dominate.

Table 3.4. Small finds, coinage by area and emperor.

Part of fort	Area	Republican	Augustus	Claudius	Domitian	Illegible	Total
Retentura	M3	–	1	6	1	5	13
Retentura	M4	–	–	2	–	2	4
External	M12	2	–	–	–	–	2
Annexe	M7	–	–	–	–	1	1
Total		**2**	**1**	**8**	**1**	**8**	**20**

Note: An Augustan denarius (Reece 2001, 72, no. 18) is present but cannot be assigned to an excavation area.

Table 3.5. Small finds, bow and disc brooches from military sites in the west midlands.

Site	Up to AD 75	M–L C1	M C1/C2	LC1/M C2	Total
Alcester	7	8	25	20	60
Chester	6	–	12	8	26
Derby	1	1	1	–	3
Droitwich	2	2	1	–	5
The Lunt	3	3	12	6	24
Metchley	–	**1**	**7**	**1**	**9**
Rocester	–	–	4	8	12
Usk	9	13	17	25	64
Wall	1	8	14	9	32
Wroxeter	15	37	61	34	147
Total	**45**	**74**	**154**	**111**	**402**

Sources for the small finds, bow and disc brooches	
Site	*Source(s)*
Alcester	Booth and Evans (2001); Cracknell (1996); Cracknell and Mahany (1994)
Chester	Kelly (1965); Newstead (1924; 1928); Newstead and Droop (1932; 1940); Petch and Thompson (1959); Richmond and Webster (1951); Thompson (1969; 1976); Thompson and Tobias (1957); Webster (1953) Also unpublished brooches from excavations by Birmingham Archaeology at Delamere St, Chester in 2006: BA n.d.
Derby, Strutt's Park	Dool (1986)
Droitwich, Dodderhill	Hurst (2006)
The Lunt	Hobley (1967; 1973)
Rocester	Bell (1986); Esmonde Cleary and Ferris (1996); Ellis et al. (unpublished)
Usk	Manning et al. (1995)
Wall	Gould (1963–4; 1966–7); Round (1983; 1992)
Wroxeter	Atkinson (1942); Barker et al. (1997); Bushe-Fox (1914; 1915; 1916); Ellis (2000); Webster (2002)

Inspection of the brooches from the earliest contexts does not cast any further light on the problem, as one is the iron brooch of unknown form discussed above, and the other from the same area was a penannular brooch, a category that is notorious for not being closely dateable. The third from a Phase 1 context in Area M3A in the *retentura* was a fragment of a Polden Hill Colchester Derivative (Mackreth 2001, 77, no. 5) and was so badly corroded that little useful could be said of it. The fact that a Colchester Derivative is coming from a Phase 1 context, though, must raise doubts about a very early date for that phase.

The vessel glass assemblage is relatively small, but still informative. Cast glass is represented by only two fragments of blue/green pillar moulded bowls (Shepherd 2001, 89, no. 3; Area M12, Macey-Bracken with Cool 2012, no. 9). Blown strongly coloured vessels come in the main from Areas M9 and M12. In the former there are Hofheim cups in emerald green and deep blue glass. Other deep blue vessels from the area include an unguent bottle, a possible cantherus, and a jug or amphorisk (Cool 2011, 59, nos 1–5). In Area M12 another deep blue Hofheim cup was recovered, together with a dark green vessel with a pad base (Macey-Bracken 2025, nos 3 and 8). Amongst the blue/green vessels there are body fragments probably from additional Hofheim cups from Areas M9 and M18 (Cool 2011, 59, no. 6; Macey-Bracken with Cool 2012). An assemblage with this range

of colours and forms certainly attests to Claudio-Neronian occupation, but some noticeable absences would argue against occupation in the earlier part of that period. There is no strongly coloured or polychrome cast glass and no blown polychrome glass, with the possible exception of the cantherus from Area M9 (these sometimes have differently coloured decoration lower down the body). Opaque blue glass is reported from M14 (outside the western fort defences, Macey-Bracken 2011, 25), but this is a fragment that has not been subject to specialist inspection. On Claudian military sites it is not uncommon to get polychrome and strongly coloured cast vessels even in very small assemblages. Two Claudian forts in Dorset are a good example of this. At Waddon Hill there was a polychrome pillar moulded bowl as well as a blue/green one, together with an opaque pale blue cast bowl (Harden 1960, 95). At Hod Hill there was again a polychrome pillar moulded bowl in addition to two blue/green ones and a blown bichrome cased vessel (Harden et al. 1968).

The proportion of polychrome to strongly coloured to blue/green pillar moulded bowls in an assemblage provides a very useful dating index from the Claudian to Flavian periods (Cool 1998, 302–3). At Metchley, it points towards a later date rather than an earlier one. Indeed, the only part of the glass assemblage that might hint at a start date within the first decade of the Roman advance is the deep blue unguent bottle from Area M9. Unguent bottles are common in the mid-1st century, but they are almost invariably made of blue/green glass. Such bottles made in other colours are rare, and might possibly indicate an early date (Cool 2007, 345, table 54) though, as examples in yellow/green and yellow/brown glass were found in the assemblage dating to the mid-1960s at Kingsholm (Price and Cool 1985, 48, nos 31 and 39), it is clear that they were still occasionally in use at that time.

The vessel glass, therefore, like the brooches, does not point to a start date in the Claudian or early Neronian period. If the earliest military occupation on the site was during the 40s to 50s, as has been previously suggested (Jones 2001, 110; 2005, 80), then it has left very little trace in these normally quite sensitive chronological indicators.

As far as the duration of the occupation goes, the regular presence of fragments of blue/green prismatic bottles (Table 3.3) indicates later 1st- or 2nd-century occupation, as it is not until the Flavian period that these become a common part of vessel glass assemblages. A collared jar from Area M18 has a *floruit* from the late Neronian period to the early 2nd century, but normally it might be expected that more Flavian forms would be present if there was military occupation of any substance in the later 1st to early 2nd centuries. Other small finds too do not necessarily indicate 2nd-century activity. As can be seen from Table 3.5, the range of brooches that start to appear in the later part of the 1st century are not common here. This can be compared to the numbers present in a site such as Rocester, where occupation did start late in the 1st century.

When originally published (Mackreth 2001), it was suggested that the variant of the omega brooch present at Metchley indicated a late 1st-century date and later. A complete silver example came from a Phase 3A context in Area M2, and the hoop only of a copper alloy brooch came from an unphased context in Area M3 (Mackreth 2001, 77, nos 9 and 10). In discussing these, Mackreth listed the dated *comparanda* that he knew of in 1996. He noted the presence of examples with smooth hoops in Claudian pits, but thought the dating evidence for the ridged hoop section forms pointed to the later date. He quoted Riha's first study of the brooches from Augst and Kaiseraugst published in 1979, but the second study published in 1994 was not cited. In that there is another silver omega brooch

with a similar cross-section to that of the Metchley silver brooch and with similar double knobbed additions to the omega terminals. This forms part of Riha's Variante 8.1.1, the pottery associations of which start in the AD 30s–50s. The silver brooch that is most similar to the Metchley example has pottery associations of both AD 30–50 and 130–70 (Riha 1994, 177–8, especially cat. No. 2981, taf. 47 and front cover). This dating would make it quite possible that the omega brooches were associated with the Neronian activity indicated by the other brooches and the vessel glass.

The other small finds are not particularly helpful in refining the dating, as they frequently have date ranges that span the mid-1st to mid-2nd century periods. Melon beads and glass counters are a good case in point. Table 3.6 summarizes their presence. As may be seen within the context of the relatively small assemblage of small finds from the site, they are relatively common– as is to be expected on a 1st century military site. As neither disappears from common use until the mid-2nd century, though, none is of any use in refining the duration of the occupation. Similarly, amongst the metal vessels there is the handle terminal of a dipper with a stamped maker's name (Tomlin 2011, 57). The vessel could easily have been made in the mid-1st century, but the type continues to be found in 2nd-century contexts (Koster 1997, 46–7, no. 40).

The nature of the site and the distribution of the material

Even without the structural evidence of the plans of the defences and the buildings, it would be possible to say that this was a military site. The military equipment would point towards it, but so would items such as the melon beads and counters just discussed. They can be found on non-military sites in the pre-Flavian period, but not generally in any quantity. On military sites, by contrast, they are very numerous, as here. Equally, the iron tools and knives recovered are typical of military sites, which were much better supplied with such items at this period than most other sorts of site. On a Neronian site, the presence of several metal vessels that were part of the utensils surrounding the service of wine, such as the two lids from hot-water jugs (Webster 2001, 81, no. 24; White 2012, no. 5) and the dipper handle, is also much more to be expected on a military site (Cool 2006, 140, table 15.3).

Table 3.6. Small finds, melon beads and glass counters from Metchley.

Part of fort	Area	Frit melon bead	Glass melon bead	Glass counter	Total
Retentura	M3	1	1	–	2
Retentura	M4	2	1	–	3
Praetentura	M12	–	–	1	1
External	M9	1	1	1	3
External	M12	1	–	–	1
Annexe	M7	1	1	1	3
Total		**6**	**4**	**3**	**13**

The military equipment consists of weapons and harness fittings. No obvious pieces of armour have been recovered. This in itself is very informative. The type of *lorica segmentata* worn by legionaries at that time was fastened by a large number of copper alloy buckles and fittings (Bishop 2002, 31–43, see also 91). These appear to have been in constant need of repair and refurbishment, so it is not unusual to find them on sites where legionaries have been present. Even on a site where metalwork is not in good condition, such fittings can be recognized from the combination of copper alloy and iron. At Metchley they are absent. Arguing from absence in a small assemblage always has to be done with care, but it seems reasonable to suggest here that the probability that the site was garrisoned by auxiliaries rather than units of legionary soldiers is high.

The presence of harness fittings (Webster 2001, 81 nos 18–21; White 2012, no. 1; 2025, no. 1) points to a cavalry presence, though it may be noted that even infantry units would have needed horses for officers' mounts, communications, etc. Such fittings, therefore, need not always indicate the presence of a cavalry unit. This material is quite widespread both in time and areas of the fort. The material excavated in 1967–9 and 1997 all came from Phase 2B contexts in Area M3 in the *retentura*. The item from Area M18 came from a Phase 3B–4B context in the *praetentura*. The piece from Area M12 was unstratified within the *praetentura*. That there was an infantry presence at some point is perhaps suggested by the ballista ball in the external Area M9 in a Phase B (= Phase 2B) context (Bevan 2011, 57, no. 1), given that siege weapons were not normally the preserve of the cavalry.

The other military material present, which includes spearheads, dagger and sword fittings, and various mounts and fittings with white metal and niello decoration, were commonly used by a variety of different types of soldiers in the Neronian/Flavian period, and so are not particularly helpful in respect of identifying the different sorts of garrisons present.

As explained in the introduction, the way the material is distributed in time and space means that there is not really a large enough body of data to address the question of intra-site variation in any detail. There are, however, a few features of the data that may hint at the nature of the occupation in various areas.

Table 3.7 attempts to summarize the distribution of what may be thought of as the small finds and vessel glass associated with the more elite elements of the garrisons. The vessel glass consists of tablewares. As already noted, the metal vessels are associated with the service of wine. The silver omega brooch and an agate intaglio (Area M25, Tomlin, no. 1) have also been included in the jewellery category. These are compared with the distribution of the more mundane items such as copper alloy brooches and melon beads of both frit and glass. The rows have been arranged so that the shift from areas with a higher proportion of the more elite items to those with the more mundane ones can be seen clearly. This table does indicate there is intra-site variability, with the excavations in the *praetentura* having a bias towards the 'elite' items and those in the *retentura* towards the more mundane. The external area M9 is particularly interesting, given that it has a mixture of both the 'elite' and the 'mundane' items not seen elsewhere. As with the varying proportions of decorated Samian from the various areas (Timby, below), there are hints in these finds that the different status of some types of occupation is being picked up by these finds (see also Fryer, Chapter 4 below). With a relatively small assemblage and the superimposition of different forts, however, all that can really be done is to point out these differences. Exploration of them would require a larger set of data.

Local vs long-distance supply

Various different supply mechanisms can be seen at work within the finds being considered here. Items that can be considered continental imports include the Neronian vessel glass assemblage, the metal vessel fragments (Webster 2001, 81, no. 24 and possibly 78, no. 2; Bevan 2011, 57, no. 1; White 2012, 70, no. 5), the omega brooches, and probably the ballista ball, as it is made of andesitic lava for which no good British matches were found. Amongst this material, the supply mechanism could range from personal possessions (the brooches) to army supply (the ballista ball) and possibly trade (the glass and metal vessels), though the latter category could as easily be personal possessions as well.

Table 3.7. Small finds, comparison of various categories of finds from Metchley by area.

Part of fort	Pillar moulded bowls	Blown glass cups	Metal vessels	Jewellery	Copper alloy brooches	Melon beads
Praetentura	2	2	–	2	1	–
Central range	–	–	1	–	–	–
External	–	4	1	–	1	2
Retentura	–	–	1	–	9	5
Annexes	–	–	–	–	1	2
Total	2	6	3	2	12	9

There is also a strong regional supply element. Six of the seven Colchester Derivative brooches have the Polden Hill method of spring fastening (spring bar lodged in the perforated ends of the wings). This is the typical method used by native brooch manufacturers in the west of Britain. Only one (Mackreth 2001, 76, no. 1) has the spring mounted in the Harlow method (spring bar through the lower part of a double perforated lug), the method favoured in the east of the country. Another product of a regional craftsman is one of the harness fittings (Area M12), which was not a typical 'Roman' military fitting but instead has close parallels with a piece in the Seven Sisters Hoard from Glamorgan.

Another local/regional supply preference can be seen in the quernstones, which are made of millstone grit from the Derbyshire/Staffordshire/Pennine area (Turner 2001, 86–8, nos 1–7; Bevan and Ixer 2005, 46, nos 3–5). This latter fact is of especial interest, as on Neronian military sites it is normal to find imported lava querns. Numerous fragments were found in the fortress pits at Usk, and it was suggested that the soldiers there were using lava querns exclusively (Manning et al. 1995, 214). Clearly the supply channels to the west were well established, which makes the absence of fragments from the early contexts which produced the millstone grit querns all the more remarkable. The only lava quern recorded from Metchley comes from a late Phase 4A context in the eastern annexe (M7, Bevan and Ixer 2005, 46, no. 2). Unfortunately, quernstones and their lithologies are a class of finds that is often overlooked in excavation reports. None, for example, is published from the fortress at Wroxeter; so putting the pattern seen at Metchley into context is difficult. Further research on the quernstones from other west midlands forts would be an interesting area, as it might reflect an early recognition of the value of millstone grit and its exploitation for the flat rotary querns which are a 'Roman' rather than native form.

Conclusions

Placing this assemblage more fully within its regional contemporary context is problematic, not only because of its relatively small size due to the problems outlined in the introduction, but also because of the gaps in the publication records of other sites. It was possible to place the brooches in context because that is a category of find for which it is conventional to use a specialist for reports. Other types of copper alloy small finds have in the past tended to be selectively published, and have frequently been dealt with by people who may not have been able to recognize poorly preserved examples of items. The fort at Wall, for example, has produced a much larger small-find assemblage, but there are no items of similar metal vessels that would have been part of the wine service amongst them. Is that because they were absent – which might have interesting implications for the number from Metchley – or were they just not recognized? The problems with putting the quernstone assemblage into context have also been noted.

Probably the most useful contribution the finds can make is helping refine the date of the main occupation. As has been noted, a Claudian or very early Neronian date seems unlikely, and military occupation of any length or substance into the late Flavian period seems unlikely. The finds provide some help in refining the type of garrison the bases had. They also hint that the more elite occupation was probably in the *praetentura*, but cannot really help in defining the different functions in the different forts. Finally, the domination of the quernstone assemblage by millstone grit stones provides very useful data with which to explore the early development of that industry, which was to become an important one.

Pottery
Jane Timby

Introduction

Metchley Roman fort (Fig. 1.3) has seen a large number of archaeological interventions over the years from the 1930s on. More recent work since the early 1960s has resulted in the recovery of some 15,260 sherds of pottery weighing 252.5kg. This has been published piecemeal by various authors, starting with the 1967–9 assemblages by Green (Green et al. 2001). Each area excavated has been allocated a sequential number starting with Area M1, the latest under consideration here being Area M25. Of these areas, pottery has been analysed from 12, with some areas being amalgamated and treated as single assemblages. Unfortunately, as a consequence of the way in which the work has been undertaken over the years and the actual ground layout of the trenches, it is not possible to characterize the pottery from individual areas of the Phase 1 and Phase 3A forts other than in general terms. Several trenches, for example, cut across the defences into the interior and/or exterior of the fort.

The Roman pottery from Metchley is, almost without exception, extremely poorly preserved. Sherds are often much abraded, with the loss of surface treatments such as slips or colour-coats. The soft nature of the local wares with few distinctive inclusions has made it difficult to distinguish products which might have been produced within or near the fort from the more widely available Severn Valley wares. It is thus quite possible that certain elements, or less distinct fabrics, have been completely missed or under-represented. Precise identification of Samian forms has also been severely compromised by the poor state of the sherds. The condition of the coarse ware and fine ware (Samian) assemblage has also somewhat limited the chronological precision that can be applied to elements of the assemblage. On a positive note, all the pottery from the fort since the 1967–9 campaign of work has been systematically recorded and quantified throughout, making it almost unique in terms of a fully recorded assemblage from a fort in the midlands and allowing a greater level of interrogation not possible elsewhere at present. The quantity of pottery recorded overall exceeds most other military sites in the west midlands.

History of work (Fig. 1.3)

Pottery from the 1963–9 excavations (Areas M1–M5) was originally reported on in the mid-1980s and subsequently updated by the various contributors in 2001 (Green et al. 2001). The assemblage was treated as a single group. Specialist reports were prepared by Hedley Pengelly, Brian Hartley, and Brenda Dickinson on the Samian; Kay Hartley on the mortaria; and David Williams on the amphorae. Areas M1 and M3–M5 were focused in the northwest corner of the fort, encompassing material from the defences and the interior, whilst Area M2 was located in the opposing southeast corner and included the Phase 3A fort rampart in part of the interior. Added to the Area M1–M5 pottery analysis was a report on the Area M6 pottery by Hancocks (2001). This excavation, adjacent to Area M2, extended over the Phase 1 and Phase 3A fort defences. Quantification of the stratified coarse wares for Areas M1–M5 was by count and weight, excluding all the specialist wares reported on separately. Fabric and form catalogues were produced. The quantification for Area M6 included estimated vessel equivalents and minimum vessel count. Overall, Areas M1–M6 produced approximately 81.23kg of pottery.

In 1998–2000 and 2002, excavations were undertaken on the eastern and southern annexes and fort defences (Areas M7–M8 and M10), and trial trenching was carried out in the north of the fort interior (Area M11). The pottery from the former was reported on by Hancocks (2005) and the latter by Evans and Hancocks (2005). Areas M7–M8 produced just over 2,000 sherds weighing c.24.3kg (Table 3.8). Unlike previous groups, the Area M7–M8 assemblage contained significant quantities of post-AD 80 material, probably relating to civilian occupation. Specialist reports were prepared on the Samian (Willis 2005), mortaria (Hartley 2005a; 2005b), and amphorae (Williams 2005a; 2005b).

The trial trenches (Area M11) yielded a very small group of just 215 sherds (c.6kg). Compared to other Metchley assemblages, the overall average sherd weight was quite high, suggesting better preservation of material. The coarse ware assemblage is accorded a pre-Flavian date (Evans and Hancocks 2005, 108), but there appear to be at least two sherds of later mortaria present (Hartley 2005b, 107), albeit from Phase 4A contexts.

Areas M9, M13–M14, M15–M16, and M18 were located across the western defences and extended into the external area to the west of the fort, including a livestock complex. The pottery from Areas M9, M14, and M15–M16 has been reported on by various authors: Evans et al. (2011) (Area M9); Evans (2011) (Area M14); and Timby (2011) (Areas M15–M16); (2012) (Area M18).

Area M9 produced some 1,870 sherds of pottery weighing c.27.8kg. The Samian suggested a date range from mid- to late 1st century, with the emphasis on sherds of Claudio-Neronian date (Willis 2011), whilst the mortaria includes pre-Flavian and Flavian forms (Hartley 2011a).

Area M14 also produced a fairly modest assemblage of 643 sherds (11.6kg). Just four sherds of mortarium were recovered, at least two of which are likely to be locally produced (Hartley 2011b), and all the Samian is likely to be pre-Flavian (Wild 2011). A similar-sized assemblage of some 549 sherds but weighing just 6.4kg, was recovered from Areas M15–M16. Area M18, located across the western defences and fort interior, produced some 3,825 sherds weighing c.52kg (Timby 2012). This is the second largest group to be analysed from the fort, and mainly comprised material of pre-Flavian date with at least three new imported wares present not previously recorded.

The final excavation in this sequence (Area M25), undertaken in 2010, was across the Phase 3A fort within the original Area M2. This produced a very small assemblage of just 166 sherds (1.5kg) (Timby 2025), with a very limited range of wares and no Samian.

Composition

Table 3.8 provides a distilled quantified summary by sherd count and weight of the main ware groups drawn from the 10 pottery reports available for Metchley. Pottery studies are rapidly evolving, particularly in terms of fabric recognition and an appreciation of the value of quantification. To a certain extent this development is reflected in the sequence of reports undertaken for Metchley, where certain identifications have become more specific through time – for example, sourcing the mortaria and identifying more exotic wares. Many of the rarer fabrics, represented by single sherds only, feature in more recent reports, suggesting the possibility that some have been overlooked in the past. Some identifications, particularly some of the North Gaulish white wares and Gallo-Belgic *craquelée bleutée*, might now be questionable.

The assemblage from Metchley comprises a mixture of domestic coarse wares, fine wares, and transport containers. As is typical of a military establishment, there are a large number of specialist wares such as tableware, mortaria, and flagons. Some of these are clearly regional or continental imports, others may have been locally made. Tables 3.9a and 3.9b summarize the named traded wares recorded from each area. Most of the early military establishments in Britain appear to have brought potters with them to provide the range of vessels familiar to a Roman but not yet available from the British domestic market. Local pottery available in Britain in the pre-Flavian period was still very entrenched in later Iron Age traditions, where jars dominate, accompanied by bowls, beakers, and lids. New forms reflecting a Mediterranean cuisine and dining habits include flagons and jugs for the dispensing of liquids; table wares for serving and eating of food and drink; and cups, platters, and mortaria for food or medical preparations. Other

Table 3.8. Pottery, quantified summary of the main wares from the different excavated areas.

Wares	Area M1–M5				Area M2				Area M6			
	No.	No. %	Wt	Wt%	No.	No. %	Wt	Wt%	No.	No. %	Wt	Wt %
Samian	103	1.8	170	0.1	0	0.0	0	0.0	13	3.6	40	0.2
Amphorae	873	15.2	7,630	6.4	2	1.2	137	9.0	17	4.7	8,330	47.4
Imported mortaria	8	0.1	0	0.0	0	0.0	0	0.0	2	0.6	79	0.4
Imported fine ware	17	0.3	30	0.0	0	0.0	0	0.0	0	0.0	0	0.0
Imported coarse ware	29	0.5	80	0.1	0	0.0	0	0.0	0	0.0	0	0.0
Regional	0	0.0	0	0.0	0	0.0	0	0.0	0	0.0	0	0.0
Regional mortaria	71	1.2	5,600	4.7	0	0.0	0	0.0	0	0.0	0	0.0
Severn Valley ware	587	10.2	14,141	11.8	59	35.5	517	33.9	0	0.0	0	0.0
Native	183	3.2	5,125	4.4	1	0.6	9	0.6	0	0.0	0	0.0
Local/unknown	3,759	65.6	86,366	72.1	103	62.0	792	51.9	331	91.2	9,118	51.9
White-slipped wares	0	0.0	0	0.0	0	0.0	0	0.0	0	0.0	0	0.0
White wares	98	1.7	650	0.5	1	0.6	71	4.7	0	0.0	0	0.0
TOTAL	**5,728**	**100.0**	**119,792**	**100.0**	**166**	**100.0**	**1,526**	**100.0**	**363**	**100.0**	**17,567**	**100.0**

Wares	Area M7–M8				Area M9				Area M11			
	No.	No. %	Wt	Wt%	No.	No. %	Wt	Wt%	No.	No. %	Wt	Wt %
Samian	93	4.6	942	3.9	59	3.2	400	1.4	8	3.7	68	1.1
Amphorae	141	6.9	9,656	39.7	354	18.9	14,026	50.4	27	12.6	1,476	24.3
Imported mortaria	6	0.3	48	0.2	8	0.4	977	3.5	0	0.0	0	0.0
Imported fine ware	176	8.7	329	1.4	24	1.3	54	0.2	0	0.0	0	0.0
Imported coarse ware	0	0.0	0	0.0	0	0.0	0	0.0	0	0.0	0	0.0
Regional	3	0.1	93	0.4	24	1.3	120	0.4	0	0.0	0	0.0
Regional mortaria	2	0.1	187	0.8	3	0.2	200	0.7	2	0.9	15	0.2
Severn Valley ware	1,026	50.5	6,968	28.7	681	36.4	6,436	23.1	26	12.1	354	5.8
Native	230	11.3	2,592	10.7	62	3.3	1,625	5.8	47	21.9	2,547	41.9
Local/unknown	352	17.3	3,471	14.3	650	34.8	3,938	14.2	105	48.8	1,612	26.5
White-slipped wares	0	0.0	0	0.0	0	0.0	0	0.0	0	0.0	0	0.0
White wares	1	0.0	28	0.1	5	0.3	42	0.2	0	0.0	0	0.0
TOTAL	**2,030**	**100.0**	**24,314**	**100.0**	**1,870**	**100.0**	**27,818**	**100.0**	**215**	**100.0**	**6,072**	**100.0**

Wares	Area M14				Area M15–M16				Area M18			
	No.	No. %	Wt	Wt%	No.	No. %	Wt	Wt%	No.	No. %	Wt	Wt %
Samian	27	4.2	110	0.9	22	4.0	78.5	1.2	147	3.8	886	1.7
Amphorae	112	17.4	5,791	49.9	48	8.6	2,685	40.0	444	11.6	23,288	44.8
Imported mortaria	1	0.2	22	0.2	8	1.4	378	5.6	14	0.4	815	1.6
Fine wares	4	0.6	13	0.1	2	0.4	2	0.0	20	0.5	6.5	0.0
Imported coarse ware	0	0.0	0	0.0	2	0.4	5	0.1	5	0.1	193	0.4
Regional	0	0.0	0	0.0	10	1.8	125	1.9	0	0.0	0	0.0
Regional mortaria	3	0.5	280	2.4	0	0.0	0	0.0	10	0.3	441	0.8
Severn Valley wares	122	19.0	1,488	12.8	187	33.6	1,348	20.1	1,015	26.5	9,817	18.9
Native	43	6.7	544	4.7	9	1.6	87	1.3	128	3.3	3,194	6.1
Local/unknown	325	50.5	3,282	28.3	265	47.7	1,970	29.4	1,920	50.2	12,638	24.3
White-slipped wares	0	0.0	0	0.0	2	0.4	27	0.4	94	2.5	477	0.9
White wares	6	0.9	70	0.6	1	0.2	1	0.0	28	0.7	204	0.4
TOTAL	**643**	**100.0**	**11,600**	**100.0**	**556**	**100.0**	**6,706.5**	**100.0**	**3,825**	**100.0**	**51,959.5**	**100.0**

vessels with military associations include honey pots, face pots, tazzae, and lamps. Most of the early forts have produced evidence for production of most of these types of vessel, such as Kingsholm (Darling 1985); Usk (Manning 1993); Longthorpe (Dannell and Wild 1987); Wroxeter (Darling 2002); London (Davies et al. 1994); Colchester (Symonds and Wade 1999); and Exeter (Bidwell 1979). Hartley (2001, 98; 2011b) notes that the 'local' mortaria from Metchley are very reminiscent of mortaria from Longthorpe (Dannell and Wild 1987, 127, nos 1–4), concluding that they are likely to be local products made by potters within, or associated with, the army. Many of the fine oxidized and fine grey wares recorded from Metchley may also be local military products: distinctive forms include the collared-rim (Hofheim) flagons (cf. Green et al. 2001, fig. 33.F1–6), flat-rimmed jars (Green et al. 2001, fig. 38.B17), jars with upright rims (Green et al. 2011, fig. 35.J1–13), dishes (Green et al. 2001, fig. 38.B16, B20), tazzae (Hancocks 2005, fig. 24.13), and possibly the rusticated wares noted on various sites.

Samian is well represented on all the sites, and forms the basis of much of the chronology. In all cases South Gaulish wares from La Graufesenque dominate with an overall date range from *c.*AD 40–110. As Willis (2005) notes, the Samian shows considerable typological variety characteristic of 1st-century military sites. The quantity of Samian present as a percentage of the overall assemblage can be an indicator of the status and identity of a site, as can the relative proportion of decorated ware present (Willis 1998). Willis (2005, 63) notes that military sites and major civil centres consistently have a higher proportion of decorated forms compared to other forms of settlement. Detailed analysis has suggested that a typical military site will have around 27% (Willis 2005, 63). Areas M7–M8 had 38.3% decorated wares, which is comparable to other Claudio-Neronian military assemblages, such as that from Brandon Camp, Herefordshire (Hartley 1987). Areas M1–M4 had around 34% decorated ware, but in Area M18 there was just 23% decorated ware. All other groups were too small for such analyses. It would appear, therefore, that there may be some differences across the fort areas. Analysis of the distribution of Samian across the 2nd-century fort at Bearsden (Breeze 1977), based on quite a small sample, showed a concentration of sherds within, or immediately adjacent to, the officers' quarters of the barrack blocks, suggesting that in addition to the commanding officer, only the officers used Samian ware.

Other imported fine wares are surprisingly rare, and largely limited to Lyon ware and North Gaulish white wares. The Lyon ware features both as cups and beakers, and is a familiar presence on most Claudio-Neronian military sites, suggesting specific military contracts operating with the producers. The North Gaulish white wares may include other white wares and possibly Gallic amphorae, and may thus be rather over-represented. It is particularly well represented in the assemblage from Areas M7–M8 (Table 3.9a), but the illustrations of a butt beaker (Hancocks 2005, fig. 25.42) and ring-necked flagon (fig. 26.79) are not typical forms from North Gaul at this time. Butt beakers tend to conform to the Cam 113 style, and the ring-necked flagon, generally a Flavian to early 2nd-century development, was being widely made in Britain, for example at Mancetter-Hartshill. No other imported fine wares have been recognized to date in the assemblages from Metchley.

There are a small number of imported coarse wares other than mortaria which are present, perhaps more likely to be personal possessions than to come from military stores. These include three sherds of white ware flagon with a black-sand fabric likely to have originated from Campania, southern Italy (Areas M15–M16 and Area M18, Table 3.9b). Also present but surprisingly rare are vessels of Campanian Pompeian red ware. Three sherds from an unslipped lid were noted from Area M18. A group of red-slipped flagon sherds recorded from Areas M1–M5 (Green et al. 2001, fabric 4.3. fig. 33.F9) are also probably from an imported vessel, perhaps from Central Gaul. The only other import recognized to date is a distinctive barley-twisted handle from Area M18, possibly from southern Italy or the eastern Mediterranean.

Although not prolific, a variety of mortaria were reaching the site with a mixture of imported continental, British regional, and local types recorded. The continental types include examples from North Gaul and the Rhône Valley, the latter being the most frequently recorded. A small number have been identified as coming from the west midlands and/or Wroxeter, and from the Mancetter–Hartshill, Verulamium, and Oxfordshire areas. The latter three are more likely to date from the Flavian period, and the numbers are very low. The mortaria include a small number of wall-sided forms, a type characteristically associated with Claudio-Neronian military assemblages, with further examples from Wroxeter and Brandon Camp (Frere 1987b, fig. 20.25). Hartley (2001, 98) has suggested that the 'local' mortaria are likely to be local products made by potters within, or associated with, the army.

Amphorae form a significant component of most military assemblages, bringing in essential goods such as olive oil, wine, fish-based products, and perhaps other goods. Dressel 20 amphorae from Southern Spain used for transporting olive oil completely dominate the Metchley assemblage. The oil would have been used for cooking, lighting, and perhaps bathing. A small number of other amphorae, as well as the globular Dressel 20, were imported from southern Spain, probably forming part of the same consignments. These include the Haltern 70, which on the basis of phytolith analyses was probably used for olives in *defrutum* or wine (Carreras 2003; Carreras et al. 2005), and the Camulodunum type 186 from the Cadiz region, generally used to transport fish products.

Table 3.9a. Pottery, quantified summary of named traded wares from Areas M1–M5, M7–8, and M9.

	Fabric	Description	Area M1–M5				Area M2				Area M7–8				Area M9			
			No.	No. %	Wt	Wt %	No.	No. %	Wt	Wt %	No.	No. %	Wt	Wt %	No.	No. %	Wt	Wt %
Imported fw	LGF SA	South Gaulish Samian	103	10.0	170	2.2	0	0.0	0	0.0	80	19.0	875	7.9	59	12.5	400	2.5
	LEZ SA	Central Gaulish Samian	0	0.0	0	0.0	0	0.0	0	0.0	13	3.1	67	0.6	0	0.0	0	0.0
	LYO CC	Lyon ware	17	1.6	30	0.4	0	0.0	0	0.0	9	2.1	10	0.1	3	0.6	19	0.1
	NOG WH	North Gaulish white ware	0	0.0	0	0.0	0	0.0	0	0.0	167	39.8	319	2.9	21	4.5	35	0.2
Imported cw	ITA WH	Campanian coarse ware	0	0.0	0	0.0	0	0.0	0	0.0	0	0.0	0	0.0	0	0.0	0	0.0
	CAM PR1	Pompeian redware fabric 1	0	0.0	0	0.0	0	0.0	0	0.0	0	0.0	0	0.0	0	0.0	0	0.0
	IMP MISC	?Central Gaulish flagon	29	2.8	80	1.0	0	0.0	0	0.0	0	0.0	0	0.0	0	0.0	0	0.0
	IMP MISC	Imported flagon	0	0.0	0	0.0	0	0.0	0	0.0	0	0.0	0	0.0	0	0.0	0	0.0
Mortaria	NOG WH4	North Gaulish white ware	2	0.2	0	0.0	0	0.0	0	0.0	0	0.0	0	0.0	5	1.1	292	1.9
	CNG OX	Central Gaulish (Rhône Valley)	3	0.3	0	0.0	0	0.0	0	0.0	6	1.4	48	0.4	3	0.6	685	4.4
	MAH WH	Mancetter–Hartshill	3	0.3	0	0.0	0	0.0	0	0.0	0	0.0	0	0.0	0	0.0	0	0.0
	OXF WH	Oxfordshire white ware mortar	0	0.0	0	0.0	0	0.0	0	0.0	0	0.0	0	0.0	0	0.0	0	0.0
	WRXWH	?Wroxeter/west midlands mortar	0	0.0	0	0.0	0	0.0	0	0.0	0	0.0	0	0.0	1	0.2	20	0.1
	VER WH	Verulamium white ware mortaria	2	0.2	0	0.0	0	0.0	0	0.0	2	0.5	71	0.6	1	0.2	115	0.7
Amphorae	BAT AM	Baetican amphorae	808	78.3	7,200	91.4	2	100.0	137	100.0	141	33.6	9,656	87.2	336	71.3	13,206	84.1
	CAD AM	South Spanish (Cadiz) amphora	7	0.7	100	1.3	0	0.0	0	0.0	0	0.0	0	0.0	0	0.0	0	0.0
	CAM AM	Campanian amphorae	0	0.0	0	0.0	0	0.0	0	0.0	0	0.0	0	0.0	0	0.0	0	0.0
	CAT AM	Catalan amphora	0	0.0	0	0.0	0	0.0	0	0.0	0	0.0	0	0.0	4	0.8	253	1.6
	GAL AM	Gallic amphorae	1	0.1	10	0.1	0	0.0	0	0.0	0	0.0	0	0.0	0	0.0	0	0.0
	AMP2-4	Dr 2-4	9	0.9	60	0.8	0	0.0	0	0.0	0	0.0	0	0.0	0	0.0	0	0.0
	RHO AM	Rhodian style	7	0.7	40	0.5	0	0.0	0	0.0	0	0.0	0	0.0	0	0.0	0	0.0
	AMP	Unidentified amphorae	41	4.0	190	2.4	0	0.0	0	0.0	1	0.2	?	0.0	14	3.0	567	3.6
Regional	DER CO	Derbyshire coarse ware	0	0.0	0	0.0	0	0.0	0	0.0	0	0.0	0	0.0	6	1.3	42	0.3
	DOR BB1	Dorset Black Burnished ware	0	0.0	0	0.0	0	0.0	0	0.0	1	0.2	22	0.2	0	0.0	0	0.0
	OXF WH	Oxfordshire white ware	0	0.0	0	0.0	0	0.0	0	0.0	0	0.0	0	0.0	4	0.8	19	0.1
	VER WH	Verulamium white ware	0	0.0	0	0.0	0	0.0	0	0.0	0	0.0	0	0.0	14	3.0	59	0.4
TOTAL			1,032	100.0	7,880	100.0	2	100.0	137	100.0	420	100.0	11,068	100.0	471	100.0	15,712	100.0

Table 3.9b. Pottery, quantified summary of named traded wares from Areas M11, M14, M15–M16, and M18.

	Fabric	Description	Area M11				Area M14				Area M15–M16				Area M18			
			No.	No.%	Wt	Wt%	No.	No.%	Wt	Wt%	No.	No.%	Wt	Wt%	No.	No.%	Wt	Wt%
Imported fine ware	LGF SA	South Gaulish Samian	8	21.6	68	4.4	27	18.8	110	1.9	22	30.6	88	3	147	23.0	886	3.5
	LEZ SA	Central Gaulish Samian	0	0.0	0	0.0	0	0.0	0	0.0	0	0.0	0	0	0	0.0	0	0.0
	LYO CC	Lyon ware	0	0.0	0	0.0	1	0.7	1	0.0	2	2.8	2	0	20	3.1	7	0.0
	NOG WH	North Gaulish white ware	0	0.0	0	0.0	3	2.1	12	0.2	0	0.0	0	0	0	0.0	0	0.0
Imported coarse ware	ITA WH	Campanian coarse ware	0	0.0	0	0.0	0	0.0	0	0.0	2	2.8	5	0	1	0.2	9	0.0
	CAM PR1	Pompeian red ware fabric 1	0	0.0	0	0.0	0	0.0	0	0.0	0	0.0	0	0	3	0.5	47	0.2
	IMP MISC	?Central Gaulish flagon	0	0.0	0	0.0	0	0.0	0	0.0	0	0.0	0	0	0	0.0	0	0.0
	IMP MISC	Imported flagon	0	0.0	0	0.0	0	0.0	0	0.0	0	0.0	0	0	1	0.2	137	0.5
Mortaria	NOG WH4	North Gaulish white ware	0	0.0	0	0.0	0	0.0	0	0.0	3	4.2	17	1	5	0.8	249	1.0
	CNG OX	Central Gaulish (Rhône Valley)	0	0.0	0	0.0	1	0.7	22	0.4	5	6.9	361	12	9	1.4	566	2.2
	MAH WH	Mancetter–Hartshill	1	2.7	11	0.7	0	0.0	0	0.0	0	0.0	0	0	9	1.4	341	1.3
	OXF WH	Oxfordshire white ware mortaria	1	2.7	4	0.3	0	0.0	0	0.0	0	0.0	0	0	0	0.0	0	0.0
	WRXWH	Wroxeter/west midlands mortaria	0	0.0	0	0.0	0	0.0	0	0.0	0	0.0	0	0	1	0.2	100	0.4
	VER WH	Verulamium white ware mortaria	0	0.0	0	0.0	0	0.0	0	0.0	0	0.0	0	0	0	0.0	0	0.0
Amphorae	BAT AM	Baetican amphorae	27	73.0	1,476	94.7	112	77.8	5,791	97.6	26	36.1	1,809	61	372	58.1	2,1780	85.0
	CAD AM	South Spanish (Cadiz) amphora	0	0.0	0	0.0	0	0.0	0	0.0	1	1.4	182	6	0	0.0	0	0.0
	CAM AM	Campanian amphorae	0	0.0	0	0.0	0	0.0	0	0.0	5	6.9	325	11	1	0.2	41	0.2
	CAT AM	Catalan amphora	0	0.0	0	0.0	0	0.0	0	0.0	0	0.0	0	0	0	0.0	0	0.0
	GAL AM	Gallic amphorae	0	0.0	0	0.0	0	0.0	0	0.0	2	2.8	87	3	70	10.9	1,435	5.6
	AMP2–4	Dr 2–4	0	0.0	0	0.0	0	0.0	0	0.0	0	0.0	0	0	1	0.2	32	0.1
	RHO AM	Rhodian style	0	0.0	0	0.0	0	0.0	0	0.0	0	0.0	0	0	0	0.0	0	0.0
	AMP	Unidentified amphorae	0	0.0	0	0.0	0	0.0	0	0.0	3	4.2	60	2	0	0.0	0	0.0
Regional	DER CO	Derbyshire coarse ware	0	0.0	0	0.0	0	0.0	0	0.0	0	0.0	0	0	0	0.0	0	0.0
	DOR BB1	Dorset Black Burnished ware	0	0.0	0	0.0	0	0.0	0	0.0	0	0.0	0	0	0	0.0	0	0.0
	OXF WH	Oxfordshire white ware	0	0.0	0	0.0	0	0.0	0	0.0	0	0.0	0	0	0	0.0	0	0.0
	VER WH	Verulamium white ware	0	0.0	0	0.0	0	0.0	0	0.0	1	1.4	38	1	0	0.0	0	0.0
TOTAL			37	100.0	1,559	100.0	144	100.0	5,936	100.0	72	100.0	2,974	100	640	100.0	25,630	100.0

By contrast, other wine amphorae are less well represented and come from a variety of sources in Italy, Gaul, and the Aegean. Rhodian amphorae have been identified at Metchley along with Dressel 2–4 from Campania, Italy, and a small number of Gallic flat-bottomed types. This latter type although documented elsewhere in pre-Flavian deposits, did not appear to be a significant import into the province until after the Boudiccan revolt (Peacock 1978). The soft nature and the pale colour of the fabric may have caused it to be overlooked in the assemblages.

British regional imports at Metchley are extremely rare, and probably in most cases come from post-Flavian contexts. Amongst those recorded are Derbyshire coarse ware (DER CO), Dorset black burnished ware (DOR BB1), Oxfordshire white ware (OXF WH), and Verulamium white ware (VER WH).

The remaining assemblage comprises handmade 'native' wares, Severn Valley wares, presumed local wares, and wares of unknown source, but probably local. The native wares mainly include grog-tempered wares, handmade grey sandy wares, and Malvernian rock-tempered wares. The latter form a very distinct component and are present in most of the assemblages (e.g. Green et al. 2001, fig. 37; Hancocks 2005, fig. 26.76–7), mainly as tubby or everted-rim jars. It has been suggested that they may reflect trade in a commodity such as salt from Droitwich, rather than the pots themselves being the product (Green and Evans 2001, 106). The vessels often show signs of sooting (Hancocks 2005, 55), so they may have been particularly good cooking vessels with a high thermal shock capacity. The industry dates back to pre-Roman times, but vessels continued to be made and distributed into the 2nd century across the region.

Severn Valley wares form a major component of the Metchley assemblages. This is a widespread and quite dispersed industry with numerous kilns, only some of which have been located. Production sites are known from Perry Barr, Birmingham (Hughes 1959), the Malverns (Evans et al. 2000), and Alkington, Gloucestershire (Fowler and Bennett 1973). The earlier phases of the industry are characterized by a wide range of fabric variants, with wares variously tempered with charcoal, grog, and/or fine sand. Two of the more distinctive and better-represented forms from Metchley are large storage jars and tankards. In addition there is a variety of wide-mouthed jars, narrow-necked jars, dishes, and bowls.

A significant part of all the assemblages is a range of fine grey (reduced) or oxidized wares. These occur in various forms: jars, bowls, dishes, flagons, and beakers. It is quite likely that many of these wares may be local military products. In particular, the collared-rim (Hofheim) flagons (cf. Green et al. 2001, fig. 33.F1–6), flat-rimmed jars (fig. 38.B17), dishes (fig. 38.B16, B20), and mortaria are all classic military types. Other wares which may or may not belong to this possible production include the white-slipped flagons, which will be under-represented due to loss of the slips.

Table 3.10. Pottery, distribution of forms (by EVE) for Areas M7–M8 and M18 compared with Wroxeter.

Forms	Area M7–M8	Area M18	Wroxeter
	% EVE	% EVE	% EVE
Jars	56	50.9	57.2
Honey pot	0	0	1.4
Bowls/dishes	c.17	7.4	12.5
Flagon	9	18.9	12
Beakers	6	3.9	5.7
Cups	2	8.1	5.9
Tankards	2	8.2	0
Platters	3	0	0
Mortaria	<1	2.3	1.7
Lids	<1	<1	0.6
Amphorae	c.4	not inc.	not inc.
Lamp	0	0	2.6
Unclassified	0	0	0.4
Total	**100**	**100**	**100**

In terms of forms, very few of the Metchley assemblages have been quantified in such a way as to allow direct comparison within or between sites. In most cases the individual assemblages are too small for statistical validity. Table 3.10 summarizes the forms for Areas M7–M8 and M18, the only two areas with such data. In both cases, jars dominate. For Areas M7–M8, this is followed by bowls/dishes at around 15% EVE (Estimated Vessel Equivalent) and then flagons at 9%. By contrast, in Area M18 flagons were the second commonest type (18.9% EVE), followed by tankards and platters each at around 8% and then bowls/dishes at 7.4%. This might suggest further potential in the future for looking at the distribution of forms across the site for possible functional variability.

Intra-site comparisons

The data in Table 3.8 has been used to create a series of pie-charts for each of the analysed assemblages, showing the relative proportions of the main wares (expressed as a percentage number) (Figs 3.1a–i). There are a number of differences across the areas. For Areas M1–M5, M2 (M25), M6, M11, M14 and M18 local or unknown wares dominate. For Area M9, Severn Valley wares take up a marginally larger proportion of the chart, whilst for Areas M7–M8, Severn Valley ware dominates. The proportion of Samian present varies from 1.8% (by number), from Areas M1–M5, to a maximum of 4.6%, for Areas M7–M8. Other excavations where it is 4% or over of the total assemblage include Areas M14 and M15–M16. For Areas M6, M9, M11, and M18, the proportion ranges between 3.2 and 3.9%, and none was recorded from the small assemblage from Area M2. Overall, this shows quite a high level of consistency, immediately defining a site of some status and one which is commensurate with a 1st-century military site.

(a)

Relative proportions of main wares from Area M1, M3–M5 (expressed as % no)

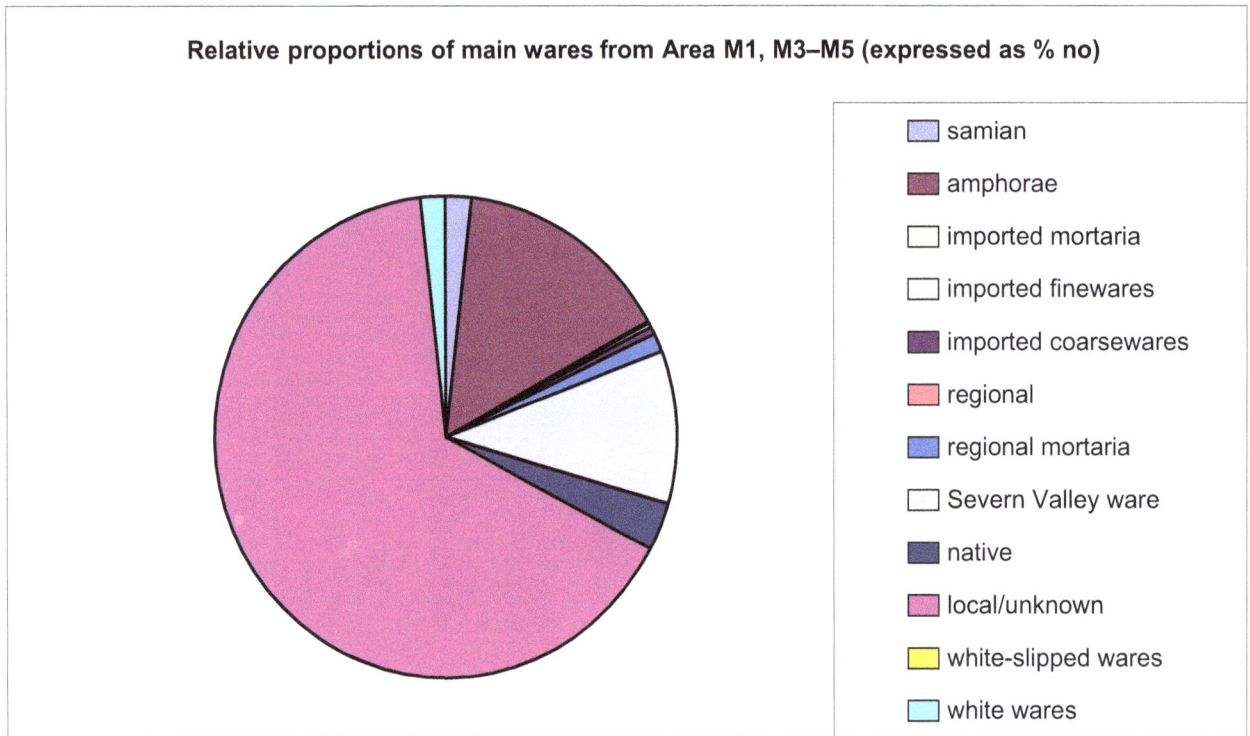

- samian
- amphorae
- imported mortaria
- imported finewares
- imported coarsewares
- regional
- regional mortaria
- Severn Valley ware
- native
- local/unknown
- white-slipped wares
- white wares

(b)

Relative proportions of main wares from Area M2 (expressed as % no)

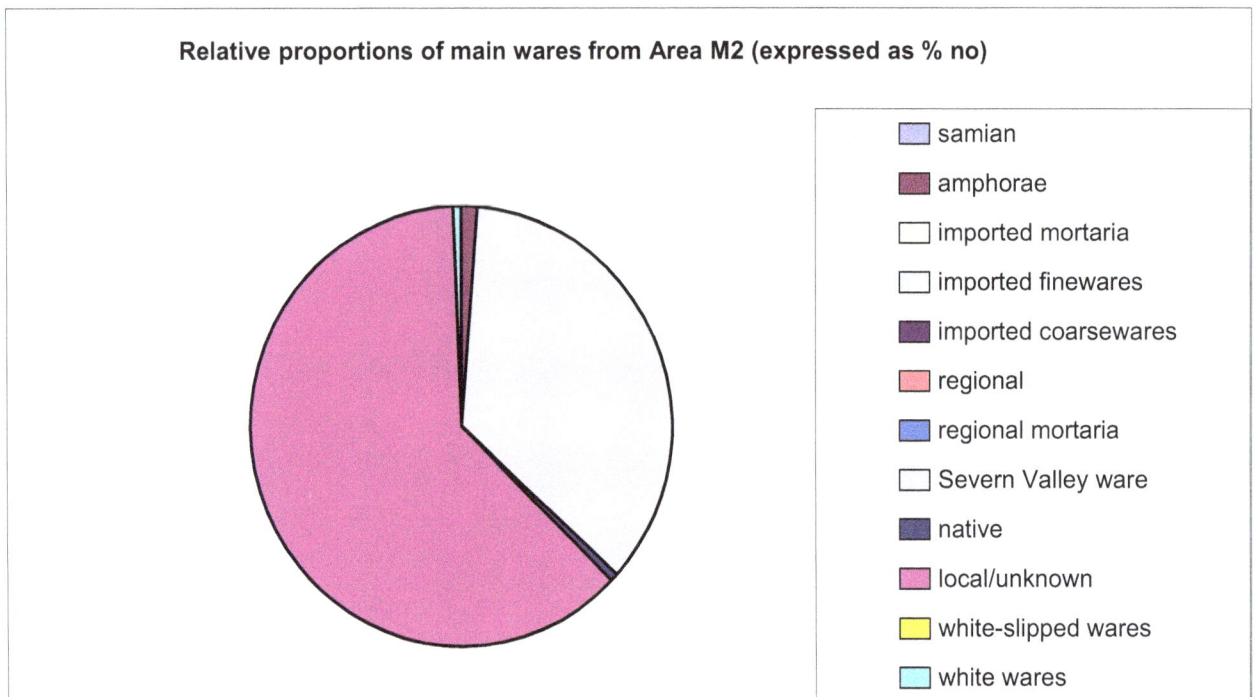

- samian
- amphorae
- imported mortaria
- imported finewares
- imported coarsewares
- regional
- regional mortaria
- Severn Valley ware
- native
- local/unknown
- white-slipped wares
- white wares

Figure 3.1. Relative proportions of main wares from different areas of the site.

(c)

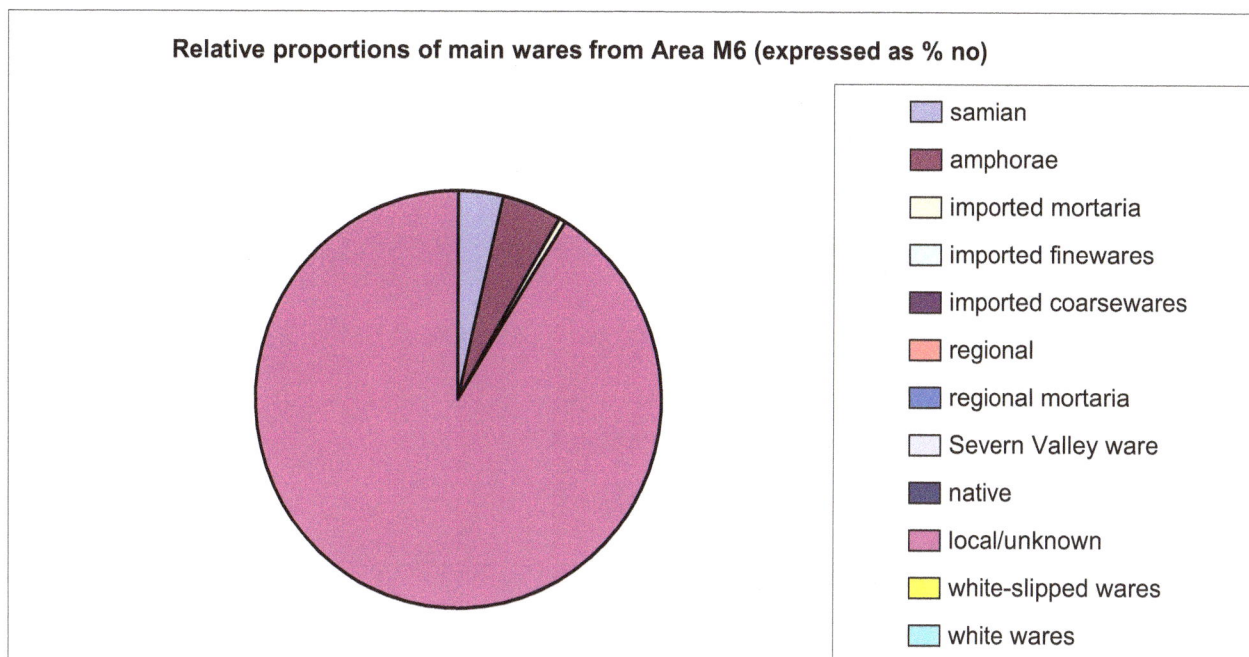

Relative proportions of main wares from Area M6 (expressed as % no)

Legend:
- samian
- amphorae
- imported mortaria
- imported finewares
- imported coarsewares
- regional
- regional mortaria
- Severn Valley ware
- native
- local/unknown
- white-slipped wares
- white wares

(d)

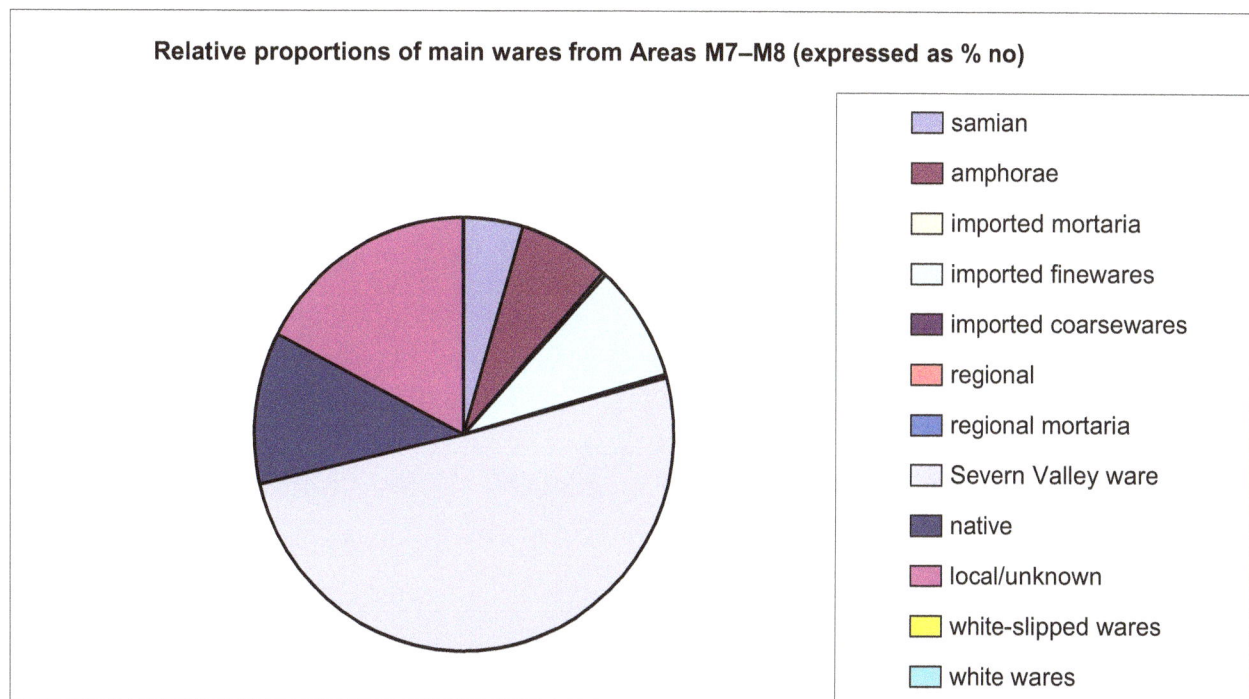

Relative proportions of main wares from Areas M7–M8 (expressed as % no)

Legend:
- samian
- amphorae
- imported mortaria
- imported finewares
- imported coarsewares
- regional
- regional mortaria
- Severn Valley ware
- native
- local/unknown
- white-slipped wares
- white wares

Figure 3.1. (*Continued*)

(e)

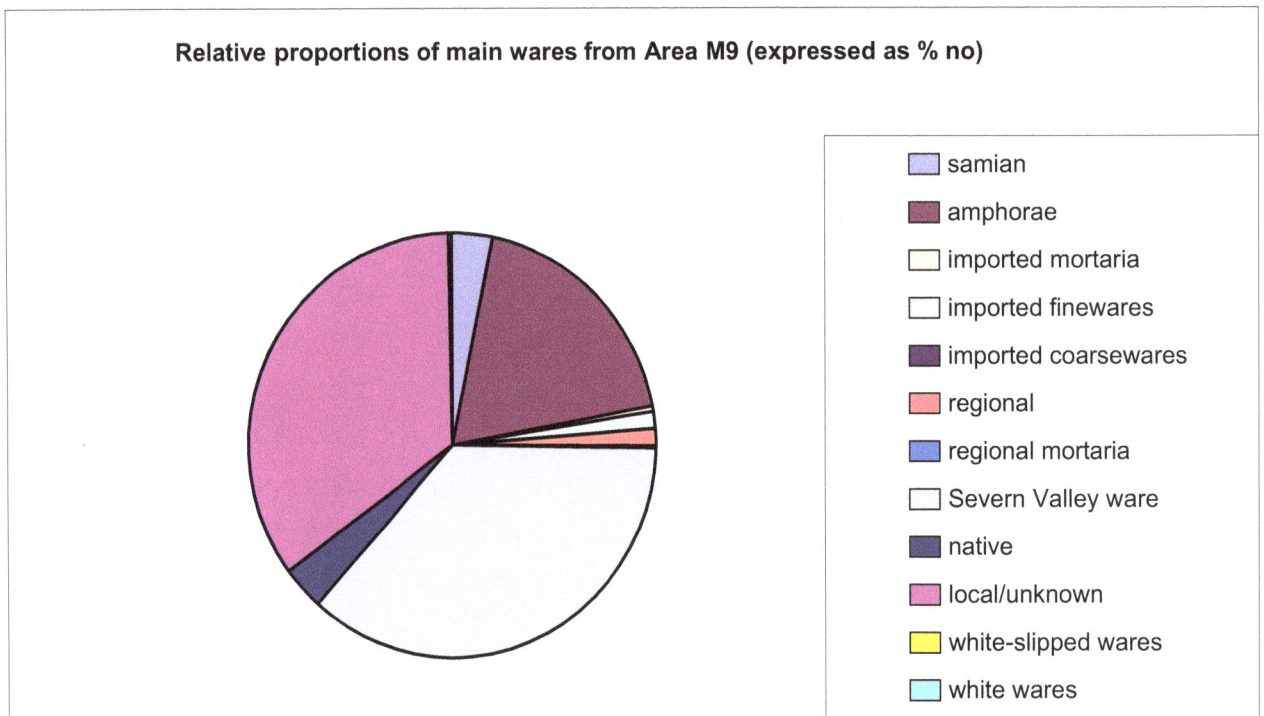

Relative proportions of main wares from Area M9 (expressed as % no)

samian
amphorae
imported mortaria
imported finewares
imported coarsewares
regional
regional mortaria
Severn Valley ware
native
local/unknown
white-slipped wares
white wares

(f)

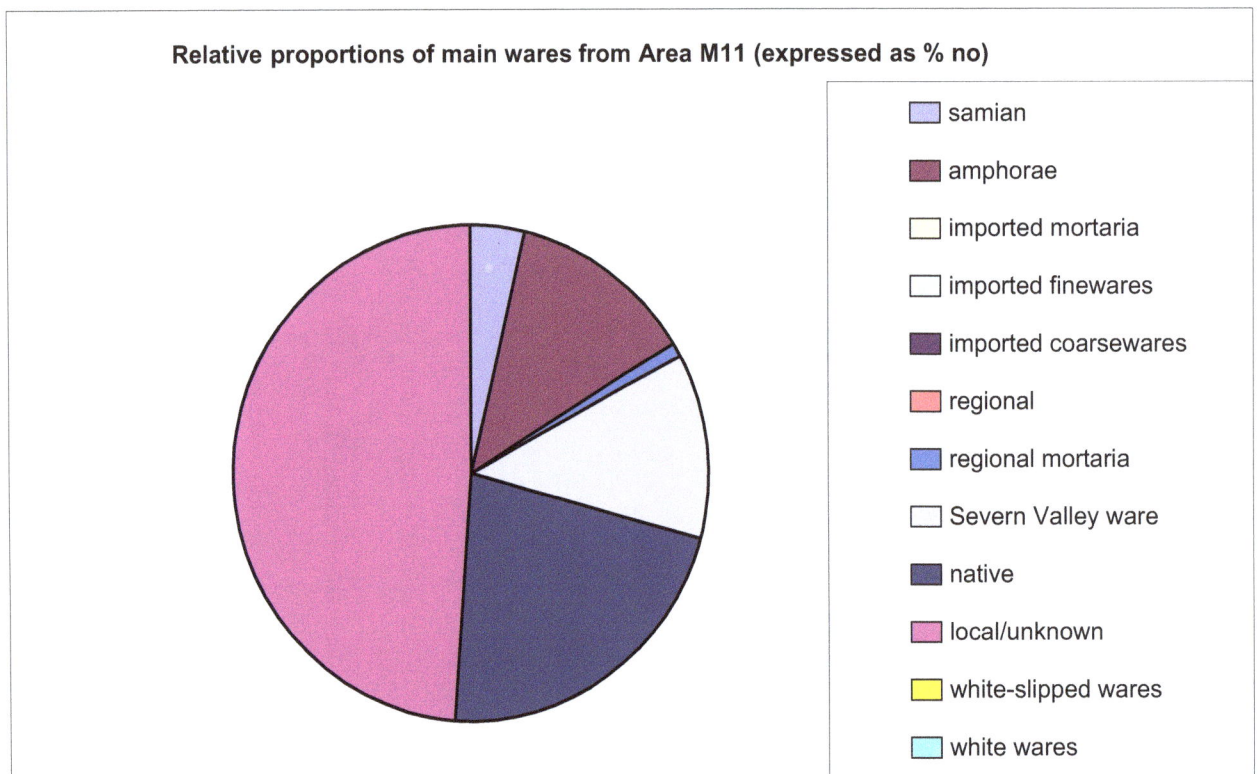

Relative proportions of main wares from Area M11 (expressed as % no)

samian
amphorae
imported mortaria
imported finewares
imported coarsewares
regional
regional mortaria
Severn Valley ware
native
local/unknown
white-slipped wares
white wares

Figure 3.1. (*Continued*)

(g)

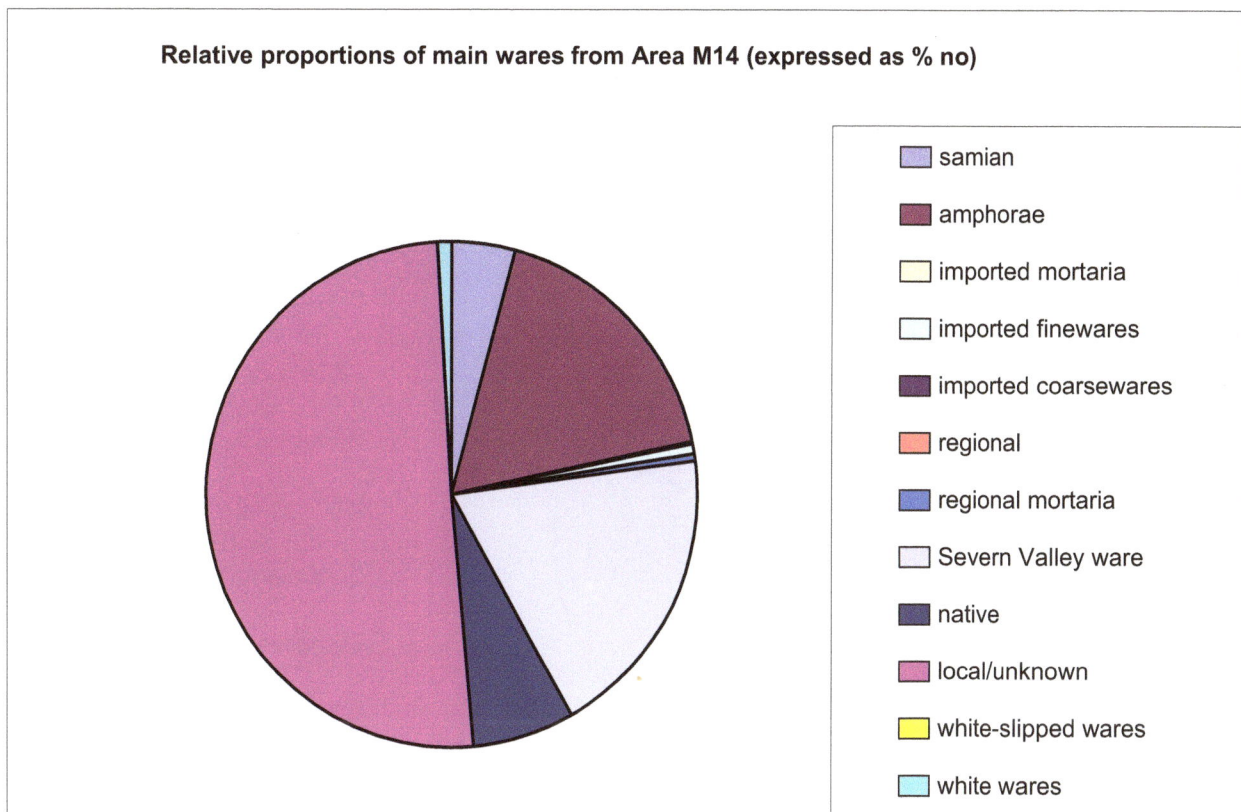

Relative proportions of main wares from Area M14 (expressed as % no)

Legend:
- samian
- amphorae
- imported mortaria
- imported finewares
- imported coarsewares
- regional
- regional mortaria
- Severn Valley ware
- native
- local/unknown
- white-slipped wares
- white wares

(h)

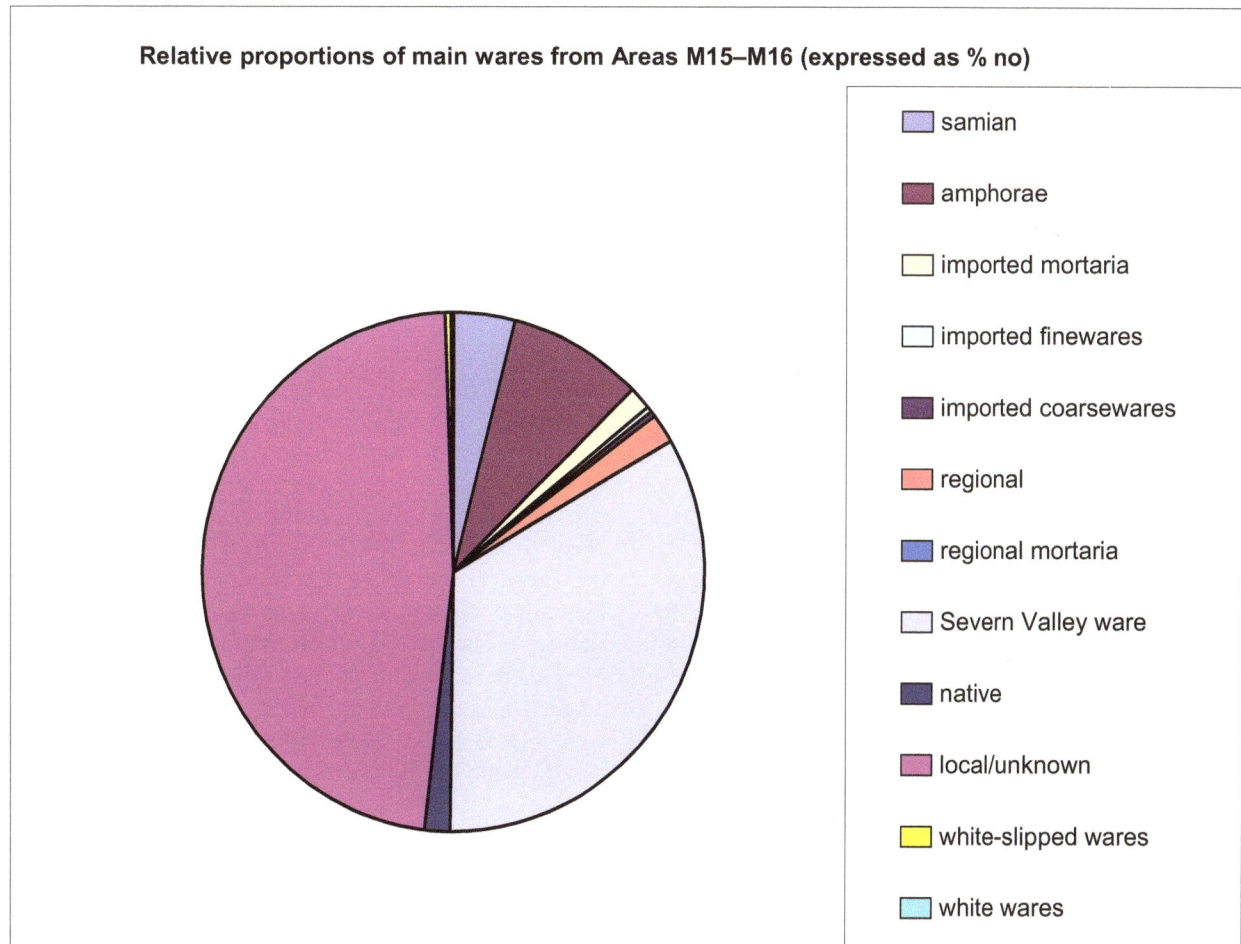

Relative proportions of main wares from Areas M15–M16 (expressed as % no)

Legend:
- samian
- amphorae
- imported mortaria
- imported finewares
- imported coarsewares
- regional
- regional mortaria
- Severn Valley ware
- native
- local/unknown
- white-slipped wares
- white wares

Figure 3.1. (*Continued*)

(i)

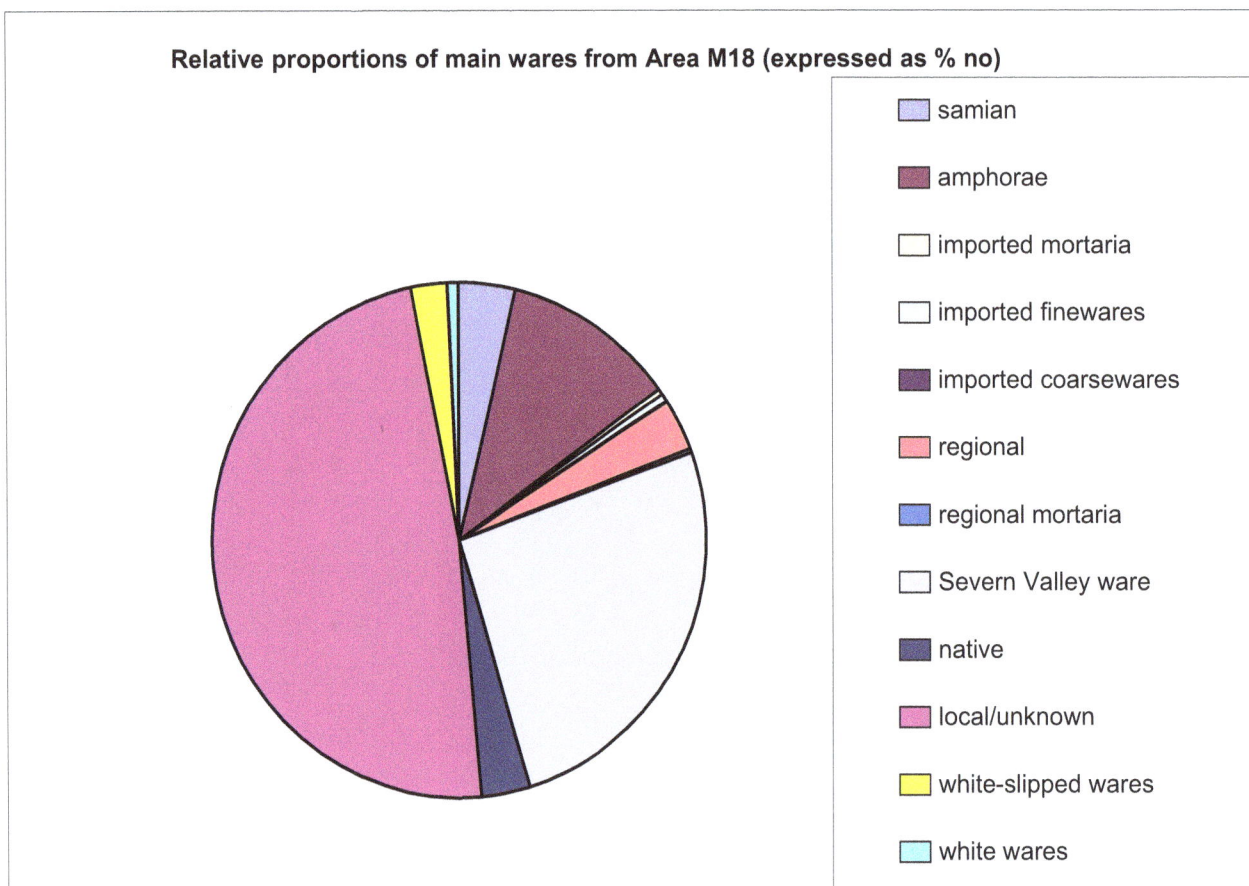

Figure 3.1. (*Continued*)

Amphorae are very well represented at Metchley, in particular the heavy Dressel 20 form. The sherd count ranges from 6.9% (Areas M7–M8) to a maximum of 18.9% (Area M9) (Area M2 not included). In terms of weight, it forms around 50% of the assemblages from Areas M14 and M9 and between c.40% and 50% of the material from Areas M6, M7–M8, M15–M16, and M18. This covers material from both the eastern and western sides of the fort and does not, on present evidence, suggest a central storage or warehouse area.

Imported mortaria, other fine wares, and coarse wares are present in very low amounts, and tend to feature more prominently in the larger assemblages. Similarly, regional wares and mortaria are in insufficient quantities to suggest any patterning. Native wares, on the other hand, are particularly prominent in Area M11, the trial-trenches in the north of the fort, where they make up 21.9% by count and 41.9% by weight of the assemblage. The second highest incidence of such material is from Areas M7–M8, much of which also lies outside the defences, but within annexed ground, where they contribute 11.3% count, 10.7% by weight. At the other investigations they contribute less than 5%.

Inter-site comparisons (Table 3.11)

The earliest military activity at Metchley (Chapter 1 above) is likely to be of mid-Neronian date. Other contemporary

military occupation in the west midlands is suggested at The Lunt, Greensforge, Mancetter, and Droitwich, northeast of Dodderhill. Unfortunately there is no detailed information available about the pottery assemblages recovered from many of these sites, but pottery has been recorded in more detail from Alcester (Booth and Evans 2001) (although largely for the later Roman assemblages) and Dodderhill (Rees 2006). The military fort at Wall was probably a Neronian foundation which continued in use into the Flavian period (Round 1983). The garrison fort at Metchley was replaced in the late Neronian period by a military stores depot (Phase 2B), followed by a new small garrison fort to be located there in the early Flavian period (Phase 3A). Similarly, the second fort at Alcester is dated to the AD 60s (Booth and Evans 2001, 301). Military occupation continued into the 2nd century at Alcester and Droitwich. Further afield, a postulated legionary base was established at Kingsholm in the Neronian period, to be abandoned c.AD 66/67, and subsequently replaced by a later Flavian fortress at Gloucester. Similarly fortresses were located at Usk, South Wales (Manning 1981), which was probably in full occupation from around c.AD 55 until c.AD 66/67 and Wroxeter, also probably initially established in the Neronian period.

The pre-Flavian period is one when the military situation appears very fluid, with much movement and reorganization of troops connected with the conquest of

Wales; the departure from Britain of the XIVth legion in AD 66 and the Boudican revolt in AD 60. The evidence for pre-Flavian supply is less certain, but it has been suggested that the long-distance supply arrangements were basically an extension of those used in the Rhineland (Hurst 1985, 124). Work recently carried out on the earliest military occupation levels at Head Street, Colchester, showed a remarkable paucity of imported finewares and mortaria, apart from Samian, along with a low incidence and restricted diversity of amphorae. Samian accounted for *c*.4.6% of the early groups, and Dressel 20 dominated the amphorae (Timby 2004). Present from the earliest layers, however, were examples of locally made Colchester mortaria, colour-coated ware, fine black and grey ware, oxidized cream and orange tablewares, and coarser oxidized and grey wares. The repertoire of forms and technology all point to the presence of potters among the arriving army. The assumption has long been made that military pottery was made by serving soldiers (Breeze 1977; Greene 1993) and it is clear from the forms at Colchester, Usk, Kingsholm, and elsewhere that these are potters – whether serving soldiers or appropriated civilians – with firm continental traditions and origins, seen in the particular range of forms produced. This highlights two things: first, the two most important ceramic products for the invading army were Samian table wares, presumably for the officer class and the foodstuffs contained in the amphorae; and second, the army was able to furnish its own pottery supplies. The Samian and amphorae from Colchester could have been part of the baggage train of the invading army, as it seems unlikely that a supply network would have been established at such an early date.

This very much seems to be the situation hinted at from Metchley, where the most significant imports are the Samian wares, averaging around 3% by count overall (see Tables 3.9a, b) and the Dressel 20 amphorae (12% count; 24.2% weight). A few other imports seem quite typical of Neronian sites in the west. Table 3.12 provides a presence/absence checklist of continental and regional imports for eight selected sites with Neronian occupation in the west. Rocester is added for comparison, although the assemblage is slightly later, dating to the Flavian–Trajanic period (Leary 1996).

The range of wares identified is to a certain extent dictated by when the reports were compiled, and for older reports, wares have been identified from illustrations or descriptions, so some types may easily have been overlooked. As can be seen from Table 3.11, Metchley compares well with Kingsholm and Wroxeter in terms of the different types/sources of import represented, 19 wares compared to 20 and 23 respectively. Usk ranks highest, with at least 30 different sources/wares represented. Brandon Camp, Herefordshire, is also moderately close, with 13 types, but this report was prepared some time ago, so other wares may also be present (Frere 1987b). All nine sites shown on Table 3.12 have produced South Gaulish Samian, and seven have sherds of Lyon ware. No Lyon ware is recorded from Alcester and Rocester – the former probably due to the very small Claudio-Neronian assemblage, the latter probably due to chronology.

With the exception of Usk, other imported fine wares appear quite sporadic. All the sites have sherds of North Gaulish white ware mortaria and at least six, perhaps seven, have Central Gaulish (Rhône Valley) vessels. Other types are documented, but never in any significant quantities. The amphorae present a similar story, with Baetican wares present on every site, Gallic wine amphorae on seven sites, Rhodian wine amphorae on at least five sites, and Cadiz fish-sauce examples from six sites. Rhodian amphorae are generally seen as specifically associated with early military supply. Williams (2001, 104) notes that they are particularly common in sites in Germany and Britain in the 40s and 50s, and may represent the payment of a tribute of wine, some of which was allocated to the army (Peacock 1977).

Many of the sites in Table 3.12 have produced evidence for pottery production; that from Kingsholm, Wroxeter, and Usk has been well documented (Darling 1985; 2002; Greene 1993). As noted above, there is some likelihood that there was pottery production at Metchley. The pottery from The Lunt includes distorted vessels which may indicate wasters (Webster 1973, fig. 18.211–12), and at Wall, wasters were found in a fine grey ware (Leary 1998, 36).

From the Flavian period onwards, literary and archaeological evidence shows the legions to have been responsible for their own supplies (food and equipment) either through on-site production and manufacture or through established supply systems (Hurst 1985). Rocester has the least diversity of wares present, with very few continental imports, demonstrating a change compared to the pre-Flavian sites. By the Flavian period there were a large number of industries established in Britain to supply military establishments, for example at Mancetter–Hartshill, Derby, and Verulamium/London. The sources of continental wares have also changed, with Argonne and Cologne beakers and other fine wares replacing the Lyon ware. For this reason one should be cautious of coming to spurious conclusions when trying to compare components of pre-Flavian assemblages with later groups.

It is suggested that the road linking Sea Mills to Gloucester, and continuing northwards to the Birmingham area, has a military origin (Hurst 1985, 119). Sea Mills, with an abundance of evidence for Claudio-Neronian and later occupation, was probably a supply depot from the Neronian period. The site has produced a diverse range of imports and very high levels of early Samian. This may have been one route by which continental supplies were reaching Metchley and other sites in the west midlands.

The range of forms present from Metchley appears significantly more limited compared to (for example)

Table 3.11. Pottery, quantified comparison of all pottery from Metchley, compared with data from Kingsholm, Wroxeter, and Dodderhill.

Category	Fabric	Description	Metchley No.	Metchley No. %	Metchley Wt	Metchley Wt %	Kingsholm No.	Kingsholm No. %	Kingsholm Wt	Kingsholm Wt %	Wroxeter Wt %	Dodderhill No.	Dodderhill No. %
Imported fine ware	LGF SA	South Gaulish Samian	459	3.0	2,627.5	1.0	300	7.9	5,432	3.6	2.4	121	7.5
	LEZ SA	Central Gaulish Samian	13	0.1	67	0.0	0	0.0	0	0.0	0.5	0	0.0
	LYO CC	Lyon ware	52	0.3	69	0.0	159	4.2	725	0.5	0.4	4	0.2
	LEZ CC	Lezoux colour-coated ware	0	0.0	0	0.0	30	0.8	97	0.1	0.4	0	0.0
	NOG WH	North Gaulish white ware	191	1.3	366	0.1	0	0.0	0	0.0	0.3	0	0.0
	GAB TN	Gallo-Belgic terra nigra	0	0.0	0	0.0	5	0.1	22	0.0	0	8	0.5
	NOG RE	Gallo-Belgic beakers	0	0.0	0	0.0	32	0.8	125	0.1	0	0	0.0
	ITA EG	North Italian fineware	0	0.0	0	0.0	12	0.3	23	0.0	0	0	0.0
	CNG GL	Central Gaulish glazed ware	0	0.0	0	0.0	4	0.1	24	0.0	0.1	0	0.0
	MICA	Imported mica-dusted ware	0	0.0	0	0.0	1	0.0	1	0.0	0	0	0.0
Imported coarse ware	ITA WH	Campanian coarse ware	3	0.0	14	0.0	0	0.0	0	0.0	0	0	0.0
	CAM PR1	Pompeian red ware fabric 1	3	0.0	47	0.0	244	6.5	5,017	3.3	0.1	0	0.0
	CAM PR2	Pompeian red ware fabric 2	0	0.0	0	0.0	37	1.0	206	0.1	0	0	0.0
	CNG CW	?Central Gaulish coarse ware	29	0.2	80	0.0	11	0.3	146	0.1	0.1	0	0.0
	IMP MISC	Imported flagon	1	0.0	137	0.1	0	0.0	0	0.0	0	0	0.0
Mortaria	AOI WH	Aoste, Isere white ware (ATISI)	0	0.0	0	0.0	1	0.0	75	0.0	0	0	0.0
	CNG OX	Central Gaulish oxidized	27	0.2	1,682	0.7	15	0.4	3,110	2.1	0	1	0.1
	NOG WH4	North Gaulish white ware	15	0.1	558	0.2	9	0.2	2,045	1.3	0.8	1	0.1
	MAH WH	Mancetter–Hartshill	13	0.1	352	0.1	0	0.0	0	0.0	0	0	0.0
	OXF WH	Oxfordshire white ware mortaria	1	0.0	4	0.0	0	0.0	0	0.0	0	0	0.0
	WRX WH	?Wroxeter/west midlands mortaria	2	0.0	120	0.0	0	0.0	0	0.0	6.3	0	0.0
	VER WH	Verulamium white ware mortaria	5	0.0	186	0.1	0	0.0	0	0.0	0.8	2	0.1

Amphorae	BAT AM	Baetican amphorae	1,824	12.0	61,055	24.2	292	7.7	42,388	28.0	33.2	98	6.1
	CAD AM	South Spanish (Cadiz) amphora	8	0.1	282	0.1	76	2.0	7,264	4.8	6	0	0.0
	CAM AM	Campanian amphorae	6	0.0	365	0.1	0	0.0	0	0.0	0	0	0.0
	CAT AM	Catalan amphora	4	0.0	253	0.1	0	0.0	0	0.0	0	0	0.0
	GAL AM	Gallic amphorae	73	0.5	1,532	0.6	51	1.4	3,509	2.3	1.9	2	0.1
	P&W AM12	Carrot amphora (Cam 189)	0	0.0	0	0.0	349	9.2	7,994	5.3	0.8	0	0.0
	AMP2–4	Dr 2–4	10	0.1	92	0.0	0	0.0	0	0.0	0.7	0	0.0
	RHO AM	Rhodian style	7	0.0	40	0.0	336	8.9	30,776	20.3	1.1	1	0.1
	AMP	Unidentified amphorae	59	0.4	817	0.3	269	7.1	15,622	10.3	2.8	0	0.0
Regional	DER CO	Derbyshire coarse ware	6	0.0	42	0.0	0	0.0	0	0.0			0.0
	DOR BB1	Dorset Black Burnished ware	1	0.0	22	0.0	13	0.3	61	0.0	0	0	0.0
	OXF WH	Oxfordshire white ware	4	0.0	19	0.0	0	0.0	0	0.0	0	0	0.0
	SAV GT	Savernake ware	0	0.0	0	0.0	1	0.0	20	0.0	0	0	0.0
	SVW OX	Severn Valley wares	3,703	24.3	41,069	16.3	109	2.9	2,403	1.6	1.3	804	49.7
	VER WH	Verulamium white ware	15	0.1	97	0.0	16	0.4	205	0.1	0.6	0	0.0
Native	NAT	Handmade native wares	703	4.6	15,723	6.2	15	0.4	462	0.3	0.3	97	6.0
Local/other	LOC	Local/other wares	8,023	52.6	124,748	49.4	1,387	36.8	23,833	15.7	38.5	479	29.6
TOTAL			15,260	100.0	252,466	100.0	3,774	100.0	151,585	100.0	99.4	1618	100.0

63

Table 3.12. Presence/absence of well-known traded wares from a range of early military sites.

	Fabric	Description	Metchley	Kingsholm	Wroxeter	Usk	Dodderhill	Alcester	Wall	Brandon	Rocester
Imported fw	LGF SA	South Gaulish samian	Y	Y	Y	Y	Y	Y	Y	Y	Y
	LYO CC	Lyon ware	Y	Y	Y	Y	Y		Y	Y	
	CNG CC	Lezoux colour-coated ware		Y	Y	Y					
	NOG WH	North Gaulish white ware	Y		Y	Y			Y	Y	
	GAB TN	Gallo-Belgic terra nigra		Y	Y	Y	Y				
	NOG RE	North Gaulish blackware				Y				Y	
	ITA EG	North Italian fineware		Y		Y				Y	
	CNG GL	Central Gaulish glazed ware		Y	Y	Y			Y	Y	
	SOG CC	South Gaulish colour-coated				Y					
	LRH CC	Lower Rhineland colour-coated				Y					
	ITA CC	Italian colour-coated				Y					
	SPA CC	Spanish colour-coated ware				Y					
	MICA	imported mica-dusted ware		Y		Y					
	LAMP	lamp		Y	Y	Y				Y	
Imported cw	ITA WH	Campanian coarseware	Y								
	CAM PR1	Pompeian redware fabric 1	Y	Y	Y	Y					
	CAM PR2	Pompeian redware fabric 2		Y		Y					
	CAM PR3	Pompeian redware fabric 3		Y	Y	Y					
	IMP MISC	imported flagon	Y								

			18	20	23	30	10	7	10	13	8
Mortaria	AOI WH	Aoste, Isere		Y	Y	Y					
	CNG OX	Central Gaulish oxidised	Y	Y	Y	Y	Y		Y	Y	
	COL WH	Colchester mortaria				Y					Y
	NOG WH4	North Gaulish white ware	Y	Y	Y	Y	Y	Y	Y	Y	Y
	ITA WH	Italian mortaria				Y					
	MAH WH	Mancetter-Hartshill	Y						Y		
	RHL WH	Upper Rhineland/Eifel				Y					
	WRX WH	?Wroxeter/W Midlands mortaria	Y		Y			Y	Y	Y	Y
	VER WH	Verulamium white ware mortaria	Y		Y	Y		Y	Y		Y
Amphorae	BAT AM	Baetican amphorae	Y	Y	Y	Y	Y	Y	Y	Y	Y
	CAD AM	South Spanish (Cadiz) amphora	Y	Y	Y	Y				Y	Y
	CAM AM	Campanian amphorae Dr 2-4	Y		Y	Y				Y	
	CAT AM	Catalan amphora	Y		Y						
	GAL AM	Gallic amphorae	Y	Y	Y	Y	Y	Y			Y
	P&W AM12	Carrot amphora (Cam 189)		Y	Y	Y					
	RHO AM	Rhodian style	Y	Y	Y	Y	Y				
	Dressel 7-11	Dressel 7-11			Y						
	EMED AM	East Mediterranean			Y						
	AMP	unidentified amphorae	Y	Y	Y		Y	Y			Y
Total			18	20	23	30	10	7	10	13	8

Kingsholm, Usk, or Wroxeter. This may be a reflection of the legionary status of these other sites, compared to Metchley, or to do with the length of occupation. To date, certain forms that might have been expected at Metchley are absent, most noticeably closed or open lamps, honey pots, and carrot amphorae (Camulodunum type 189). Table 3.10 compares the breakdown of forms (% EVE) from the Wroxeter military phase against Metchley Areas M7–M8 and M18. The relative proportions are very similar to Metchley, with jars dominating, followed by bowls/dishes and flagons in almost equal amounts and then drinking vessels. Unfortunately, comparable data are not available from the other sites discussed above to extend the comparison.

There is very little evidence for any later prehistoric or non-military 1st-century occupation near Metchley. A ditched enclosure of mid- to late Iron Age date followed by Roman activity from the late 1st–2nd century through to the 4th century was excavated at Langley Mill along the M6 Toll to the north of Birmingham (Powell and Ritchie 2008, Site 29). The site produced no South Gaulish Samian and few other specialist wares (Leary 2008a). A Romano-British livestock complex was excavated at Kings Norton, Birmingham (Jones et al. 2008), but most of the activity here dated to the 2nd–4th century. These 'rural' sites, in contrast to the military establishments, appear to show a low consumption of Samian and limited or no access to other imported wares (Leary 2008b).

Conclusion

A high proportion of the pottery from the Metchley excavations is pre-Flavian. The most dateable material in the recovered assemblages is the Samian, Lyon ware, mortaria, and Dressel 20 amphorae rims. Lyon ware is traditionally regarded as a pre-Flavian (AD 40–70) import in southern and central Britain. Flagons also provide another chronological marker, with the collared (Hofheim-type) flagons being typical of the pre-Flavian period, to be gradually replaced from the early Flavian period by ring-necked forms. Some of the vessels from Areas M1–M6 included material assigned a late 1st- or early 2nd-century date, but only one sherd of Samian was thought to be Flavian and there was no later datable Samian (Green and Evans 2001, 105). Some of the mortaria is dated to the Flavio-Trajanic period. Later activity was also documented in Areas M7 and M8, which featured amongst other types ring-necked flagons.

The range of forms and fabrics appears very typical of any early pre-Flavian military establishment where supplies are being drawn from the indigenous native industries, in this case the Severn Valley ware potters and Malvernian kilns supplemented by imported specialist vessels – fine wares, mortaria, and amphorae probably coming through the military supply system. It has been suggested that changes in the pottery present observed between different military occupations over time at all these various military sites might suggest that different army units controlled their own supplies (Hurst 1985, 125). This may also be due to changes in Roman military central administration and available supplies, or may reflect the previous locality the new garrison had been moved from. As with many other military establishments, it is extremely likely that Metchley was also producing its own wares to supplement what was locally available. This is likely to have included mortaria, flagons, jars, dishes, and perhaps drinking vessels. The restricted repertoire of forms compared to other military production elsewhere at the time might suggest a very short period of production.

4

Environmental Evidence

Val Fryer

This chapter was compiled in 2010, and has not been updated.

Introduction

Although the latter stages of work at Metchley saw the introduction of a systematic regime of sampling for plant macrofossils, pollen, charcoal, and insect remains, excavations prior to 1970 were conducted before the value of environmental analysis was recognized. Therefore, evidence from the fort interior and other areas investigated prior to 1970 was very limited. In addition, the acidic nature of the soil, and the fact that the area had been greatly disturbed by various groundworks over the years, generally meant that the few remains which were recorded were very poorly preserved, with some groups of material, for example bone and molluscs, being almost entirely absent. Notwithstanding these issues, however, the environmental evidence from the fort and its surroundings is of interest, with the pollen and charcoal data in particular clearly illustrating how the day-to-day life of the fort impacted on the area, and how the environment developed in the later Roman and post-Roman periods.

Methodology

Standard methods of sampling and processing were used throughout. The plant macrofossil samples were processed using water flotation, with the flots being collected in either 300- or 500-micron mesh sieves. Most flots were dried prior to sorting, although some wet retents were stored in water to maintain the equilibrium of the material. Both dried flots and wet retents were sorted under a binocular microscope at ×10 magnification. Non-floating residues were collected in a 1mm-mesh sieve and sorted when dry. Insect samples were processed using paraffin flotation as outlined in Kenward et al. (1980), and the flots were sorted at ×20 magnification. Charcoal fragments >2mm in radial cross section were selected for identification, with fragments from each sample being fractured to expose fresh transverse surfaces. The material was sorted using a ×20 hand lens. Representative fragments were selected for detailed study at magnifications up to ×400. Pollen samples were processed using fine filters to concentrate the size fraction of the pollen, followed by swirl separation and filtration on a 10-micron mesh. The material was acetolysed to remove cellulose, stained with safranin, and mounted on microscope slides using glycerol jelly. Identifications of all categories of material were done by comparison with modern reference specimens.

Charcoal and seeds from the basal deposits within Phase 3A fort ditch F252.05 (Area M8) were submitted to the radiocarbon laboratory at the University of Waikato, New Zealand. The AMS radiocarbon date for this material was 180 cal BC–cal AD 70. Two samples from Phase 4C deposits in Area M18 (Jones 2012, table 4.6) were dated cal BC 50–AD 90 and cal BC 60–AD 80 (Beta Analytic).

Results

Full lists, tables, and discussions relating to all categories of environmental evidence can be found within the individual reports (Monckton 2001; Greig 2002; Ciaraldi 2005; Greig 2005; Smith 2005; Ciaraldi 2011; Greig 2012a; 2012b; McKenna 2012; Ciaraldi 2025; Greig 2025a; 2025b; Hopla and McKenna 2025).

Although a number of samples for the retrieval of both charred and waterlogged plant macrofossils were taken, remains were generally very scarce and preservation was frequently quite poor. Charred grains of wheat (*Triticum* sp.), barley (*Hordeum* sp.), and oats (*Avena* sp.) were recorded, but in many instances the cereals were too poorly preserved for close identification. Of the identifiable grains, emmer (*T. dicoccum*), spelt (*T. spelta*), and bread (*T. aestivum/compactum*) type wheats were recorded, along with asymmetrical grains of six-row barley (*H. vulgare*). However, cereal chaff was consistently scarce.

With the exception of occasional pieces of hazel (*Corylus avellana*) nutshell, which almost certainly represented the remains of casual gathered foods or snacks, evidence of other charred food plants was limited. De-watered/waterlogged fig (*Ficus carica*) seeds and grape (*Vitis vinifera*) pips were noted within a sample from Structure 12.5 in Area M12 (Ciaraldi 2025), and further grape pips were recorded from beam-slot 105 within Area M25 (Hopla and McKenna 2025) and feature F422 within Area M14 (Smith 2011, 36). Lentils (*Lens esculens*), which are rarely recorded, were noted within post-pit 4165 in Area M20 (Greig 2025b).

Charred seeds also occurred very infrequently, with most being of common grassland herbs. Taxa noted included meadow/creeping/bulbous buttercup (*Ranunculus acris/repens/bulbosus*), bedstraw types (*Galium* sp.), dock (*Rumex* sp.), medick/trefoil/clover (*Medicago/Lotus/Trifolium* sp.), stitchwort (*Stellaria graminea*), vetch/vetchling (*Vicia/Lathyrus* sp.), sedge (*Carex* sp.), spike-rush (*Eleocharis* sp.), and various grasses (Poaceae).

Occasional seeds of weeds more commonly found on disturbed ground (e.g. fat-hen type (*Chenopodium* sp.)) were recorded, but at an insufficient density to indicate that any agricultural production was occurring within the immediate vicinity of the fort. Waterlogged plant assemblages were only recorded on three occasions (fort ditch F250.05, Greig 2005) and features within Area M12 (Ciaraldi 2025) and Area M25 (Hopla and McKenna 2025). The results were somewhat limited but, as with the charred assemblages, they did appear to indicate that damp, slightly overgrown grassland conditions were prevalent within the vicinity of the fort.

Detailed analysis of charcoal residues was undertaken on material recovered from Areas M7–M8 (Gale 2005), Area M12 (Gale 2025), and Area M25 (Hopla and McKenna 2025). The evidence from all areas was broadly similar, with examples of oak (*Quercus*), ash (*Fraxinus*), hazel, birch (*Betula*), willow/poplar (*Salix/Populus*), alder (*Alnus*), sloe (*Prunus spinosa*), and hawthorn/*Sorbus* type (Pomoideae) charcoal occurring throughout. However, in most instances, oak charcoal was predominant, suggesting both that oak was the preferred fuel for the various activities conducted on or near the fort and, in the case of beam-slot F168 (Area M12), that it was sufficiently plentiful locally to provide largewood for structural use.

Only three samples, from waterlogged deposits within the Area M8 southern fort ditches, produced insect remains (Smith 2005), and even here the faunal assemblages were very small and poorly preserved. The majority of the insects present, in particular the water beetles such as *Hygrotus inequalis* and the *Ochthebius* and *Enochrus* species, and the larval resting stage of the Daphnia water flea, are associated with areas of slow-flowing, still, or temporary water. Other habitats indicated by the insect remains included detritus-covered muddy ground adjacent to water, pasture, and grassland, but it was noted that few species normally associated with human settlement or activity were recorded.

Pollen from the Phase 3 rampart in Area M3, dug in 1968 (Strachan 2001, 107–8), was dominated by species which indicated a fairly damp woodland environment, but also contained heathland and grassland species. Evidence for erosion, in particular within Area M19 (Fig. 1.3), may have derived from stripping turf for use in rampart construction (Jones 2011, 105). The felling of timber for the construction of timber-framed buildings will have caused a significant change in the local landscape.

Two detailed pollen sequences were obtained, one from the backfill deposits within Area M8 fort ditch F252.05 (Greig 2005) and one from Area M25 ditch 132/re-cut 147 (Hopla and McKenna 2025). Both sequences were from deposits which accumulated when the second fort was established (Phase 3A ditch 132, and Phase 4A re-cut 147), or at the end of its functional life (Phase 4A–5 fills within ditch F252.05 in Area M8), and both showed that tree/shrub species, including alder, hawthorn (*Crataegus*),

sloe, hazel type, elder (*Sambucus nigra*), willow (*Salix*), oak, and birch were, somewhat surprisingly, locally predominant. Herbaceous pollen indicative of unwooded open grassland was also recorded along with pollen of wetland/aquatic plants and cereals, although the latter was limited. As the ditch F252.05 sequence continued into the post-fort period, it showed an initial increase in oak and ash woodland, followed by limited woodland clearance during the post-Roman period and the beginnings of the cultivation of rye (*Secale cereale*). Woodland management followed, and the end of the sequence showed an increase of herb pollen, possibly suggesting that the nearby land was being farmed in the medieval and post-medieval periods.

Discussion

In the following discussion, only the broad phase divisions have been used. Further subdivision was largely impossible, as the corpus of environmental evidence was so limited.

Phase 1: Construction camp and first fort (mid-Neronian)

Phase 1 saw the establishment of the first fort on a gravel ridge with a nearby water supply. The fort superseded a construction camp. A small civilian settlement was also established outside the western defences.

Very few samples were taken from features associated with this phase of activity, and those assemblages studied mostly contained very low densities of plant remains. Scattered refuse, including cereal grains, weed seeds, and fragments of charcoal/charred wood, appeared to be predominant, but although both wheat and barley were represented, chaff was entirely absent. This appeared to indicate that the processing of cereals for both human and animal consumption did not occur within the immediate vicinity, implying that the cereal requirements of the fort were met by the importation of semi-cleaned or prime grain from elsewhere. Similar evidence has been recorded at the Roman fort of Rocester (Moffett 1996, Ciaraldi unpublished). Somewhat unusually in a Roman context, barley was predominant within the Phase 1 assemblages. Although almost certainly used in bread and porridge, Caesar (cf. Davies 1971) states that it was given to soldiers as a form of punishment, and it certainly is more commonly seen as being used for animal fodder. Structure 12.1 is interpreted as a stable and Structure 12.4 (also in the central range) is interpreted as a barn or stable. However, barley was also widely used for brewing (cf evidence from a later 3rd-century 'brewery' at St Albans, Fryer 2006).

The few seeds recorded within the Phase 1 features were mostly of grasses and grassland herbs, with segetal taxa occurring very infrequently. It is assumed that many of these seeds were derived from burnt fodder or from the use of grassland herbs as kindling, although it should be noted that tracts of grassland outside the fort area were almost certainly being utilized for the digging of turf to be used for the construction of the ramparts – although the latter would leave little evidence within the charred plant macrofossil record. A moderate density of sedge fruits noted within Area M9 pit F260 may have been indicative of burnt flooring, bedding, or thatching materials. Assuming that such materials were harvested locally, these may imply that some features within the civilian settlement area were seasonally wet or waterfilled during the Roman period.

Analysis of the assemblages from beam-slots F183.01 and F183.02, both in the *praetentura* (Area M12), appeared to indicate that both contained possible industrial residues in the form of charcoal and slag. Similar material was also recorded from ditch F169.01 in the right *praetentura* and beam-slot F110 towards the centre of Area M12, possibly suggesting that smithing hearths were a feature within the fort and its environs at this time. The charcoal was predominantly of oak, although other species included, somewhat unusually, ivy (*Hedera helix*). Charcoal made from oak heartwood from wide poles/trunk wood or cordwood appears to have been favoured as an industrial fuel, as the density and weight of the wood provided a greater weight of carbon per volume. Essentially, it lasted longer and provided a higher heat energy source. Comparable use of oak as the dominant fuel for industrial purposes is known from Biddlesdon Road, east of Banbury, Oxfordshire (Gale unpublished), Watchfield, Oxfordshire (Gale 2001), Creeton, Lincolnshire (Cowgill in preparation), and Hatton–Silk Willoughby (Rackham 1999).

Phase 2B: Military stores depot (later Neronian)

During Phase 2A, the fort was supplemented by the addition of external annexes, and in Phase 2B the fort interior was cleared prior to the establishment of a military stores depot. Morphologically, many of the Phase 2B features appeared to be designed specifically for the management of livestock, but as little or no animal bone survives, there is little corroborative evidence. By this stage, Metchley was part of a network of forts, and because of its location near to a major road junction, it was particularly well placed as a supply depot.

Evidence from the Phase 2B contexts was again sparse, with most of the available data coming from a very few features. The fills within oven F206 (Area M7), which was situated within the eastern *intervallum* area, contained a moderate to high density of oak charcoal along with a lesser quantity of ash, hazel, and hawthorn/*Sorbus* type. However, much of this material was from the backfills of the structure and was, therefore, in a secondary context. A large quantity of charcoal was also present within the primary fill of the innermost eastern fort ditch in Area M7 (F250.02), and other rich deposits were noted within the eastern and southern fort ditches within Area M8, possibly indicating that some materials cleared from the fort interior were being dumped within the ditch fills.

In all instances oak charcoal was predominant. Heartwood was also abundant, suggesting common usage of wide roundwood, cordwood, or poles from reasonably mature trees. As small wood appears to have been rarely used, and as a fort of this size almost certainly required huge quantities of wood for both fuel and construction purposes, it is probably reasonable to assume that a certain amount of timber was requisitioned, over and above that which could be locally supplied. Only rarely were other plant macrofossils noted within these deposits, although the assemblages were often seen to contain small pieces of coal and black tarry residues (the latter probably being derived from wood, charcoal, or other organic remains, which were exposed to high temperatures for a prolonged period of time). The coal could have been obtained from local surface deposits and would almost certainly have been used as a direct heat source (e.g. for cooking, heating, or industry). It is therefore probably reasonable to assume that a proportion of the charcoal associated with the coal was probably used for similar purposes. However, one Phase 2B charcoal layer (context 1094) within Area M12 was consistent with a spread of burnt remains from a structural fire. Such conflagrations were probably a common occurrence when open fires were being used in close proximity to wooden buildings, some of which almost certainly contained highly combustible materials like fodder or grain. Alternatively, it is possible that the structure was burnt as part of a process of clearance of the military stores depot interior, under military control.

Plant macrofossils other than charcoal fragments are again scarce within the Phase 2B deposits. Ditch F250.04 contained a moderate density of cereal grains, with barley again being predominant. Spelt grains were also identified. However, as with the Phase 1 assemblages, cereal chaff was almost entirely absent, implying that the occupants of the fort were still reliant on imported grain to meet their everyday requirements. Area M9 pit F267 contained a fill which consisted almost entirely of the well-preserved grains of both spelt and bread wheat, an unusual assemblage within the overall context of the fort. The excellent condition of the grains suggested that they had undergone slow charring, although how this occurred is not known. Similar mixed wheat assemblages have also been noted from other contemporary deposits within the midlands, including some military contexts, although it would appear that during this early Roman period, the production of bread wheat was based largely in central, southern, and eastern Britain, with little evidence coming from the more northerly sites.

The F267 assemblage from Area M9 was also of note, as it contained a small number of fruits of soft brome or rye brome (*Bromus* sp.), a grass which is commonly seen as a persistent contaminant of both Iron Age and Roman grain deposits. As the seeds are of a similar size to the grains, they were difficult to separate out, and as they affected neither the palatability nor the storage potential of the crop, it appears that they were frequently tolerated.

As has been stated above, the Romans primarily saw barley as a fodder crop. Therefore, a charred layer (1092), rich in charcoal and barley grains, which formed part of the floor of Phase 2B Structure 12.4 (Area M12), may indicate that this building functioned as a barn, fodder store, or stable. This hypothesis is probably supported by the number of seeds of fodder plants (namely grasses and grassland herbs) also present within the assemblage. The inclusion of some wetland plant fruits may also suggest that this hay was gathered from the nearby stream valley. It is possibly also of note that this assemblage contained the only examples of beech (*Fagus sylvatica*) charcoal recorded from the entire fort area.

The composition of an insect assemblage recovered from Area M8 ditch F250.05 (layer 1741) indicated that the ditch was muddy or possibly seasonally water-filled. As few species associated with human settlement were recorded, it would appear that rubbish from the fort was not accumulating within this segment of ditch.

Phase 3A: Second fort (early Flavian)

Phase 3A witnessed the establishment of a second, smaller fort within the footprint of the original Phase 1 fort. Although the primary Phase 3A turf rampart was partly rebuilt as a timber-framed box rampart, very few contemporary buildings have survived.

Much of the evidence for the Phase 3A occupation of the fort complex is in the form of scattered refuse or material within secondary contexts. Therefore, a precise interpretation of the day-to-day functioning of this fort is, at best, tenuous. For example, samples taken from industrial features in the southern *intervallum* (Area M6), comprising gullies, ovens, and hearths, and from southern Phase 3A fort ditch F400, produced assemblages which were relatively uniform in composition, with most containing a low density of charcoal, grains, and grassland weed seeds. Although some of these remains were possibly derived from scattered or wind-dispersed fuel waste, others may have been residual remains from Phase 1 features, which were disturbed during the construction of the Phase 3A fort. Pollen from the Phase 3A rampart included alder, birch, hazel, grass, bracken, and heather.

A possible cookhouse (Structure 2.4), with ashy deposits across some of the internal floor areas, was recorded within Area M2 in the extreme southeastern corner of the Phase 3A fort. Plant macrofossil samples were not taken from the structure itself (dug in 1967). However, investigation of nearby features during the Area M25 excavation (Hopla and McKenna 2025) did recover cereals at varying densities, and it is perhaps reasonable to assume that some of these were derived from activities conducted within the cookhouse. That the material was charred may suggest that some cereals were accidentally burnt during culinary preparation, whilst it is also possible that left-over food waste was burnt at the end of each meal.

Much of the charcoal from the Area M12 assemblages appeared to be related to debris from industrial fuel residues. However, the charcoal from Structure 12.5 (F165) and associated beam-slot F168 was of more significance. The charcoal assemblage from this beam-slot was entirely composed of oak largewood, much of which was probably derived from the timbers used to construct the building. However, a wider range of species, including oak, hazel, alder, hawthorn/*Sorbus* type, and possibly willow or poplar was obtained from samples within the structure, and it is perhaps most likely that these are derived from internal structural elements, for example wattle fences or panels in timber-framed buildings, or from portable artefacts like baskets.

Although many of the Phase 3A plant macrofossil assemblages are somewhat mundane, a sample from Structure 12.5 within Area M12, and more specifically from the possible loading platform F158, was potentially of some importance. Although small, it contained charred grains along with waterlogged/de-watered seeds of grape and fig. Such high-status foodstuffs are probably indicative of a diet reserved for senior officers of the Roman army. Although recent investigations in the Nene Valley (Brown et al. 2001) have established the presence of Roman vineyards within the area, given the date of the Metchley material it is, perhaps, more likely that these are the remains of exotic imports from the Mediterranean.

A pollen monolith (Hopla and McKenna 2025) taken through deposits within the eastern Phase 3A ditch (132) in Area M25 and its Phase 4A re-cut (147) was of note, as it suggested that this area at the southeastern corner of the Phase 3A fort was dominated by stands of alder, a tree which is commonly found on damp, marshy ground. Other wetland/bank-side flora represented within the monolith included sedges (Cyperaceae). Beyond this area, the wider landscape consisted of hazel/birch/oak woodland, with areas of open heath and grassland. Interestingly, few anthropogenic indicators were recorded. Insect evidence from Area M8 ditch F252.05 (layer 1722) was also suggestive of the presence of wetland plants, pasture and nettles (*Urtica dioica*).

Phase 4: Later Roman activity (later Flavian–late 2nd century AD)

Phase 4 activity was limited. After the abandonment of the second fort, the fort area and its environs was used for small-scale civilian activity, possibly including livestock herding.

Very few Phase 4 features were sampled for the retrieval of plant macrofossils, and of those which were, the recovered assemblages were generally very sparse. Some day-to-day activity was indicated in the form of charred deposits of charcoal, cereals, and weed seeds, but evidence was very limited. Samples taken from eastern annexe ditch F140 (Area M7) and Area M8 ditch F319 contained assemblages which were essentially similar to those from other phases of activity within and around the fort, probably suggesting that the utilization of plant resources by the occupants changed little over time. However, it should be stressed that because of the general paucity of plant remains, some trends – for example, food preferences or sources of supply – could be under-represented or completely masked within the record. Cereals were again predominant within the ditch F140 and F319 assemblages, and it was possibly of note that a small number of barley grains within ditch F319 showed clear signs of germination. Although this may have been achieved deliberately as part of the malting process prior to brewing, given the small number of grains, it was possibly more likely to be a result of accidental germination due to inadequate storage conditions.

By around AD 200, all activity, both civilian and military, may have ceased, and the areas adjacent to the fort had begun to revert to scrub. Evidence for this comes from the base of a pollen sequence taken through the backfill deposits of fort ditch F252.05 (context 1722), which showed that by Phases 4 and 5 the land around the fort was supporting a number of species of colonizing trees/shrubs including willow, hawthorn, sloe, and elder. Evidence for oak, birch, and alder woodland was also recorded along with pollen from species indicative of un-wooded open grassland including grasses, plantain (*Plantago lanceolata*) and knapweed (*Centaurea nigra*).

Phase 5: Post-Roman activity

Evidence for the development of the local landscape during the post-Roman and later periods came almost exclusively from the pollen monolith taken from ditch F252.05 in Area M8. Shortly after the abandonment of the site at the end of the 2nd century AD, the habitat developed from scrub to secondary or pioneer woodland, with an increase of species like hazel, alder, ash, and birch. An increase in oak pollen indicated that mixed oak woodland was also developing nearby. Herb pollen started to decrease, and fluctuations in the incidence of plants associated with human and animal activity suggested that such activity was greatly reduced at this point in time.

By the post-Roman/early Saxon period, the pollen indicated that reasonably well-established woodland was locally prevalent, and a slight increase in herb pollen was suggestive of the resumption of a degree of human/animal activity. Of particular note was the incidence of rye pollen, which, although scarce, possibly indicated that some limited cultivation of the land for crop production was occurring locally. An increase of rye pollen has been noted at other sites of Saxon date (Greig 2004; 2005; and in preparation).

The early medieval period saw a change in the composition of the local woodland, with a marked increase in the incidence of holly (*Ilex* sp.) along with birch, alder, and oak. This was possibly indicative of the development of wood pasture, where the trees were pollarded to promote fresh growth, providing forage for stock (Rackham 1980).

An increase in the pollen of cornflower (*Centaurea cyanus*, a common weed of arable fields, especially during the medieval period) and hemp (*Cannabis*) type possibly indicated that some areas were still being cultivated, although it would appear most likely that the area was still predominantly wooded and sparsely settled.

By the later medieval and post-medieval periods, beech woodland had replaced the holly woods. An increase in herb pollen suggested that more open land was being farmed, and there was continued evidence for the limited cultivation of hemp.

Conclusions

In summary, the plant macrofossil evidence from Metchley is somewhat sparse, almost certainly in part because samples were not taken from the early phases of the excavations, which examined key areas of the fort's interior. Despite this, it is possible to make a number of broad statements about the fort and its environs.

Firstly, even allowing for the fact that the overall assemblage may not be complete, the density of material recovered is exceptionally low for an area of Roman occupation, especially given the size of the fort. Many of the assemblages appear to be composed of little more than scattered refuse, and only in rare instances can evidence of specific activities or incidents be seen. The reasons for this paucity of data are unknown, but possible explanations may include the fact that, soon after construction, the fort was restructured as a stock-holding facility, thereby decreasing the incidence of anthropogenic remains. A number of the recorded assemblages do appear to be derived from small deposits of burnt animal fodder including barley, a cereal which was little used for human consumption during the Roman period. A further possible reason for the apparent 'cleanliness' of the site is the desire to minimize the risk of catastrophic fires within a structure largely built of wood.

The cereals which were used at Metchley for both animal and human consumption, were almost certainly being imported to the site as batches of either semi-cleaned or prime grain, as both chaff and segetal weed seeds are virtually absent. How this grain was being stored, and in what quantity, is not known, but it is possibly of note that evidence for the storage of glumed wheat in the spikelet, which is seen at other contemporary sites in the west midlands (Carruthers and Hunter Dowse 2019), is completely absent at Metchley.

Military complexes the size of Metchley fort would have required huge quantities of structural materials, in the form of both timber and turf. A campaigning army would, of necessity, have sourced all of this material locally, and there is evidence in both the charcoal and pollen assemblages that the fort was situated within a landscape which included stands of reasonably mature mixed oak woodland. Such woodland would almost certainly have been managed, although direct evidence for either coppicing or pollarding has been difficult to establish. Turf, which was a principal component of the early fort ramparts, was probably cut from grassland areas which occupied parts of the nearby river valley.

As the latest civilian settlement in the vicinity of Metchley gradually fell into disrepair, and may have finally ceased to be used at the end of the 2nd century AD, pollen evidence suggests that areas of local scrub and woodland slowly encroached on the site. At some point during the early Saxon period, limited cultivation of the land commenced, with some evidence for the production of rye. Agricultural usage of the land continued into the medieval period, although woodland areas remained predominant. However, the composition of the woods had changed, with a marked increase in the incidence of holly. By the later medieval/ post-medieval period, it would appear that the nature of the landscape had changed once again. More land was coming under cultivation, and the woodland, which had remained throughout, was now dominated by beech.

It has proved very difficult to assess the information from Metchley in terms of its regional or national importance, largely because the sampling strategy was not comprehensive, thereby leaving crucial gaps in the recovered data. In addition, Metchley is unusual, as it was specifically restructured to be a military supply depot, and comparative material from such sites is particularly scarce. Whilst there do appear to be some similarities with the assemblage from Rocester, including evidence that the garrison did not engage in cereal production/ processing but relied on imported grain, it should be noted that the Rocester data predominantly comes from deposits of later Antonine date. However, this was probably a relatively common pattern for a military base, where raw materials of all types were almost certainly being requisitioned from the surrounding area. The charcoal recovered from Metchley corresponds with the list of species known to have been present within early Roman Britain (Greig 2002), and the industrial residues also have parallels elsewhere.

Probably the best corroborative evidence for the Metchley assemblage comes from a number of contemporary written sources. The use of barley as animal fodder is known from the Vindolanda tablets (Bowman and Thomas 1983), and both Vegetius and Caesar (Davies 1971) state that cereals were the mainstay of the Roman military diet, where they were supplemented by sour wine, wine, salt, and (occasionally) meat. These sources also mention that fodder for the animals was of particular importance, and it would appear that one of Metchley's key roles was to supply these provisions to an increasing Roman garrison via the network of newly laid-out roads..

5

Overview and Synthesis

Introduction

The excavations at Metchley have been extensive (Fig. 1.3), comprising a total of approximately 2.7ha (from 1963 to 2010), cumulatively amounting to over 25% of the forts, annexes and external settlements, by area. The location and extent of excavation was determined by the location and extent of proposed development and the timing by the programme of development. Within the areas investigated, archaeological survival has been variable, for example within Area M18 (Jones 2012), the largest of the most recent investigations. Survival of the Phase 1 structural remains has generally been good, while the more ephemeral remains of the Phase 2B military stores depot have survived better when protected from disturbance by the overlying Phase 3A rampart. Few buildings associated with the Phase 3A fort have survived later disturbance, possibly because they too were constructed on shallow foundations.

An important feature of the investigations has been the opportunity to investigate external areas, where several annexes belonging to different phases; two ditched livestock complexes and civilian settlements have been uncovered, together with evidence for the latest Roman activity within the complex overall. Survival within these external areas has generally been good. Modern land use has often involved deep terracing-up of the natural slope away from the fort, covering and protecting the external Roman military remains from modern intrusion.

A disappointing aspect of the investigations has been the limited dating evidence recovered – so that the phasing is largely based on the recorded stratigraphy. Some of the pottery has been abraded by the acid soil conditions. Animal bone has not survived.

Sequence

In places, the excavations at Metchley have identified a complex sequence of activity – including repeatedly re-cut ditches (e.g. Figs 2.3 and 2.7), and some vertical stratigraphy (beneath/adjoining later ramparts), albeit often associated with limited dating evidence (see below).

Phase 1A

This earliest Roman activity was ephemeral, only surviving where the later Phase 1B fort rampart had provided protection from later truncation. The excavated Phase 1A features comprised slight ditched defences, post-holes, and parts of two timber-framed buildings (Fig. 2.1). These remains are interpreted as forming part of a construction camp approximately coincident with the western defences of the later fort (Phase 1B), and which could also have included the first cutting of the *clavicula* outside the later *porta principalis dextra*.

First fort (Phase 1B–1E)

The remains of the succeeding first fort are more coherent. The Phase 1B rampart sealed the Phase 1A features. The primary Phase 1B turf rampart was rebuilt in places with a timber revetment. The Phase 1B fort may have been contemporary with the later use of the western *clavicula*, and the western external settlement.

The evidence from the fort interior is more complex (Fig. 2.2). Several layouts or rebuilding episodes are recorded within the fort interior, articulated by slightly different alignments, although this fort was comparatively short-lived overall. The more complex sequences of timber-framed building were located in the central range (Fig. 2.4). Here, the three earliest buildings (Phase 1D) were poorly preserved (Structures 18.12 and 18.14, Jones 2012, fig. 2.6; Structure 20.5, Jones 2025, chapter. 3, fig. 3.2). Within part of the right *praetentura* (Area M12, Fig. 2.5), the earliest activity was industrial, not structural, in nature. In the central range, the later buildings (Phase 1E, Fig. 2.4), respected the location of their Phase 1D predecessors, if not their alignment. Phase 1E Structure 18.15 (Fig. 2.4), located in the left side of the central range, is interpreted as the *praetorium*. This building was rearranged during the later use of the first fort. Parts of two further Phase 1E buildings were recorded within the *praetentura* (Structures 12.1 and 12.2, Fig. 2.5).

Other excavated buildings which cannot be related to the distinct Phase 1D or Phase 1E alignments represented the earliest structures within other parts of the fort interior (Figs 2.4, 2.5). Within the left *retentura* these buildings comprised parts of two facing barrack-blocks (Structures 3.1 and 4.1). The northern barrack-block was partially rearranged, to increase the accommodation available, while in the southern barrack-block (Structure 3.1) a number of the *contubernia* had been later converted for storage, reducing the number of *contubernia* available. Parts of two further buildings were excavated in the right side of the central range (Structure 20.1) – a possible *principium*, and also a second building (Structure 20.3). The latter was later extended to the south, reducing the width of the *via principalis*. A difference of 3° was recorded between the alignment of the primary build and the rebuild. Part of a possible *fabrica* (Structure 2.1) was recorded in the right *praetentura*.

A small-scale settlement (Fig. 2.5) was established to the west of the *porta principalis dextra* during the use of the first fort. It overlay the backfilled Phase 1A *clavicula*. The layout of this settlement, in particular of the buildings, was irregular, possibly suggesting rearrangement over time. One of the roadside buildings (Structure 9.6) post-dated a disused boundary ditch.

Also contemporary with the first fort was the western annexe or enclosure (Phase 1C, Fig. 2.2), which was probably associated with pottery production. It could not be related stratigraphically to the *clavicula* or the western settlement.

Phase 2A (Fig. 2.6)

Excavation at the junction between the northwestern corner of the Phase 1B fort defences and the southwestern corner of the northern annexe established that the annexe ditches were cut into the fort ditches during their continued use (Fig. 2.3.S.1). The southern annexe may have been contemporary, although its junctions with the first fort defences were not available for excavation. Similarly, the relationship between the fort defences and the eastern annexe could not be established.

Phase 2B (Fig. 2.8)

It is probable that at least part of the Phase 1E *principia* and *praetorium* were retained during the early part of the Phase 2B military stores depot sequence. Elsewhere, the Phase 1 fort buildings were levelled (Period 1 of the Phase 2B sequence). Four further periods (2–5) of activity have been distinguished within the later occupation of the military stores depot. In Period 2, new, irregular timber-framed buildings were laid out, often following the earlier foundation trench lines, suggesting that demolition and rebuilding was part of a single operation, carried out under military control. These buildings included a possible granary (Structure 3.4), a store building (Structure 3.5), and a building of unidentified function (Structure 3.6) in the former *retentura* (Fig. 2.9). In the former central range Structures 18.9–18.11 adjoined the retained Phase 1E *praetorium*, and Structure 20.2 adjoined the retained Phase 1D/1E *principia* (Structure 20.1, Fig. 2.10). Within the former right *praetentura* (Fig. 2.11), a clay-floored barn/stable (Structure 12.4) was succeeded by a building of unidentified function (Structure 12.3). A possible stable/grooms' quarters (Structure 2.3) was also recorded.

There were also scattered lengths of beam-slots following different alignments, none securely stratified, suggesting continued building of temporary structures after the fort alignment ceased to be respected.

Period 3 of Phase 2B activity was represented by ovens and hearths (Figs 2.8 and 2.9). Their location in the left side of the former *retentura* could suggest that Structure 3.5 remained in use. Elsewhere, ovens and hearths cut Phase 2B Period 2 foundation trenches (e.g. in the right

side of the former central range (Fig. 2.10) and in the right side of the former *praetentura* (Fig. 2.11)). The largest complex of Phase 2B industrial features encroached upon the western *intervallum* in the left side of the former central range (Fig. 2.10). Pit group C166 (Jones 2012, fig. 2.15) was cut into the later Phase 1B rampart timber revetment, and several associated features were cut across the western *via sagularis*. Significantly, the backfills of this pit group contained fragments of high-status Samian, interpreted by Wild (2012, 76) as associated with the commander's table. Assuming this pottery does not represent redeposited midden material, its place of deposit suggests that the *praetorium* was only finally cleared out when the industrial features went out of use, indicating that the later use of this building was contemporary with Periods 1–3 of the military stores depot. This deposit also indicates that the building function was unchanged in the early part of Phase 2B.

The fourth period of Phase 2B activity was represented by livestock pens, recorded within the former *retentura*, and a 'funnel' (Structure 18.4, Fig. 2.9) was inserted into the retained Phase 1B *principalis dextra* to facilitate the herding of livestock into the fort interior. A complex of contemporary ditched enclosures for livestock, and a further 'funnel', were located outside the western fort defences (Fig. 2.11). This livestock complex overlay the remains of the abandoned Phase 1D/1E western civilian settlement.

The final episode (Period 5) of Phase 2B activity was represented by the deposition of a charcoal-rich deposit representing clearance of the military stores depot interior by fire (either deliberate or accidental) and the slighting of the fort defences prior to the first military abandonment of the site.

Phase 3A

The second fort (Phase 3A) marks the military reoccupation of the site (Fig. 2.12). Forts in the west midlands are rarely single-phase (White 2018, 24). Its defences included the re-excavation of the inner Phase 1B defences to provide an additional line of defence. The original Phase 3A turf rampart was later rebuilt with a timber revetment.

Comparatively little is known about the fort interior. Of the four internal buildings that have been identified, three are granaries. The foundation trenches of these buildings are cut through the Period 5 Phase 2B destruction deposit, and into the Phase 2B Period 2 internal buildings, and the subsoil. There is no surviving evidence of rebuilding within the Phase 3A fort interior, except along part of the defences.

The eastern annexe ditch was re-cut (Fig. 2.13, Fig. 2.7.S.6), and this annexe was brought back into use. Two parallel north–south ditches and the base of a turf rampart (Fig. 2.7.S.9) to the south of the southern Phase 3A defences (in Area M6) could have formed part of the eastern defences of a further (southern) annexe, not otherwise recognized, which could not be related to any other Roman military features. A similar double-ditched arrangement in Area M30 (Fig. 1.3) (although unexcavated) could represent the eastern side of a northern annexe (Jones 2025, chapter. 6, fig. 6.1). The eastern defences of the possible Phase 3A southern annexe which were located inside the Phase 1B southern fort defences could be related to the re-cutting of the Phase 1B fort defences in this phase (Fig. 1.3) to provide an additional line of defence.

Phase 3B–4B

The Phase 3A *porta principalis dextra* was rebuilt to provide an L-shaped building (Structure 18.5, Fig. 2.14) which formed an integral part of an arrangement of livestock enclosures defended by palisade trenches located outside the western defences of the former fort. These succeeded scattered hearths/ovens. The latest external activity was formed by palisade trenches cut following different alignments, and an irregularly planned timber-framed building (Structure 18.3), also misaligned with the fort, and cut through the backfilled livestock enclosure palisade trenches. Finally, extensive cobbled surfaces were laid out overlying the abandoned palisade trenches and industrial features.

Phase 4A

In this phase the fort and annexe ditches were re-cut, and practice trenches were cut in the south of the complex (Fig. 2.15). No contemporary internal features could be identified.

Phase 4C

A three-sided ditched enclosure, possibly for livestock, was recorded in the northwestern angle of the fort interior (Fig. 2.15). The Phase 3A *porta principalis dextra* was partially blocked by ditches and pits, to form a 'funnel' for livestock. Two parallel palisade trenches were dug in the east of the abandoned Phase 3A fort, one cutting the fort rampart at a slight tangent.

Chronology

Small finds

The dating evidence from Metchley is limited, perhaps reflecting the comparatively short periods of occupation of the site by a garrison fort. Based on analysis of the small finds, Cool (Chapter 3 above) dates military occupation from the mid-Neronian period to the early Flavian period. Cool notes that the coin list is typical of a military complex of the Claudian–Neronian period, although the coin evidence for pre-Neronian occupation is not clear. She observes that brooches of mid-1st century date, belonging to the Aucissa and Hod Hill types, which normally predominate on Claudian–early Neronian forts, are scarce. Many of the brooches from

Metchley are Colchester derivative types, not usually found in a Claudian fort, and are more usually associated with a fort of mid- to later Neronian date (Cool, Chapter 3 above). Similarly, comparison of the proportions of polychrome and blue/green pillar moulded glass bowls from the site suggests that the fort was occupied from the mid Neronian period onwards. This could place the establishment of the fort in the period around the Boudiccan revolt, or slightly later. Another feature of the glass assemblage is the lack of military forms of later 1st- and early 2nd-century date, indicating that the Flavian military occupation of the complex was comparatively shortlived.

This chronology could suggest that the first fort at Metchley post-dated the fort at Droitwich (Hurst 2006), but was contemporary with the first fort at Wall (Round 1983), although the Claudian or Neronian origins of this site have been the subject of much debate (e.g. Round 1993; Gould 1993). At Wall, the later, smaller Flavian fort was located within the interior of the earlier fort.

Whilst not chronological indicators in themselves, a number of characteristics of the Phase 1B fort could hint at hurried construction, perhaps in response to the Boudiccan uprising. In particular, the layout of the double barrack-block (Structure 4.1, Fig. 2.4), formed of two barrack-blocks constructed without an intervening passageway, may suggest pressure for space – an unusual layout signalling the requirement to maximize the size of the garrison, whilst minimizing the length of the encircling defensive perimeter. A double barrack-block would also result in a saving of material (i.e. timber) compared to two free-standing single barrack-blocks. The provision of a western gatehouse with only a single guard chamber (Structure 18.2, Fig. 2.4) may be another indicator of hurried construction, albeit a layout which was repeated in Phase 3A (Structure 18.6, Fig. 2.12).

Pottery

The majority of the pottery (Timby, Chapter 3 above), including the Samian, is pre-Flavian in date. The Samian provides the most accurate pottery dating overall. The Samian from Phase 1A contexts to the west of the fort (Willis 2011, 68, Area M9, Phase A) was generally Claudian in date, although some sherds of possible Neronian date were also included. Samian from the western settlement was Claudian–early Neronian in date (Willis 2011, 68, Area M9, Phase B). The succeeding western livestock enclosures contained Samian of mid- to late Neronian to early Flavian date (Willis 2011, 68, Area M9, Phase C). In her assessment of one of the largest groups of Samian from the complex (Area M18), Wild (2012, 75) notes that the earliest pieces are consistent with a Claudian date, although the material overall is best described as pre-Flavian. She also notes that this collection includes very few pieces which are more likely to be Flavian than Neronian – again suggesting the probable brevity of the Flavian military reoccupation of the site (Phase 3A).

Pengelly et al. (2001, 101) suggested that significant supply of Samian to the fort ended around A D 70, or soon after. Similarly, Green and Evans (2001, 105) in their discussion of the pottery from Areas M1–M5 identify the presence of Hofheim-type flagons, but not ring-necked flagons, a Flavian type. Lyon ware is also generally datable to the pre-Flavian period. Overall, the range of forms and fabrics is considered typical of a pre-Flavian military establishment (Timby, Chapter 3 above).

Area M6 (Hancocks 2001, 97) notably produced necked jars of Flavian–Trajanic date from a zone of Phase 4 civilian occupation adjoining the southern defences. Similarly, later civilian use of the eastern and southern annexes (Areas M7–M8) produced 2nd-century Samian, including pieces from Lezoux, although activity was much less intensive in the 2nd than in the preceding century (Hancocks 2005, 65–7). These post-Flavian ceramics may reflect the civilian rather than military use of the complex (see below), unless the site continued in at least occasional use for military requisition and supply.

Mechanisms of military supply

The dating evidence provided by the small finds and the pottery need not be contradictory. As observed by Hanson (2007, 647), a military garrison would not have arrived at a new fort equipped with 'new' pottery and other objects. They would have brought with them pottery and glass acquired over the previous 10 years, as illustrated by the range of pottery from southwestern England associated with the early Flavian advance into Scotland (Swan and Bidwell 1998). As noted by Hanson (2007, 647), it is unwise to use a few 'earlier' sherds of pottery to date fort occupation. The presence of a few 'old' heirlooms would also not be unexpected. As observed by Timby (Chapter 3 above), most early military establishments in Britain would have brought potters with them to provide the range of vessels required by the army, which were not available in the pre-Flavian period from native British production. Similarly, the locally made mortaria found at Metchley are likely to be the products of potters within or associated with the army (Hartley 2011b, 32–3).

These mechanisms could provide a context for the Claudian Samian found at Metchley. It would not explain why no other objects (e.g. brooches) of Claudian date were brought to the site, except perhaps to suggest that the mechanisms of supply for pottery, and non-pottery items could have differed. Brooches and similar items which were easily carried were perhaps more likely to be retained by their owners when they left the site, while pottery may have been discarded when broken or at a site abandonment. Millett (1990, 45) highlighted the different type of supplies for a mobile army (e.g. metal cooking utensils) – which are unlikely to be dumped as rubbish and therefore unlikely to enter the archaeological record – while fort garrisons used pottery which was deposited as rubbish, providing useful dating evidence.

The possibility of an earlier temporary military occupation at Metchley (e.g. a marching camp) is considered later in this chapter.

Layout and function

Location

Metchley may have been located close to an important road junction (Fig. 1.1), although precise details of the local routes remain to be established. The dates of the main Roman roads are largely unknown. It is possible that the Roman military could have utilized existing roads or trackways, as is suggested in Cornovian territory (White and Wigley 2018, 119). Roman roads would initially have been constructed to military requirements (Margary 1973, 18). The layout of new roads and the construction of forts (and fortresses) were interlinked (White 2018, 19), since the roads made possible the rapid deployment of large numbers of troops at a time of crisis, such as the Boudiccan revolt of A D 60.

Ryknield Street (Fig. 1.5) linked Alcester to the south and Wall and Watling Street to the north (Margary 1973, route 18b). Margary describes two further routes, linking Metchley with Droitwich to the south (route 180) and Greensforge and Kinvaston to the north (route 190). Another route, linking Metchley with settlement around the Roman temple at Coleshill, has also been suggested (Booth 1996, 28). Despite this evidence for convergence or near-convergence of several roads, there is no overwhelming evidence for the Claudian military occupation of the site that its central position within the road network might justify. Such early military occupation could have been temporary in nature (e.g. marching camp), leaving no trace despite the extensive excavations. The earliest military occupation at Wall, also located near an important road junction, was represented by marching camps (Welfare and Swan 1995, 175–6), recorded by aerial photography, a form of evidence which is not so useful at Metchley. R. H. Jones (2012, 24 and fig. 2) observes that the distribution of marching camps flank the routes of Roman roads, 'because they represent the best ways through territory'.

Leather (1994, 9) suggests that a road junction may have been located at Selly Park, 3km to the southeast of Metchley (Fig. 1.1B). This theory could explain the apparent lack of evidence for early, Claudian military occupation at Metchley. In their discussion of forts in Wales and the Marches, Burnham and Davies (2010, 68) draw attention to the frequent bypassing of a site by the road network. Forts, including Metchley may have been connected to the road network by a spur road, in the case of Metchley leading to Ryknield Street to the northeast. The line of a suggested Roman spur road to the northeast and also to the southwest of the fort has been tentatively identified from early 19th-century field boundaries (in red on Fig. 1.1B, after Baker 2008) also identified by trenching (Jones 2019a; Jones 2025, chapter. 6).

Johnson (1983, 36) observes that ease of communications, a good water supply, and timber for building and firewood were important factors in the location of a fort. The preferred location was at the end of a spur, or on a small plateau with ground falling away on three sides, commanding extensive views. At Metchley, aside from its possible location near an important road junction, useful for military supply and to control the road network, the site may have been chosen for its topography: on a spur, with nearby supplies of water and timber. The natural gravel plateau was defined on its eastern and western sides by streams which would have provided an additional line of defence from attack. The ground to the south was probably marshy (see Fryer, Chapter 4 above), and although the forts were overlooked by slightly higher ground to the north (Fig. 1.2), this area may also have been marshy in places.

Located at or near the tribal boundaries of the Cornovii, Dobunni, and Corieltauvi (Fig. 1.5; Millett 1990, fig. 12), the earliest garrison fort at Metchley could have provided a base for the 'supervision' of these tribes, and possibly for a westwards advance into the territory of the Cornovii. The former is the more likely alternative, given the mid-Neronian date suggested for the foundation of the complex. By analogy with the positioning of Alchester near the border of the Catuvellauni and Dobunni, interpreted as being chosen to control and draw upon food supplies from those two tribes (Sauer 2001, 40), Metchley could have been located to control and requisition supplies from all three surrounding tribes, thereby reducing the burden on the 'friendly' Dobunni to the south and southwest. The military sought to avoid discontent caused by placing excessive demands for military supplies on the immediate native population (Millett 1992, 56). Like Alchester, Metchley was located near a strategically important cross-roads.

There is growing evidence for Roman military deployment in particular to 'control the spaces between the major British peoples rather than occupying their heartlands' (Mattingley 2006, 146) for the purpose of segregating civitas groups and supervising their contacts. The vexillation fortresses at Lake Farm and Longthorpe, both located on a tribal boundary, were suggested by Millett (1990, 50) to have provided a base for campaigns in the adjoining tribal areas. Although not a vexillation fortress, Metchley may have fulfilled the functions Mattingley and Millett describe. Further, Millett (1990, 51) suggests that Roman forts were placed to oversee territorial gains where centres of Late Iron Age power were absent. This may explain the apparent density of Roman military complexes in the vicinity of Metchley, including Greensforge, Kinvaston, and Wall, but excluding Alcester (Booth and Evans 2001) and Droitwich (Hurst 2006), where later Iron Age occupation is attested.

Phase 1A

The earliest Roman military features at Metchley, comprising shallow ditches and parts of two timber-framed

buildings, are attributed to a construction camp (Fig. 2.1). These features are overlain by the eastern and western Phase 1B ramparts, suggesting that the area occupied in the two phases was roughly coincident, although the full extent of the construction camp has not been found by excavation. An external Phase 1A *clavicula* outside the western defences was also recorded.

Phase 1B

The fort (Fig. 2.2) was located close to a water supply (two streams which drained into the Bourn Brook to the south of the forts) and plentiful supplies of timber (see Fryer, Chapter 4 above). The alignment of the fort at a right-angle to the natural slope suggests that the intention was to ensure that the *via principalis* occupied level ground, as at Pen Llystyn (Hogg 1968, 109).

From the Claudian period, forts conformed to a regular 'playing-card' or square shape (Johnson 1983, 234). The layout of Metchley in three divisions (*retentura*, central range, and *praetentura*) reflects the development of a new fort layout first seen at Obserstimm (Germany), built around AD 40 (Johnson 1983, 238 and fig. 180). The earlier Roman forts in Britain were also divided into two halves by a principal street (e.g. Hod Hill, Gosbecks, and Longthorpe, Johnson 1983, figs 182, 184, and 185).

The first fort measured 210 m² (inside the rampart), an area of 4.4ha, or 240 m² (from the outside of the outermost ditch), an area of 5.76ha. The fort gates were probably positioned centrally along the four sides. The square shape of the Metchley fort, and the central positioning of the gates along each side is the same as the arrangement recorded at the Flavian fort of Elginhaugh (Hanson 2007, fig. 12.3) and at Caerhun (Burnham and Davies 2010, 217, and fig. 7.44).

At Metchley (Fig. 2.2), the *praetentura* occupied the southern half of the fort interior, and the central range and the *retentura* combined the remainder. The central range and *retentura* measured 52m and 42m in length respectively (north–south). At Elginhaugh (Hanson 2007, fig. 12.3) the *praetentura*, central range, and *retentura* measured 50m, 25m, and 33m respectively in length. At Pen Llystyn (Hogg 1968), where the *portae principalis dextra* and *sinistra* were located off-centre, the *praetentura*, central range, and *retentura* occupied 35m, 28m, and 47m respectively in length.

The Phase 1 Metchley fort was defended by double ditches. Traces of corner towers were recorded at the northwestern and southeastern corners. The gatehouse (Structure 18.2) at the *porta principalis dextra* was furnished with only a single guard chamber. Single portal gates are recorded at Caerhun (west) and Castell Collen (northwest, primary and secondary structures) (Burnham and Davies 2010, 74). This is unusual, particularly for a gate along the *via principalis*. As Metchley was not located at a road junction, being merely linked to Ryknield Street by a spur road, the *via principalis* would not have functioned as a through route.

Phase 1C western annexe or enclosure

The re-cut palisade trench defining the western annexe or enclosure (Fig. 2.2) lay just 19m to the west of the outer fort ditch (measured centre-to-centre). This palisade boundary was not a defensible feature (Fig. 2.3.S.4–S.5), but may have defined an area used for the production of mortaria. It could not be related to the external western settlement.

Phase 1 internal buildings

Retentura (Fig. 2.4)

Parts of two Phase 1D/1E barrack-blocks arranged *per scamna* were excavated in the left side of the *retentura* (Structures 3.1 and 4.1), forming a *hemistrigium* pair. In each case the excavated part of the building mainly comprised the men's quarters; the officers' quarters in the west of the building were mostly unexcavated. The northernmost barrack-block (Structure 4.1) was a double barrack-block, divided by a midrib, and (unusually) not including an intervening passageway. The southernmost of the pair was a single *contubernium* in width (Structure 3.1). The right side of the *retentura* was not investigated.

Comparative layouts

A greater density of building is possible by building *per strigas* (at a right angle to the *via principalis*) rather than *per scamna* (Hanson 2007, 99), as at Metchley which suggests a lack of pressure for space at the site. In contrast, the double barrack-block at Metchley is a space-saving arrangement (as well as saving material – timber) (Davison 1989, type 2). Thus, a saving in materials could have been more important than a saving in space.

The *retentura* at Elginhaugh contained three barrack-blocks/stables, a *hemistrigium* pair on the left side (possibly stable-barracks, Hanson 2007, 67), and a pair of barrack-blocks, with conjoined officers' quarters (Hanson 2007, fig. 5.4). Similarly, the *retentura* at Caerhun contained two paired barrack-blocks (Burnham and Davies 2010, fig. 7.44). The *retentura* at Pen Llystyn contained a total of eight or nine buildings, mostly barrack-blocks, but also included a possible administration building (Hogg 1968, fig. 20). The *retentura* at Fendoch (Richmond and McIntyre 1939, fig. 2) contained six barrack-blocks, arranged in two facing pairs, and two single barrack-blocks. At Strageath the *retentura* of the Flavian fort contained seven barrack-blocks (Frere and Wilkes 1989, fig. 66), and a possible stable. At Gelligaer II the *retentura* contained two barrack-blocks, a possible *fabrica*, and a building of unidentified function (Ward 1903, facing p. 114).

Central range (Fig. 2.4)

Three buildings belonging to the earliest fort layout (Phase 1D) were recorded in the central range, including two in the left side of the central range. One may be interpreted as the *praetorium* (Structure 18.14), by analogy with the similar positioning of its Phase 1E successor (see below). The second building (Structure 18.12), represented by a single wall only, is not easily interpretable. The third contemporary building comprised three (or five) pits (Structure 20.5), perhaps forming part of an ambulatory, a feature which would not be unexpected in this part of the fort.

The westernmost Phase 1D/1E building in the central range was a granary (Structure 3.2), together with an associated loading-bay (Structure 3.3), both located immediately to the south of the *via quintana*. The Phase 1E *praetorium* (Structure 18.15) occupied much of the remainder of the left side of the central range. The eastern wall of the Phase 1D/1E *principia* (Structure 20.1) was located approximately 66m to the west of the eastern fort defences, amounting to approximately one third of the width of the fort. No other outer walls of this building were excavated, although Trench B2 (Fig. 1.3) may have sampled part of its internal arrangement. Occupying part of the right side of the central range was a building laid out in two stages (Structure 20.3), the latter build unusually also extending across part of the *via principalis*. The different alignments suggest piecemeal reconstruction.

The central building was the *principia* (Structure 20.1), represented by its excavated eastern wall. To the west was the *praetorium* (Structure 18.15). Further to the west, adjoining the western defences, was a granary (Structure 3.2/3.3). The layout of the right side of the central range is less well understood. Here the only partly excavated building (Structure 20.3) was rebuilt in stages, later extending across part of the width of the *via praetoria*.

Comparative layouts

The layout of the central range at Metchley appears to follow the traditional central range pattern, with the *principia* at its centre. The *praetorium* was located to the west of the taller *principia*, in order to receive the maximum sunlight (Johnson 1983, 139). The *praetorium* may have occupied the whole of one side of the central range, unless this space was shared with one or more granaries (Johnson 1983, 139), as at Metchley (see below). In Britain, the *praetorium* was most usually located to the left of the *principia* (as at Metchley), while the reverse was true in Germany (Marvell and Owen-John 1997, 182).

At Elginhaugh (Hanson 2007, fig. 12.3), Pen Llystyn (Hogg 1968, 111), Caerhun (Baillie Reynolds 1929), and Strageath (Frere and Wilkes 1989, figs 17, 28, 66), the *praetorium* lay to the left of the *principia*. At The Lunt a *praetorium* (or officer's house) was located on the left side of the central range (Hobley 1973, 25; 1975, 8). A possible *praetorium* or *fabrica* lay to the left of the *principia* at Carlisle (Zant 2009, 420).

Conversely, at Fendoch (Richmond and McIntyre 1939, fig. 2), Gelligaer (Ward 1903, facing p. 114), and Pen-Llwyn (geophysical survey, Burnham and Davies 2010, fig. 7.94), the *praetorium* was located to the right of the *principia*, with granaries at the former site located to the left of the *principia*, in the location more usually occupied by the *praetorium*.

Structure 20.3 at Metchley to the right of the possible *principia* most closely resembles a courtyard building, such as a *fabrica* (e.g. Llanfor, Hopewell 2005, 249–50, fig. 11), a building often conforming to a courtyard pattern when built in the central range (e.g. Johnson 1983, 185–6), although this interpretation would not explain its apparent later encroachment over the *via principalis*. Granaries are recorded to the right of the *principia* at both Elginhaugh (Hanson 2007, fig. 12.3, 54–6) and Pen Llystyn (Hogg 1968, fig. 19). Other building types recorded within the central range include store buildings, barrack-blocks, and hospitals (Johnson 1983, 35 and fig. 19).

Praetentura (Fig. 2.5)

Whilst the Metchley *praetentura* occupies the largest part of the fort interior, its internal arrangement is poorly understood because of limited excavation.

The earliest layout in the right side of the *praetentura* included six ovens (Area M12), adjoining the eastern frontage of the *via praetoria*. Fragments of two Phase 1E buildings were also recorded adjoining the *via praetoria*, the easternmost (Structure 12.1) a possible stable, the westernmost (Structure 12.2) of unidentified function. The most extensive excavated Phase 1D/1E building in the right side of the *praetentura* was a workshop (Structure 2.1), containing a number of pits of likely industrial function. A fragment of a possibly associated building (Structure 2.2) of unidentified function was excavated further to the south. Few interpretable features were recorded within the other areas excavated within the left side of the *praetentura*.

At Metchley, the *praetentura* was also characterized by the recovery of a number of finds or environmental evidence of high-status association, including grape pips and date figs (Chapters 3 and 4 above). There are some forts where two *praetoriae* have been identified (Johnson 1983, 139), the second building often located in the *praetentura*, for example when mixed garrisons of auxiliaries and legionaries were present. At The Lunt (Hobley 1973, 25ff.; 1975, 11–12), a larger *praetorium* or prefect's house may have housed the officer commanding cavalry practice. Whilst the Metchley finds suggest higher-status occupation, there is no corroborative structural evidence from admittedly limited excavation, concentrated within the right side of this part of the fort. Individual finds or environmental evidence of possible high-status association have also been found in other parts of the military complex – which may of course belong to secondary contexts.

Comparative layouts

At Elginhaugh the *praetentura* contained eight barrack-blocks/barrack-block/stables, including three paired buildings (Hanson 2007, fig. 12.3). At Pen Llystyn, the *praetentura* contained four barrack-blocks and two store buildings/workshops (Hogg 1968, 110). Barrack-blocks have also been excavated in the *praetentura* at Carlisle (Zant 2009, 430ff.). Three excavated barrack-blocks and an undivided possible store building were recorded in the *praetentura* at Caerhun (Burnham and Davies 2010, fig. 7.44). The *praetentura* at Gelligaer comprised four barrack-blocks, two possible store buildings, and another building (Ward 1903, facing 114). The *praetentura* at the Flavian fort of Strageath contained two granaries, five barrack-blocks, and a possible store building (Frere and Wilkes 1989, fig. 66). At Fendoch (Richmond and McIntyre 1939, fig. 2), a total of four barrack-blocks, arranged in two facing pairs with store buildings, were found within the *praetentura* adjoining the *via praetoria*.

It seems reasonable to suggest that whilst barrack-blocks were not excavated within this part of the fort interior at Metchley, it is likely that they would have been present, outside the areas excavated.

Phase 1 civilian settlement (Fig. 2.5)

The western civilian settlement was laid out along the roughly east–west aligned trackway entering the *porta principalis dextra*. A maximum of six buildings were recorded at excavation. Their layout with long axes along the trackway suggests a lack of pressure for space. Two open-fronted buildings were interpreted as shops or booths (Structures 9.5 and 9.6). The small size of this settlement is all the more surprising since it is possible that the roughly east–west trackway may have joined the spur road (Fig. 1.1B, in red) off Ryknield Street with the *via principalis*, creating opportunities for trade in the external area.

External civilian settlement is likely to have been more extensive. Webster (2001, 78ff.) identified a group of copper alloy objects from Area M1A (Fig. 1.3) in the north of the western fort defences as being civilian in association. This may hint at a more extensive civilian settlement outside the western fort defences, beyond the zone excavated in Area M9. Only limited investigation has been undertaken to the east of the fort (Jones 2025, chapter. 6, fig. 6.2). A road, gulleys, and possible post-holes have been identified, but this activity is difficult to interpret in detail, and impossible to phase within the Roman period.

One category of evidence is absent despite extensive excavation outside the fort: burials. This is perhaps not surprising, since cemeteries may have been located beyond the outer settlement limits and alongside approaching roads. Very little excavation has been undertaken along nearby road alignments. As noted above, bone does not survive in the acid subsoil, although this should not affect the survival of cremated bone. None has been found to date.

The relative paucity of finds in Phase 1 (and other contexts) at Metchley suggests a careful clearance of the site before abandonment at the end of Phase 1.

Phase 2A annexes (Fig. 2.6)

The northern annexe extended along the whole of the fort's northern side, enclosing an area measuring 210m × 75m, comprising 1.57ha. It occupied the highest ground within the military complex overall. Within the areas excavated, no buildings or other structures were found.

The eastern annexe was misaligned with the eastern side of the Phase 1 fort. It is not known if the annexe extended along the full length of this side of the fort. The excavated part of the annexe interior contained a number of ovens, cut into the back of the eastern rampart and internal pebble surfaces.

The southern annexe extended for the full length of the fort's southern side, but its excavated eastern side was cut at a tangent to the southeastern angle of the fort, following the line of the natural topography. It is not known if this annexe contained any internal features. The interior of this annexe has been subject to severe modern disturbance.

Phase 2B military stores depot (Fig. 2.8)

Period 1: Destruction of Phase 1 buildings

The earliest event in the reuse of the fort interior as a military stores depot was the clearance of most of the Phase 1 buildings, possibly leaving only the *principia* and *praetorium* standing.

Period 2: Timber-framed buildings (Figs 2.8–2.11)

A notable feature of several of these buildings, particularly within the *retentura* (Fig. 2.9), is that they followed the line of the dismantled Phase 1 buildings, suggesting that dismantling and the layout of Period 2 buildings were part of the same operation, without an intervening gap in occupation. This suggestion is supported by the apparent retention of at least part of the *principia* and *praetorium*, which would be unlikely to be left standing after a total site abandonment.

Three partly excavated timber-framed buildings were recorded in the left side of the former *retentura*. One may be interpreted as a store building (Structure 3.5), and the second was a possible small granary (Structure 3.4); the function of the third building (Structure 3.6) is unknown.

Three Period 2 temporary buildings were partly excavated in the left side of the former central range (Fig. 2.10, Structures 18.9–18.11). They respected the location of the Phase 1E *praetorium* (Structure 18.15), which continued to be maintained. Similarly, in the right side of the former central range Period 2 Structure 20.2 probably respected the eastern side of the Phase 1 *principia* (Structure 20.1),

which may also have been retained in this period. Parts of two other temporary buildings belonging to this period were recorded in this part of the military stores depot interior (Structures 20.4 and 20.6), but neither can be interpreted.

Two intercutting Period 2 buildings were recorded in the right side of the former *praetentura*. The earlier of the two was a stable/fodder store (Structure 12.4), but the function of the later building (Structure 12.3) could not be identified. The other building identified in the right former *praetentura* was a second stable/fodder store (Structure 2.3).

Parts of the northern and western Phase 1 *intervallum* roads went out of use, and were encroached upon by buildings and industrial activity.

This group of small and irregularly planned timber-framed buildings may be paralleled by small and irregularly shaped buildings at Brandon Camp, Herefordshire (Frere 1987b, fig. 2), including a granary, dated to the early Neronian period. These buildings were interpreted by the excavator as representing temporary structures, including a possible small barrack-block and small structures suitable for offices or accommodation for very small groups of solders (Frere 1987b, 63). In the alternative, Frere also suggests that they could represent the combined living quarters and offices of officials supervising stocks of timber or reserve camp wagons, although the similarity to structures found in external civil settlements is also noted. By analogy with the evidence from Brandon Camp, in the former *retentura* at Metchley these small structures could represent the offices/living quarters of supply officials involved in the military requisition of livestock. Thus, Periods 2 and 4 could be related to the same activity, despite the intervening period (3) in which continued activity at the site is represented by hearths or ovens. The other Period 2 buildings at Metchley were combined stables and fodder stores.

Period 3: Ovens or hearths (Figs 2.9–2.11)

The remains of Period 3 comprised ovens or hearths, some cut into the ground surface, others (e.g. Area M3, Fig. 2.9) built above ground level. In the left side of the former *retentura* their location appears to respect the Period 2 structures, which may have continued in use. In contrast, in the former central range, the industrial features sealed the demolished outer walls of the Period 2 structures, indicating their abandonment. In the left side of the former central range, large pit C166 was cut into the western Phase 1B rampart timber revetment, providing evidence that the rampart was reduced in width during this phase. Little evidence of this period has been found within the right former *praetentura*.

Period 4: Livestock pens (Fig. 2.9–2.11)

The remains of this period comprised livestock pens. A four-sided enclosure (Enclosure 1) was recorded within the left side of the former *retentura*, along with part of a second enclosure (Enclosure 2). A 'funnel' was inserted into the *porta principalis dextra* to facilitate the herding of livestock within the fort interior. The best parallel for this arrangement is the 'funnel' inserted into an annexe at Elginhaugh (Hanson 2007, fig. 12.2). No other evidence of this activity was found within the interior of the former central range, or in the former *praetentura*. An extensive ditched livestock complex, incorporating a second 'funnel', was recorded to the west of the fort. The two presumably contemporary 'funnels' suggest that traffic into the *porta principalis dextra* was limited. One possibility is that local traffic, which could have entered the fort at this gate, was diverted around the outside of the fort.

This period post-dated the clearance of the *praetorium*, represented by the dumping of Samian from the demolition of this building into disused Period 3 pit C166. This does not necessarily suggest the military abandonment of the site prior to Period 4. In this period, the commanding officer may have been relocated elsewhere within the fort interior, perhaps within a smaller building, reflecting a smaller military garrison during Period 4. In an alternative interpretation, the clearance of the *praetorium* could represent the formal military abandonment of the site, later only used as a base for occasional military foraging and the requisition of livestock in Period 4 (e.g. Elginhaugh, Hanson 2007, 652).

Phase 3A (Fig. 2.12)

This fort marks the military reoccupation of the Metchley site. The Phase 3A fort was rectangular in plan, with its long axis aligned north–south. It measured 165m × 150m (from the inside of the ramparts) and 186m ×172m (from the outside of the ditch), 2.47ha and 3.19ha in area, respectively. The fort was defended by a single ditch, supplemented by re-cutting of the innermost Phase 1B fort ditch.

Davies (2009, 45) has suggested that forts measuring up to 3ha in area may have held a single unit in garrison, whilst those of greater size may have included vexillations of a number of different units. In the absence of any completely excavated barrack-block accommodation at Metchley it is impossible to accurately estimate the size or composition of the garrison (see below). Forts constructed after AD 70 were generally smaller in size than earlier military installations, and were usually intended to house individual auxiliary units (Mattingley 2006, 153).

The *viae principales* of the first and second forts were coincident; presumably the earlier road was resurfaced for the later fort. The *porta decumana* and the *porta praetoria* were positioned medially along the northern and southern sides respectively of the second fort, as in the case of the Phase 1B fort. Unlike the Phase 1B fort, the *via principalis* of the Phase 3A fort divided its interior into two unequal halves. Measuring north–south, the *praetentura* occupied 70m (from the southern rampart tail to the *via principalis*) and the *retentura* and central range combined measured

90m (including the width of the *via quintana*). The positioning of the Phase 3A fort within the Phase 1B fort was intended to ensure that the Phase 3A internal roads retained their original position, as well as maintaining the *via principalis* on level ground.

Comparatively little is known about the overall layout of the second fort. Reconstruction of the earlier turf rampart with a timber revetment suggests that occupation was not confined to a single season. In contrast to the Phase 1 fort, the Phase 3A buildings were mostly arranged *per strigas* (north–south).

The only building excavated within the left side of the *retentura* (Structure 3.4) was interpreted as a granary. As excavated it measured 8m by 3.5m.

A second granary was the only internal building located in the left side of the central range (Structure 18.8). It was sited to the west of the presumed central location of the *principia* (not itself identified at excavation). The location of Structure 18.8 suggests that the contemporary *praetorium* was located to the right of the *principia*, since this building was often sited on the opposite side of the *principia* to the granaries. This positioning would be unusual, but not without precedent (see above).

The right side of the *praetentura* contained a third granary (Structure 12.5), and part of a possible cookhouse (Structure 2.4).

A number of ovens were cut into the tail of the northern rampart, but no trace of any adjoining barrack-blocks could be identified. Other industrial features were recorded along the southern *intervallum*.

An explanation should be sought for the small number of internal buildings associated with the second fort, and the apparent predominance (admittedly from a very small excavated sample) of granaries. It is possible that the granaries were more deeply founded than other building types, which therefore did not survive disturbance – in which case the number of excavated granaries would be more apparent than real. At Elginhaugh, the granary beam-slots measured 0.17–0.4m in depth (Hanson 2007, 59), compared with the beam-slots of the adjoining *principia* (0.5–0.8m, p. 40), and 0.3–0.9m for the *praetorium* (p. 50), which could suggest the contrary, although the depth of truncation at this site was admittedly variable. Alternatively, it is possible that the Phase 3A fort had a specialist function for the storage/supply of grain, so that this building type predominated within the fort interior (e.g. South Shields, Dore and Gillam 1979). The suggested identification of northern and southern annexes (Fig. 1.3) could support this argument for a specialist function.

Phase 3B–4B fort (Fig. 2.14)

A small area of external settlement outside the *porta principalis dextra* was fortuitously protected from modern disturbance. It contained a number of ditched livestock pens. Other features included an irregularly-shaped fragment of a timber-framed building and a number of hearths/ovens. By analogy with the evidence from Elginhaugh (Hanson 2007, 650), this could represent the occasional use of the site for the military supply of livestock, perhaps on a seasonal basis. It need not be interpreted purely as evidence of Roman civilian occupation, in particular because of the continued respect for the military alignment and western fort entrance.

Phase 4A fort (Fig. 2.13)

The re-cutting of the Phase 3A fort ditch could not be related to any internal structures.

Garrison

Comparative evidence

All forts were different in size, as they were built for different units at different times (Hanson 2007, 653). Fort size would have been related to the composition of the garrison, but not the precise garrison type (Jones 1975, 49). The former assumption that there was a direct correlation between garrison and fort internal area and barrack provision (e.g. Breeze and Dobson 1974) has now been challenged. Mattingley (2006, 153) suggests that the Roman army may have deliberately created over-capacity in forts, to imply the garrison was larger than was actually the case.

Forts built for a single unit were the exception and not the rule (Davies 2009, 46) in the case of forts greater in size than 3.1ha. A total of 45 out of all forts (excepting coastal forts and vexillation fortresses) enclose more than 3.1ha (20% of the total) – a group including the Phase 1 fort at Metchley. Davies (2009, 48) argues that these forts were designed for composite units, either on campaign (forming winter quarters or *hibernia*) or where it was necessary to occupy a tactical position with a force capable of a rapid response (such as a combination of cavalry and infantry). Within Wales and the Marches, the dimensions of campaign bases and early forts at Rhyn Park I and II, Clifford, Clyro, and Cardiff I (of a similar size to Metchley) suggest the brigading together of units of different composition and numbers (Burnham and Davies 2010, 70). Such 'larger' forts are generally of pre-Flavian date, and are replaced, as at Metchley, with forts of more 'normal' size, reflecting changes in military deployment. Davies (2009) argues that most forts of 3.1–6ha in size occupied up to the Flavian period are the bases of the army on active campaign, or bases occupied in the primary stages in the subjugation of newly conquered territory. The smaller sites may be type-sites for individual units (Burnham and Davies 2010, 70).

The practice of supplying vexillations for service elsewhere hampers the identification of the units present, since accommodation may have been provided only for the manpower not deployed for service elsewhere, and not based on the theoretical full strength of the unit (Hassell 1998, 37). He concluded that detachments were frequently divided to operate independently, as is illustrated by evidence from Vindolanda (Bowman and Thomas 1983). Less than half of the unit may have been based at that site, although it is also possible that part of another unit was also based there.

Since forts were rarely constructed for a single unit (Maxfield 1986, 59; Hassell 1998) the barrack accommodation provided may not fit the hypothetical strength of any unit. At Metchley and elsewhere, where drains are not provided, stables may also be difficult to distinguish from barracks in terms of their internal arrangement (Hanson 2007, 656) (see below).

Doubling or pairing units of identical type (Hassell 1998, 31) was also commonplace (e.g. Pen Llystyn, Hogg 1968; two quingenary cohorts, Hassell 1998, 33). At Haltern, two courtyard houses were provided, one for each of the two commanding officers (Hassell 1998, 33). The pairing of dissimilar units is also recorded (e.g. Hedderheim, Hassell 1998, 34).

A further problem, as Hanson (2007, 655) explains, is that the unit sizes have not been definitively established. Following Hygenus, the number of men per infantry century and per *contubernium* is agreed, but the size of a cavalry *turma*, generally set at 32 (following Vegetius), is less clear. This figure is arrived at by dividing the overall strength of an *ala quingenaria* (512, after Arrian) with the number of *turmae* in that unit recorded by Hyginus (16), although estimates ranging from 24 to 70 have also been suggested, based on comparison of the papyrological evidence and barrack-block plans.

Metchley barrack-blocks

Only two barrack-blocks have been identified at Metchley (Structures 3.1 and 4.1), both in the left *retentura*, neither completely excavated. It is difficult therefore to identify the size and type of unit for which they were built. Estimating the total military strength of the first fort at Metchley, and the composition of its garrison is clearly not possible. Other barrack-blocks were doubtless provided within the Phase 1 fort, in areas of the fort interior which have not been excavated (e.g. in the right *retentura* and large parts of the *praetentura*). No barrack-blocks associated with the Phase 3A fort have been identified.

The overall size of the *contubernia* in both excavated barrack-blocks is larger than the average range suggested by Davison (1989, 10) for auxiliary barracks, although not totally unknown within an auxiliary context. Size is not on its own sufficient to identify legionary accommodation (Davison 1989, 178) because of the practice of garrisoning legionary and auxiliary units together, and changes in the composition of the garrison over time.

The larger size of the *arma* in Structure 3.1 and in the central unit of Structure 4.1 is usually a feature of auxiliary barracks (Davison 1989, 15, 94), which may highlight the need for additional equipment storage (Maxfield 1986, 62; Johnson 1983, 173; *contra* Davison 1989, 188).

The similar size and relative proportions of the *armae* and *papiliones* in the two barrack-blocks forming the *hemistrigium* pair, and the similarities between the arrangements at Metchley and Valkenburg Castellum I (Maxfield 1986, 62–3), may suggest that these barrack-blocks were intended for units of similar composition, if not parts of the same unit.

The arrangement of the four *contubernia* in the northern and southern parts of the central unit of Structure 4.1 could suggest occupation by two cavalry *turmae*, with the decurions accommodated elsewhere. The excavated block of four *contubernia* measured approximately 14m in length, and the flanking corridors originally measured up to 7m wide in total. Davison (1989, 79) notes that Claudian or Neronian auxiliary barracks rarely exceeded 47m in length. Similarly, the fully excavated auxiliary barrrack-blocks at Elginhaugh measured between 44.4 and 47.6m in length (Hanson 2007, 656). The overall length of barrack-blocks in relation to the width of the fort has been calculated by Davison (1989, 104). He suggests that barrack-blocks arranged *per scamna* would not exceed 38% of the width of the fort, a measurement of approximately 80m at Metchley. If four similarly sized structural units, each comprising four *contubernia*, were provided (total of 56m in length), this arrangement would leave 24m for corridors and decurions' quarters out of the hypothetical length of 80m. Davison (1989, 10) suggests that the officers' quarters occupied around 25% of the total length of a barrack-block, in the hypothetical Metchley example approximately 20m in length. At Elginhaugh, the officers' quarters comprised 22.5–25.2% of the total barrack-block accommodation (Hanson 2007, 656).

Hypothetically, it is possible therefore that Structure 4.1 contained six *turmae*, three on either side of the midrib, occupying three of the excavated structural units of the building, with the decurions accommodated at the unexcavated ends of the building. This building was clearly unusual in arrangement as a double-barrack-block, more so given the lack of a dividing double central wall, and also because of its suggested long length.

Following this hypothetical interpretation, and assuming that the provision of barrack accommodation in the left and right *retentura* at Metchley was symmetrical, each double barrack-block could perhaps have accommodated six *turmae* (each comprising 32 men) and their decurions, making a total of twelve *turmae*. This would amount to part of the compliment of 16 *turmae* in an *ala quingenaria* (a total of 512 men, Johnson 1983, 21). Although too little of Structure 3.1 was excavated to permit identification of its garrison, it is possible to speculate that it may have contained two *turmae*, and a corresponding building in the right *retentura* a further two *turmae*, so that the combined compliment of Structures 3.1 and 4.1, and their counterparts

in the right *retentura* could have amounted to the 16 *turmae* of an *ala quingenaria*. Whilst this hypothesis is purely speculative, the evidence does suggest that Structures 3.1 and 4.1 could have been occupied by troops of similar composition. There is no present evidence to suggest or refute the hypothesis that the barrack accommodation in the left and right sides of the *retentura* was the same; the right side of this part of the fort interior has been little investigated.

The two *contubernia* in the western unit of Structure 4.1 were divided in approximately inverse proportions to the *contubernia* in the central unit of that building, which could suggest that these structural units housed different troops. While noting that the excavated sample from the western structural unit is very small (one *contubernium*), it is possible to suggest that the western unit may have contained infantry, so that occupation of the building by a *cohors quingenaria equitata* (comprising six centuries of 80 infantry and 120 cavalrymen (Johnson 1983, 23)) might perhaps also be suggested.

In their survey of recently excavated barrack-blocks from Hadrian's Wall, Hodgson and Bidwell (2004, 131) highlight the identification of barracks with distinctive characteristics, including nine rather than 10 *contubernia*, and most notably a centrally placed pit in each front room, and a hearth in each back room which according to the authors is an arrangement paralleled on the continent, notably at Dormagen (Germany). At this site, environmental evidence indicated that horses were stabled there. The similar buildings at Wallsend and South Shields resemble barracks in other respects, including end rooms for officers. They are interpreted as stable-barracks, providing combined accommodation for cavalry mounts and their riders. Hodgson and Bidwell (2004, 133) suggest that three troopers were accommodated in the rear rooms, and their mounts in the front room. Nine such *contubernia* would have accommodated up to 27 troopers, with the junior officers accommodated in the end rooms with the decurion. Furthermore, Hodgson and Bidwell argue that the absence of such an arrangement is evidence for infantry rather than cavalry accommodation. *Prima facie*, following this argument, the excavated Metchley barracks should have accommodated infantry, rather than cavalry, in the absence of evidence of pits (for urine) in the front rooms. In considering the applicability of the evidence from Hadrian's Wall, it has to be borne in mind that the barrack examples considered by Hodgson and Bidwell belong to the second quarter of the 2nd century or later, around half a century after the final military abandonment of Metchley, and that many are built in stone, not timber. The right *praetentura* of the Phase 1 fort at Metchley contained a stable or store building (Structure 12.1, Fig. 2.5), identified as a stable and/or groom's quarters.

Another possibility is that the garrison included a legionary vexillation. One of the most distinctive features of Structure 4.1 are the two corridors crossing the width of the building. This feature is often associated with the

XX legion, although an example at Wroxeter (Webster 1993) is associated with the XIV legion. This feature is representative of early cohort barrack planning by Davison (1989, 24, 82), not just confined to the XX legion. Analysis of the small finds from Metchley (Cool, Chapter 3 above) does not suggest that there was a legionary detachment in garrison.

The internal changes recorded in Structure 3.1 in particular suggest a reduction in garrison, with *contubernia* replaced by store-rooms.

Metchley finds

Military equipment from the site comprised weapons and harness fittings which are not helpful in identifying the nature of the garrison. Armour fragments were not found, suggesting an auxiliary rather than a legionary garrison (Cool, Chapter 3 above). The harness fittings indicate that cavalry were in garrison, although it has to be remembered that even infantry units would have needed horses for transport. Cool notes that the harness fittings from stratified contexts predominantly derive from Phase 3B–4B features (Fig. 2.14), interpreted as associated with livestock. It is possible that these harness mounts were used by animals transporting fodder within the livestock complexes. The ballista ball indicates an infantry presence.

Some of the higher-status finds, including the agate intaglio and the silver omega brooch, were found in the *praetentura*, while the *retentura* has a bias towards more everyday objects. This distribution could suggest the presence of an elite garrison within the *praetentura*, but is not, in itself, evidence for a second *praetorium* within the *praetentura*, as recorded for example at The Lunt (Hobley 1975, 8). Similarly, the proportion of Samian within the pottery varies from 1.8% for Areas M3–M5 (the *retentura*) to between 3.2% and 3.9% in the remainder of the fort interior, suggesting higher-status deposition within the central range (not perhaps unexpected) and in the *praetentura*. Among the environmental data, 'exotics', including the fig and date pips, are found in the *praetentura*, but not generally in any number elsewhere, further strengthening the argument for elite occupation in this part of the fort.

An alternative interpretation of the excavated barrack-blocks in the left *retentura* – based on the absence of pits in the front rooms, following Hodgson and Bidwell (2004) – could suggest that these buildings held infantry rather than cavalry. In this hypothesis, the evidence for an elite element in the *praetentura* could merely highlight differences between the material culture of the cavalry in the *praetentura* and the infantry in the *retentura*.

Finally, a number of sherds from white ware flagons and Campanian and Pompeian red ware vessels are interpreted by Timby (Chapter 3 above) as representing personal possessions, rather than items derived from military supply. Could these items hint at the origins of part of the garrison?

Military supply

Analysis of the finds indicates the supply of goods from the continent, the region, and from within the local area. Early regional imports of pottery are rare, suggesting that the site conformed with the model of pre-Flavian military supply defined by Hurst (1985, 124). This identifies a 'polarity' in the use of resources, with the majority of the wares deriving from either the continent or the local area, a pattern associated with an invading army. Regional imports become more common from the Flavian period onwards.

Many early military garrisons brought a range of pottery with them, including flagons and jugs, table wares and mortaria which were not available locally (Timby, Chapter 3 above). Imported wares were limited to Samian, mostly from La Graufesenque, amphorae, mortaria from North Gaul and the Rhône Valley, Lyon ware, and North Gaulish white wares. Amphorae from southern Spain were used to transport olive oil, wine, and fish-based products. Other amphorae found at Metchley in smaller numbers derived from Gaul and Campania. Some of the imported coarse wares may represent personal possessions, including sherds which may have originated from Campania, southern Italy (Timby, Chapter 3 above). Other continental imports comprise the vessel glass, metal vessels, the omega brooches, and the ballista ball made of lava; including personal possessions, army supply, and perhaps trade. The grape pips and fig seeds (Fryer, Chapter 4 above) could provide further evidence of continental trade.

Regional supply is represented by mortaria from the west midlands, and/or Wroxeter, Mancetter-Hartshill, and the Verulamium areas (Timby, Chapter 3 above). Timby observes that regional imports are rare, with most coming from post-Flavian contexts. These included Derbyshire coarse ware, Dorset Black Burnished ware, Oxfordshire white ware, and Verulamium white ware. The Colchester Derivative brooches fastened by the Polden Hill method of spring fastening were typical of native brooch manufacturers in the west of Britain (Cool, Chapter 3 above), as well as the harness fitting which is paralleled by an item from the Seven Sisters Hoard (Glamorgan). A number of the quernstones derive from the Derbyshire/Staffordshire/Pennine area.

Local pottery supply comprises handmade 'native' wares, Severn Valley and other local wares including Malvernian rock-tempered wares. The Severn Valley industry is well represented in the assemblage. Kilns producing forms of Severn Valley type, as well as the tankards characteristic of Severn Valley ware they also produced vessels in forms similar to the non-mortarium products of Mancetter–Hartshill, have been found in Birmingham, Perry Barr (Hughes 1959), and Sutton Coldfield (Evans et al. 2014). A number of the mortaria and some of the fine oxidized grey wares from Metchley may have been made at the complex by military potters (Timby, Chapter 3 above), with the clay deriving presumably from local sources.

Other local supplies are represented by grass from the fort environs, cut for fodder and bedding (Phase 2B stable, Structure 12.3; Ciaraldi 2025), timber for building, and turf for rampart construction. Among the seeds, wheat and barley chaff were absent, indicating that the cereal requisitions of the fort originated from at least partly cleaned grain derived from elsewhere (Fryer, Chapter 4 above).

The complex may have functioned as a collection point for livestock requisitioned for local military supply in Phase 2B (Period 4) and in Phase 3B–4B. Esmonde Cleary (2011) has suggested that the west midlands region formed a 'resource procurement zone' which could have included livestock for military supply. The sources of livestock for military supply have been much debated. While animal bone does not survive in the acid soil at Metchley, analysis of patterns of age at death from other sites, and the recovery of all parts of the carcase together suggest that animals were often requisitioned locally and butchered on site or nearby (Davies 1989, 187–206; King 1999, 146; Webster 1998, 262–4). Study of animals from civilian and military contexts within the same region (King 1999, 144–5) suggests a common and local source of supply. Analysis of the animal bone from Alchester, Oxfordshire (Thomas 2008, 34), indicates that beef formed the bulk of the diet, followed by pork and then mutton, a similar pattern to that found on native sites, suggesting that in the immediate post-conquest period requisition was based on availability rather than demand. Assuming that livestock were supplied locally, such local arrangements would be sensitive to local reductions or the removal of entire garrisons, which would render this supply redundant, which could explain the disuse of the Phase 2B military stores depot after Period 4.

Other forts in the midlands were well positioned to utilize local natural resources. The fort (and settlement) at Chesterton/Holditch was engaged in the exploitation of coal, iron ore, and lead from local deposits (White and Hodder 2018a, 6). Of particular note is the evidence for lead smelting for the extraction of silver at Pentrehyling, Shropshire (White and Hodder 2018a, 6; Allen with Cane 2015, fig. 1.3). Esmonde Cleary (2011) characterizes the region as a zone of resource procurement in the Roman period – in particular for mineral, agricultural, and human resources.

External activity: civilian and military

A key feature of the evolving excavation strategy has been the opportunity to examine extensive areas outside the fort defences, in order to understand their geography, chronology and economy. In particular, examination of the external areas has contributed towards an understanding of the specialist function of the site for the supply of livestock, and the relationship between military and civilians, recently a subject of much debate (e.g. James 2001; Goldsworthy and Haynes 1999; Sommer 2006).

Annexes

The Phase 2A northern, eastern, and southern annexes define a pivotal change in the layout and function of the complex – approximately doubling the size of the defended area from 4ha to 8ha.

Of the total of 298 Roman military sites of all periods mapped by Bidwell (2000), around one third are associated with annexes, or possible annexes – a distribution which emphasizes forts associated with the Antonine Wall, which post-date the abandonment of Metchley, as well as being associated with a linear frontier. Along with Alchester (Sauer 2001), Metchley is one of very few military complexes in the midlands which are associated with annexes – possibly because excavation elsewhere has been confined within the fort perimeter.

The northern annexe ditch was cut during the continued use of the northern Phase 1 ditches (Jones 2001, 42), indicating continued demarcation between the fort and annexe. With the exception of a few industrial features identified within the eastern annexe, comparatively few features have been identified within the interiors of the Metchley annexes. This absence of evidence could be more apparent than real, as a result of limited excavation (northern, eastern, and southern annexes), poor preservation (southern annexe), or a combination of both. At Metchley, the western annexe or enclosure has been distinguished from the three annexes because of its slight defining palisade – clearly not forming a defensive obstacle. The palisade may have functioned to define an area used for pottery production (Jones 2011, 11). The quantity of amphorae recovered from the eastern annexe suggests use for storage (Jones 2005, 83). The ovens to the rear of the rampart may have been used for breadmaking.

Sommer's (1984) Group II annexes, running the whole length of one fort side (including the northern, southern, and possibly eastern annexe at Metchley), were interpreted by him as containing stores, pack animals, and wagons, as well as camp followers. Other annexes which contain few internal features are interpreted as being used for baggage trains, to provide additional security. This interpretation may be open to question on some sites, because it relies on negative evidence from often limited sampling (e.g. trenching) of annexe interiors.

Settlements are usually located on opposite sides of the fort to annexes (Sommer 2006, 121). Their different 'zoning' suggests that annexes were not fortified versions of civilian settlements (Sommer 2006, 122), with the possible exception of Elginhaugh, where possible strip houses were located within an annexe (Hanson 2007, fig. 12.4) and Newstead (Sommer 2006, 122).

Civilian settlement

The traditional interpretation of the economic basis of civilian settlements (Webster 1966) was based on the spending power of the soldiery attracting camp followers, including craftsmen, shopkeepers, merchants, and their wives (Sommer 1984, 11; Burnham and Wacher 1990, 7; Millett 1990, 75). All forts occupied for at least one season would have had a civilian settlement (Sommer 1984, 12). Understanding the economic base of the Metchley settlement is particularly important, because unlike most military sites in the midlands it failed to develop into a small town (the other exceptions are Greensforge, The Lunt, and Kinvaston near Penkridge). At Greensforge, a small settlement is recorded until the 4th century (Jones 1999). Unlike Greensforge and Kinvaston (Fig. 1.5), Metchley and The Lunt were located at a distance from the main Roman road network (Fig. 1.1B).

Abandonment of settlements in the Marches occurred soon after removal of the garrison (Sommer 2006, 131), emphasizing the economic nexus between the garrison and the settlers. At Metchley, the civilians and civilian traders probably followed the garrison to their new location when the Phase 1 fort was given up. The western external livestock complex occupied the area vacated by the western civilian settlement. It is possible that the small specialist force charged with the maintenance of the Phase 2B military stores depot might not have been of sufficient size to sustain a settlement, even of small size. Alternatively, the western settlement could have continued to be maintained during the early use of the military stores depot (Periods 1–3), and only displaced in Period 4 when the western livestock complex was laid out.

There is also evidence of later external activity, principally livestock compounds (Phase 3B–4B) associated with the Phase 3A or 4A fort (Fig. 2.14; Jones 2012, 55–63), although the remains here also included hearths and a single, irregular building. The possible continued specialist function of the site in Phase 3A associated with grain storage, and the potential brevity of its occupation, could further explain why a thriving settlement failed to develop. The spur road linking Metchley (Fig. 1.1B in red) to Ryknield Street may have suffered a reduction in traffic. After the departure of the military at the end of Phase 3A, the small size and eventual end of the civilian settlement could have been determined by cultural factors. Excavations along the M6 Toll have suggested that the pre-Roman inhabitants were living in small and comparatively widely spaced individual farming units.

Sommer (2006, 97) notes that external settlements are most usually located (as at Metchley) outside the *porta principalis dextra*, although not necessarily so (e.g. Caerhun, Baillie-Reynolds 1938, settlement adjoining the *porta principalis sinistra*). Should civilian settlement have continued at the site after the abandonment of the Phase 1 garrison fort, it would necessarily have been re-located when the plateau to the west of the fort was used for livestock. Indeed, recent trenching to the east of the fort (Jones 2025, ch. 6) has identified a few features which may be associated with a civilian settlement. The livestock 'funnels' inserted along the line of the external

road entering the *porta principalis dextra*, and also the second funnel within this gateway (Structure 18.2), suggest that traffic was restricted to livestock. Other traffic may have been rerouted, so that any civilian settlement was re-established at a new location, possibly in the south of the complex (in an unexcavated area), in order to take advantage of opportunities for trade with travellers along this major route.

Alternative locations for the Metchley settlement should also be considered. Sommer (1984, 4, 30–31) had argued that soldiers' families would not have been allowed to live inside forts, because the suggested distinction between civilian and military elements meant that 'the walls of Roman military bases marked a near perfect boundary between the private world of the army and everything else' (James 2001, 83). This is because of the assumed ban before AD 197 on soldiers below the rank of centurion getting married (Allason-Jones 1999, 45). James (2001, 80) has now suggested that non-combatants, including cavalry grooms, private servants/slaves, traders, wives, and even dependent parents may have been integrated into the life of the military community (Mattingley 2006, 17). In this interpretation, the fort defences would have mainly functioned for the surveillance of the military themselves (James 1999, 16). Following James' reinterpretation, it is perhaps possible that part of the settlement was in fact located within the fort interior. This hypothesis could help to explain the small size of the external settlement. Perhaps it could even suggest that the settlement had later contracted into the fort interior. This hypothesis would also have implications for garrison size.

The most common form of settlement type was the 'street type' or 'ribbon type' laid out along both sides of the road (at Metchley, the spur road off Ryknield Street) approaching the fort (Sommer 2006, 97, 101), as at Brough-on-Noe, Derbyshire (Dearne 1993, 152, 154). The arrangement of the Metchley settlement does not conform with the norm, because of the low building density immediately outside the fort, and in particular the arrangement of buildings side-on and not end-on to the road at Metchley, suggesting a lack of pressure for space. There was no evidence for side roads at Metchley, branching off the main road at right angles (Sommer 2006, 106). It is difficult to find parallels for the small size and arrangement of the Metchley settlement within a west midland context, because few excavations have investigated these areas. The recently excavated/surveyed settlement sites noted by Sommer (2006, appendix 1) are confined to Wales, Scotland, and northern England, with the sole exception of Richborough.

External livestock complexes

The Phase 1 and Phase 3B–4B livestock complexes adjoining the western defences may represent a continued preference for the location of livestock enclosures on level ground, adjoining the nearby water supply provided by the stream to the west.

The Phase 2B western livestock complex formed an integral part of the livestock enclosures within Period 4 of the military store depot, as is demonstrated by the external livestock 'funnel' and the 'funnel' inserted into the *porta principalis dextra* (Structure 18.4). Intriguingly, further livestock enclosures (Phase 3B–4B) were also recorded outside the contemporary *porta principalis dextra*, and are also associated with a contemporary rearrangement of entrance arrangements there.

Phase 2B: military or civilian?

One possibility to be considered is that the irregular suite of Phase 2B features within the fort interior is the result of civilian occupation within the fort, after its military abandonment. *Prima facie*, this possible 'shift' could explain the apparent abandonment of the western settlement. However, the Period 2 irregular structures, often following the earlier wall lines, suggest that demolition and rebuilding were part of one operation, carried out under military control. Equally, the apparent retention of the *praetorium*, and also possibly of the *principia*, with Period 2 temporary buildings clustered around them, suggests continuing military rather than civilian occupation.

There is no clear evidence to suggest an exclusively military or civilian context for the Period 3 industrial features. The deliberate dumping of Samian from the *praetorium* when pit C166 went out of use at the end of this period argues for continued military control of the site, as well as the continued presence of a commanding officer up to this point. The succeeding Period 4 activity is concerned with livestock herding. It is likely that these features formed part of a military collecting point for livestock. At Metchley, it is unlikely that the Period 4 activity was undertaken as a result of the civilian occupation of the site by the native population. The location of Metchley at or near three tribal boundaries would have made this site particularly suitable for military requisition from each of the three surrounding *civitates*.

Roman civilian occupation post-dating military abandonment?

The Roman military occupation of the complex probably ceased in the early Flavian period, with the abandonment of the Phase 3A fort. The finds evidence suggests at least sporadic occupation of the site until at least the end of the 2nd century. At other forts the associated civilian settlement did not long outlive the departure of the military, indicating that the economic fortunes of the civilian traders within the settlement were intertwined with the military, for example at Brompton, Shropshire (White 2015, 142). The continuation of some form of settlement here, however sporadic, suggests that the settlement may have been able to function economically without the spending power of the military. In the alternative hypothesis, this Phase 4 civilian occupation continued to be associated with the military, perhaps with the military supply of livestock,

as at Elginhaugh (Hanson 2007) after the final departure of the garrison. White (2018, 26) has suggested that this post-military Roman occupation at Metchley could have been part of a wider pattern, with former fort sites being reused for the collection of tax in kind and the holding of (presumably) livestock by state officials, represented by the six-post gate at The Lunt (Hobley 1975, 4–6) and the re-cut fort ditch at Brompton, dated by a coin of AD 340 (Allen with Cane 2015).

The Phase 4A re-cut of the western Phase 3A fort ditch may represent the final military occupation of the site, although the irregularity of the re-cut of the fort ditch at its southeastern corner suggests a civilian rather than a military context. Other features, including the partial blocking of the *porta principalis dextra*, the three-sided enclosure in the northwest of the Phase 3A fort interior, and the parallel ditches recorded in the right *praetentura* could be Roman civilian, or even post-Roman in date, and are difficult to interpret.

Except for the three-sided enclosure, the post-military features are located in the east and south of the military complex, on comparatively low-lying land. They are sited away from the former *via principalis* which may have connected the fort via a spur road (Fig. 1.1B, red line), with Ryknield Street to the north and south of the complex. Like the later Roman settlement at Longdales Road, Kings Norton, Birmingham (Jones et al. 2008), and the roadside settlement at Birdlip adjoining Ermine Street, the roadside frontage at Metchley, adjoining the *via principalis* where there could have been the greatest opportunities for roadside trade, appears to have been avoided by the post-military settlement in favour of the more lowlying land to the south of the military complex.

The later Roman roadside settlement at Longdales Road, Kings Norton, Birmingham (Fig. 1A), established from AD 120 to AD 160, which functioned as a collection point for livestock along Ryknield Street was contemporary with the later Roman civilian occupation of the Metchley complex; it is even possible that the two site economies were similar. The Phase 4A ditches at Metchley, and in particular the Phase 4C partial blocking, could have functioned for the corralling of animals. This latter activity is undated, and could also be post-Roman in context. This possible specialist function for the later Roman civilian occupation of the Metchley complex would explain the absence of other feature types (e.g. pits, post-holes) associated with settlement, although recent truncation could have scoured-out all but the deepest ditched features.

It is suggested that the location of Metchley, adjoining one or more tribal boundaries, and the strategic road network might be appropriate for the sale or exchange of livestock. The possible market at Plas Coch, Wrexham (Arnold and Davies 2000, 71) was suggested to be located at a *civitas* boundary, in order to take advantage of the monetary economy of Roman Britain and also the native barter economy (Gaffney and White 2007, 51). It is possible that the later civilian economy of Metchley could have been similar, trading with the Dobunni and the Cornovii. White and Hodder (2018a, 11) highlight the cultural differences between more or less 'Romanized' areas of the region, in particular contrasting the north of Worcestershire and Warwickshire with the southern parts of those counties. Metchley is located on the suggested 'boundary' between these two different cultural traditions.

It is notable that the proportion of Samian within Areas M7–M8 increases from 3.2% in Phase 2B to 3.76% in Phase 3A, and 6% in Phase 4 deposits (post-dating the military withdrawal from the site; in each case measured by weight, excluding amphorae). This suggests that the site functioned at the time within the wider trading network (despite a location off the main road network), also represented by Malvernian wares and Severn Valley forms within a regional context (within Area M8 in particular, Hancocks 2005, 66). In his analysis of the Samian wares from these excavations Willis (2005, 63–64) highlights the comparatively high percentage of decorated sherds at 38.3% (from Phases 2–4 inclusive), which supports the interpretation of the site as being under military control (he did not consider the different percentages of decorated sherds from each phase). In contrast, it is worth noting that the character of the pottery from the Phase C western livestock complex emphasizes storage vessels over table wares, highlighting a change of use from the preceding civilian settlement.

The latest finds are dated to the end of the 2nd century. This is not to say that all Roman activity at the site ceased around AD 200. It is possible that later Roman activity could have been sporadic (e.g. livestock herding) and aceramic. The absence of 3rd-century finds may be more apparent than real. White (2015, 142) observes that 'the 3rd century in particular is notorious for its poor artefactual evidence'. In his discussion of the Romano-British period in the M6 Toll volume, Booth (2008, 519) notes that a number of rural sites had gone out of use in the 3rd century, notably Site 34. Millett (1990, 203) notes the increased size of rural estates in the later 2nd/early 3rd century, leading to a concentration of landholdings, which could have made the Metchley civilian settlement unviable.

The military complexes at Alcester, Droitwich, Wall, and Mancetter, located on the strategic road network, became successful small towns (Burnham and Wacher 1990). By contrast, Metchley and The Lunt, both ascribed a specialist function, did not, although admittedly both sites were not located along the main road network. It is possible that Metchley was located 3km to the northwest of a road junction at Selly Park, although the proportion of Samian (6%) within Phase 4 deposits suggests that the site continued to function within the wider trading network. There is no finds evidence for the military reoccupation of the Metchley complex such as the coin of Gallienus (260–268) and Wappenbury type pottery dating to the later 3rd/early 4th century recovered from a Period IV gateway at The Lunt (Hobley 1973, 4).

Stratigraphically, one of the latest features, the Phase 4C blocking of the western Phase 3A fort entrance, produced AMS dates of cal BC 50–90 AD and cal BC 60–80 AD (Jones 2012, table 4.6). It is of course possible that the material dated was residual. The associated charred plant remains were adjudged to be typical of those found at other Romano-British sites in the region (McKenna 2012, 93).

Environment

Establishment of the military complexes at Metchley will have resulted in extensive changes in the local landscape. There will have been a significant loss of land appropriated for military cultivation (White and Wigley 2018, 119), as well as extensive felling of woodland to provide timber for timber-framed buildings and the rampart superstructure (Shirley 2001).

The plant remains from Phase 1D feature 4165 in the central range were dominated by grassy material and seeds of grassland plants. A number of plants typical of wet grassland environments were collected from a Phase 2B barn or fodder store in Area M12, which probably originated as fodder, cut within the vicinity of the fort, perhaps to the south, west, or east. A number of sedge fruits from a pit within the western civilian settlement are indicative of burnt flooring, bedding, or thatching material; they also suggest that the area could have been seasonally wet or waterfilled after the military abandonment of the site. This evidence could suggest flooding from the adjoining stream to the west.

The frequency of oak within the charcoal samples studied from Area M12 (Gale 2025b) suggests that oak was common in the surrounding environment. Other species recorded included alder, birch, hazel, beech, ash, ivy, holly, hawthorn/*Sorbus* group, lime, and elm.

The pollen profile from the southern fort ditch is important for the reconstruction of the later Roman landscape. Phase 3A deposits included pioneer shrubs and trees, not held in check by grazing, which was indicated by the presence of dung beetles. Sloe and hawthorn suggest a mixed landscape, with pasture and heathland nearby (Greig 2005). Phase 3A ditch deposits sampled along the eastern fort defences (Hopla and McKenna 2025) are dominated by arboreal pollen, principally alder, an indicator of a damp environment, perhaps reflecting the low-lying location of this area within the complex overall. In Phase 4 the pollen record from the southern defences shows a change from scrub to secondary or pioneer woodland, with a decline in herb, weed, and other plant pollen (Greig 2005, 76–81), implying that activity at the site was very much reduced after the military withdrawal. Along the eastern defences (Hopla and McKenna 2025) heaths are first recorded in Phase 4 contexts, along with a decline in herbaceous pollen. The fort would have been surrounded by scrubby woodland, including hazel, birch, and oak, with some areas of open heath.

The Area M18 excavation (Greig 2012a) contained a number of weed seeds, including plants typically growing in wet ground or adjoining streams, although some of these could be modern in origin. Pollen was abundant in Phase 4A and 4C contexts within this area. The pollen record was dominated by alder and hazel, with smaller quantities of oak and lime. Grasses and ribwort plantain were also abundant. The pollen record indicates that these areas were not kept clear, and developed open scrub.

Post-Roman

The post-Roman archaeological features at the complex are, unfortunately, undated. Some post-military activity may be dated to the later Roman or post-Roman periods. These later features include the three-sided enclosure in the northwestern corner of the Phase 3A fort (Jones 2001, fig. 19), and the Phase 4C arrangement recorded in the western entrance of the Phase 3A fort, interpreted as being used for livestock 'sorting' (Jones 2012, 64–8). The later arrangement of nine post-holes or small pits in the same entranceway could be associated with the post-medieval hunting park. The northern flanking ditch of the *via principalis* was also re-cut in this period (Jones 2012, 69); other fort ditches were also re-cut, and the Roman roads were re-surfaced (Jones 2025, chapter 6). Lengths of a palisade trench were also cut adjoining the eastern (Jones 2001, fig. 18; 2025, chapter. 4) and southern Phase 3A defences (Jones 2001, fig. 9), possibly forming a stockade for livestock.

The pollen record provides the main source of information concerning the post-Roman environment. Pollen from the southern Phase 1 ditch infills (Greig 2005, 76–81) indicates fairly well-established woodland, while a few grains of rye suggest the resumption of farming in the vicinity, an event ascribed elsewhere to the Anglo-Saxon period. The medieval environment was dominated by birch, alder, oak, and holly woodland, species often associated with pasture. Cornflower seeds date this landscape to around AD 1200. The later medieval/post-medieval landscape was increasingly dominated by beech woodland. The increase in herb pollen reflects the increased farming of the surrounding land, perhaps around the villages of Harborne and Edgbaston. Many of the villages surrounding Metchley have -ley endings (e.g. Selly, Weoley, Bartley, and Moseley) indicating wood-pasture. Harborne is among the earliest of Anglo-Saxon place names in the city. The boundary of the Hwicce may have run along the Bourn Brook, reflected in the later allocation of Harborne to Staffordshire, with the land to the south of the brook joined to Worcestershire.

The name of Metchley was first recorded in 1530 (Mawer and Stenton 1936), referring to a park which was almost certainly enclosed by the 14th century. The 1327 Lay Subsidy mentions people living in the 'hay' (Slater 2002, 11), which can refer to a woodland enclosure or game enclosure. The name Metchley means 'great enclosure' (*micel gehaeg*), an Old English word perhaps suggesting

that it pre-dated the 11th century. It is therefore possible that the name could refer to the surviving earthworks of the Roman fort.

The forts were located at a distance from the medieval village centres of Harborne and Edgbaston, to the northwest and east of the site, respectively. In the 18th century, the fort lay within a hunting park, and a lodge was built within the defences (Jones 2001, 10, fig. 4A). The line of the *via decumana* and *via praetoria* remained fossilized as a farm track leading to Metchley Park Farm in the north of the site.

The partly levelled ramparts and ditches were mapped by Sparry (1718), Finch (1822: Jones 2001, fig. 4B) and the Ordnance Survey (Jones 2001, figs 5A, 5B). The surviving earthworks would have been suitable for stock enclosures, particularly given their location in a deer park (Hodder 2018, 161). The fort earthworks were visible into the 20th century (Jones 2001, 10–12; White 2018, 17).

Conclusion

The dating evidence suggests that Metchley fort was first established as a base for the mid-Neronian reoccupation of conquered territory. The choice of the site was a strategic one. Located at or close to three *civitas* boundaries, it was sited to facilitate supervision of contacts between the Cornovii, Dobunni, and Corieltauvi, later providing a base for the requisition of supplies, most notably represented by the Phase 2A annexes and the Phase 2B military stores depot. The site was important for the military supply of livestock in particular, although the absence of animal bone must be noted. Its location close to a major crossroads facilitated both its military garrison and its military supply functions. The re-establishment of a fort here in Phase 3A underlines the continuing strategic importance of the location in the earlier Flavian period.

A small and short-lived civilian settlement was located outside the western (and also possibly outside the eastern) defences. Civilian occupation of the site continued after the military abandonment in the early Flavian period up to the end of the 2nd century, reflecting the roadside opportunities for trade. During military occupation the civilian settlement was small and probably short-lived, reflecting the comparatively brief occupation of the site by a substantial garrison. Thereafter, the small-scale nature of the specialist garrison in Phase 2B, and the brief military reoccupation of the site in the later Neronian-early Flavian period (Phase 3A) failed to provide sufficient impetus for the establishment of a substantial settlement, despite its near-roadside location. The environmental evidence, in particular, provides tantalizing glimpses of the post-military or post-Roman landscape development in the surrounding area. It is possible that later in the Roman period the site was reused for the collection of tax in kind (presumably livestock) by state officials which may be suggested at this and other fort sites in the midlands. Located within a hunting park, the site was again reused for corralling animals sometime during the post-medieval period.

The particular importance of the site to Roman military archaeology in the west midlands region lies in its specialist function for military supply, in the complex history of Roman military and civilian occupation, as well as the details of its Phase 1 internal buildings. It contributes towards the growing evidence for 'specialization' and diversity within auxiliary forts (White 2018, 23), complementing the evidence from The Lunt (possible cavalry training school) and Brompton (extraction of silver from lead). The site is important for the variety of buildings and structures associated with the military

stores depot (Phase 2B). The evidence for the Roman post-military reuse of the site is intriguing. The site is also distinctive as one of the very few forts which failed to develop into a substantial urban centre. As a result, and also because of its incorporation into a hunting park for possibly 400 years, the remains are in places particularly well preserved.

In a Birmingham context, the Metchley Roman military and civilian complex is important as the main monument of the city's pre-medieval past, constituting probably the most long-lasting group of sites of this early date (spanning up to 150 years in total) and a reminder of Birmingham's long, rich, and varied past.

References

Abbreviations

AJA   AJ Archaeology
BA   Birmingham Archaeology
BUFAU   Birmingham University Field Archaeology Unit

Allason-Jones, L., 1999. 'Women in the Roman army in Britain', in Goldsworthy and Haynes (1999, 41–51).

Allen, J., with J. Cane, 2015. 'Pentrehyling fort and Brompton camps, Shropshire: excavations 1977–98', *Transactions of the Shropshire Archaeological and Historical Society* **88** (2015), 1–151.

Arnold, C. J., and J. L. Davies, 2000. *Roman and Early Medieval Wales*, Stroud, Sutton.

Atkinson, D., 1942. 'Report on excavations at Wroxeter (the Roman city of *Viriconium* in the county of Salop 1923–1927), *Birmingham Archaeological Society Monograph.*

Baillie-Reynolds, P. K., 1929. 'Excavations on the Roman site of Caerhun', *Archaeologia Cambrensis* **84**, 61–99.

Ballie-Reynolds, P. K., 1938. *Excavations on the site of the Roman fort of Kanovium, at Caerhun*, Caernarvonshire, Cardiff.

Baker, A., 2008. *Roman Roads and Metchley*, University of Birmingham Continuing Studies/Birmingham Roman Roads Project, unpublished.

Barker, P., R. H. White, K. Pretty, H. Bird, and M. Corbishley, 1997. *The Baths Basilica Wroxeter: Excavations 1966–90*, English Heritage Archaeological Report **8**, London.

Bell, A., 1986. 'Excavations at Rocester, Staffordshire, by Fiona Sturdy in 1964 and 1968', *Staffordshire Archaeological Studies* **3**, 20–51.

Bestwick, J. D., and J. H. Cleland, 1974. 'Metal-working in the north-west', in Jones and Grealey (1974, 143–58).

Bevan, L., 2005. 'Glass objects (Area 7)', in Jones (2005, 46–7).

Bevan, L., 2011. 'Copper alloy objects', in Jones (2011, 55–7).

Bevan, L., and R. Ixer, 2005. 'Stone objects (Area M7)', in Jones (2005, 46).

Bevan, L., and R. Ixer, 2011. 'Worked stone objects', in Jones (2011, 57–8).

Bidwell, P. T., 1979. The *Legionary Bath-House and Basilica and Forum at Exeter*, Exeter Archaeological Report **1**, Exeter, Exeter City Council and University of Exeter.

Bidwell, P. T., 2000. *Roman Forts*, London, Batsford/English Heritage.

Bidwell, P. T., R. Miket, and B. Ford (eds), 1988. Portae Cum Terribus*: Studies of Roman Fort Gates*, British Archaeological Reports British Series **206**, Oxford, British Archaeological Reports.

Bird, J. (ed.), 1998. *Form and Fabric: Studies in Rome's Material Past in Honour of B. R. Hartley*, Oxford, Oxbow Monograph **80**.

Bishop, M. C., 2002. *Lorica Segmentata*, vol. 1: *A Handbook of Articulated Roman Plate Armour*, JRMES Monograph **1**, Duns.

Booth, P., 1996. 'Warwickshire in the Roman period: a review of recent work', *Transactions of the Birmingham Warwickshire Archaeological Society* **100**, 25–57.

Booth, P., 2008. 'Romano-British period discussion', in Powell et al. (2008, 516–35).

Booth, P., 2018. 'Roman Warwickshire', in White and Hodder (2018b, 33–46).

Booth, P., and J. Evans, 2001. *Roman Alcester, Northern Extramural Area: 1969–1988 Excavations*, Roman Alcester Series, vol. 3, Council for British Archaeology Research Report **127**, London, Council for British Archaeology.

Bowman, A. K., and J. D. Thomas, 1983. *Vindolanda: The Latin Writing Tablets*, Britannia Monograph Series **4**, London, Trustees of the British Museum.

Bradley, R., 2007. *The Prehistory of Britain and Ireland*, Cambridge, Cambridge World Archaeology.

Breeze, D., 1977. 'The fort at Bearsden and the supply of pottery to the Roman army', in J. Dore and K. Greene (eds), *Roman Pottery Studies in Britain and Beyond*, British Archaeological Reports Supplementary Series **S30**, Oxford, British Archaeological Reports, 133–45.

Breeze, D., and B. Dobson, 1974. 'Fort type as a guide to garrisons: a reconsideration', in E. B. Birley, B. Dobson, and M. G. Jarrett (eds), *Roman Frontier Studies 1969*, Cardiff, 13–20.

Brickstock, R., and P. J. Casey, 2002. 'Coins', in Webster (2002, 85–9).

Brown, A. G., I. Meadows, S. D. Turner, and D. J. Mattingley, 2001. 'Roman vineyards in Britain: stratigraphic and palynological data from Wollaston in the Nene Valley, England', *Antiquity* **75**, 290, 745–57.

Burnham, B. C., and J. L. Davies, 2010. *Roman Frontiers in Wales and the Marches*, Cardiff, RCAHMW.

Burnham, B. C., and J. Wacher, 1990. *The 'Small Towns' of Roman Britain*, London, Batsford.

Bushe-Fox, J. P., 1914. *First Report on the Excavations on the Roman Town at Wroxeter, Shropshire 1912*, Reports of the Research Committee of the Society of Antiquaries of London **1**, Oxford.

Bushe-Fox, J. P., 1915. *Second Report on the Excavations on the Roman Town at Wroxeter, Shropshire 1913*, Reports of the Research Committee of the Society of Antiquaries of London **2**, Oxford.

Bushe-Fox, J. P., 1916. *Third Report on the Excavations on the Roman Town at Wroxeter, Shropshire 1914*, Reports of the Research Committee of the Society of Antiquaries of London **4**, Oxford.

Carreras, C., 2003. 'Haltern 70: a review', *Journal of Roman Pottery Studies* **10**, 85–91.

Carreras, C., A. Agulera, P. Berni, E. Garrote, P. Marimon, R. Morais, J. Moros, X. Nieto, A. Puig, J. Remesal, R. Rovira, G. Vivar, X. Aquilue, J. Buxeda, P. Castanyer, J. Gonzalez, M. Gonzalez, V. Martinez, J. C. Matamala, M. Santos, J. Tremoleda, J. Juan-Tresserras, and L. Vila, 2005. *Culip VIII i Les Amfores Haltern 70*, Girona, Monografies del CASC.

Carruthers, W., and K. L. Hunter Dowse, 2019. 'A review of macroscopic plant remains from the midland counties', https://historicengland.org.uk/research/results/reports/47–2019

Ciaraldi, M., 2005. 'Charred plant remains (Areas 7–8)', in Jones (2005, 72–5).

Ciaraldi, M., 2011. 'Charred plant remains (Area M9 only)', in Jones (2011, 81–3).

Ciaraldi, M., 2025. 'Plant remains (Area M12)', in Jones (2025, 35–8).

Ciaraldi, M., unpublished. 'The plant remains from Mill Street, Rocester, Staffordshire', in Ellis et al. (unpublished).

Cool, H. E. M., 1995. 'The glass', in H. E. M. Cool, G. Lloyd-Morgan, and A. D. Hooley, *Finds from the Fortress*, The Archaeology of York **17/10**: The Small Finds, York, Council for British Archaeology.

Cool, H. E. M., 1996. 'The glass and faience objects', in Esmonde Cleary and Ferris (1996, 122–7).

Cool, H. E. M., 1998. 'Early occupation at St Mary's Abbey, York: the evidence of the glass', in Bird (1998, 301–5).

Cool, H. E. M., 2006 *Eating and Drinking in Roman Britain,* Cambridge, Cambridge University Press.

Cool, H. E. M., 2007. 'The glass vessels', in P. Crummy and A.-M. Bojko, *Stanway: An Élite Burial Site at Camulodunum*, London, Society for the Promotion of Roman Studies, 340–46.

Cool, H. E. M., 2011. 'Roman vessel glass', in Jones (2011, 58–9).

Cowgill, J., in preparation. *An Iron Age and Romano-British Smelting Site at Creeton Quarry, Lincolnshire and a Survey of Local Smelting Sites.*

Cracknell, S. (ed.), 1996. *Roman Alcester: Defences and Defended Area: Gateway Supermarket and Gas House Lane*, Roman Alcester Series 2: Council for British Archaeology Research Report **106**, York, Council for British Archaeology.

Cracknell, S., and C. Mahany (eds), 1994. *Roman Alcester: Southern Extramural Area 1964–1966 Excavations. Part 2: Finds and Discussion*, Roman Alcester Series 1, Council for British Archaeology Research Report **97**, York, Council for British Archaeology.

Cuttler, R., S. Hepburn, C. Hewitson, and K. Krawiec, 2012. *Gorse Stacks - 2000 Years of Quarrying and Waste Disposal in Chester*. British Archaeological Reports British Series **563**, Oxford, BAR.

Dalwood, H., J. Dinn, C. J. Evans, N. Holbrook, D. Hurst, R. Morton, R. Jackson, and E. Pearson, 2018. 'Worcestershire in the Roman period', in White and Hodder (2018, 47–82).

Dannell, G. B., and J. P. Wild, 1987. *Longthorpe II*, Britannia Monograph Series **8**, London, Society for the Promotion of Roman Studies.

Darling, M. J., 1977. 'Pottery from early military sites in Western Britain', in Dore and Greene (1977, 57–100).

Darling, M. J., 1985. 'Roman pottery', in Hurst (1985, 55–93).

Darling, M. J., 2002. 'Pottery', in Webster (2002, 137–223).

Darvill, T., 2000. *Prehistoric Britain*, London, Routledge.

Davies, B., B. Richardson, and R. Tomber, 1994. *A Dated Corpus of Early Roman Pottery from the City of London*, Council for British Archaeology Research Report **98**, York, Council for British Archaeology.

Davies, J. L., 2009. 'Size matters: campaign forts in Britain', in W. S. Hanson (ed.), *The Army and Frontiers of Rome: Papers Offered to David Breeze on the Occasion of His 65th Birthday and Retirement from Historic Scotland, Journal of Roman Archaeology*, Supplementary Series **74**, Portsmouth, RI, 44–54.

Davies, R. W., 1971. 'The Roman military diet', *Britannia* **2**, 122–42.

Davison, D. P., 1989 *The Barracks of the Roman Army from the First Century to the Third Century AD*, British Archaeological Reports International Series **472**, Oxford, British Archaeological Reports.

Dearne, M. J., 1993. *Navio, the Fort and Vicus at Brough-on-Noe, Derbyshire*, British Archaeological Reports British Series **234**, Oxford, British Archaeological Reports.

Dool, J., 1986. 'Excavations at Strutt's Park, Derby, 1974', in Dool and Wheeler (1986, 15–32).

Dool, J., and H. Wheeler, 1986. 'Roman Derby: excavations 1968–1983', *Derbyshire Archaeological Journal* **105**.

Dore, J. N., and K. Greene, 1977. *Roman Pottery Studies in Britain and Beyond: Papers Presented to John Gillam*, British Archaeological Reports Supplementary Series **S30**, Oxford, British Archaeological Reports.

Dore, J. N., and J. P. Gillam, 1979. *The Roman Fort at South Shields, Excavations 1895–1975*, Newcastle Society of Antiquaries, Newcastle upon Tyne Monograph Series **1**.

Duncan, M., 2008. *Queen Elizabeth Psychiatric Hospital, Vincent Drive: Phase 2 Archaeological Excavations 2008*, BA report no. 1804, unpublished.

Ellis, P. (ed.), 2000. *The Roman Baths and Macellum at Wroxeter: Excavations by Graham Webster 1955–1985*, English Heritage Archaeological Report **9**, London.

Ellis, P., J. Halsted, and B. Burrows, unpublished. *Excavations at Mill Street and Northfield Avenue, Rocester, Staffordshire 2000–2002*.

Esmonde Cleary, A. S., 2011. 'The Romano-British period: an assessment', in Watt (2011, 127–47).

Esmonde Cleary, A. S., and I. M. Ferris, 1996. 'Excavations at the New Cemetery, Rocester, Staffordshire', *Staffordshire Archaeological Historical Society Transactions* **35**.

Evans, C. J., 2011. 'Romano-British coarse pottery', in Jones (2011, 26–32).

Evans, C. J., and A. Hancocks, 2005. 'Pottery discussion', in Jones (2005, 108).

Evans, C. J., A. Hancocks, K. Hartley, R. Tomlin, S. Williams, and D. Williams, 2011. 'Roman pottery (Area M9)', in Jones (2011, 59–76).

Evans, C. J., P. Booth, and M. A. Hodder, 2014. 'A Romano-British pottery kiln at Sherifoot Lane, Sutton Coldfield', *Transactions of the Birmingham Warwickshire Archaeological Society* **117**, 1–32.

Evans, C. J., R. Gale, A. Hancocks, K. Hartley, and S. Willis, 2005. 'Pottery from Areas 7–8', in Jones (2005, 47–67).

Evans, C. J., A. Hancocks, R. Tomlin, S. Willis, and D. Williams, 2011. 'Roman pottery (Area M9)', in Jones (2011, 59–76).

Evans, C. J., L. Jones, and P. Ellis, 2000. *Severn Valley Ware Production at Newlands Hopkins: Excavation of a Romano-British Kiln Site at North End Farm, Great Malvern, Worcestershire in 1992 and 1994*, British Archaeological Reports British Series **313**, Oxford, BAR.

Fitzpatrick, A. P., 2008. 'Prehistoric discussion', in Powell et al. (2008, 503–15).

Fowler, P., and J. Bennett, 1973. 'Archaeology and the M5 Motorway', *Transactions of the Bristol and Gloucestershire Archaeological Society* **92**, 21–84.

Frere, S. S., 1987a. *Britannia: A History of Roman Britain*, London, Routledge and Kegan Paul.

Frere, S. S., 1987b. 'Brandon Camp, Herefordshire', *Britannia* **18**, 49–92.

Frere, S. S., and J. K. S. St Joseph, 1974. 'The Roman fortress of Longthorpe', *Britannia* **5**, 1–129.

Frere, S. S., and J. J. Wilkes, 1989. *Strageath: Excavations Within the Roman Fort 1973–1986*, Britannia Monograph Series **9**, London, Society for the Promotion of Roman Studies.

Fryer, V., 2006. 'Charred cereals and other remains', in R. Niblett, W. Manning, and C. Saunders, 'Verulamium: excavations within the Roman town 1986–1988', *Britannia* **37**, 173–80.

Gaffney, V. L., and R. H. White, with H. Goodchild, 2007. *Wroxeter, the Cornovii and the Urban Process: Final Report on the Wroxeter Hinterland Project 1994–1997*, vol. 1: *Researching the Hinterland*, *Journal of Roman Archaeology*, Supplementary Series **68**, Portsmouth, RI.

Gale, R., 2001. 'Charcoal', in V. Birbeck, 'Excavations at Watchfield, Shrivenham, Oxfordshire, 1998', *Oxoniensia* **66**, 284–7.

Gale, R., 2005. 'Charcoal residues (Areas 7–8)', in Jones (2005, 68–71).

Gale, R., 2025. 'Charcoal analysis (Area M12)', in Jones (2025, 32–35).

Gale, R., unpublished. *Charcoal from Biddlesdon Road, west of Banbury, Oxfordshire*.

Glasbergen, W., 1972. *De Romeinse Castella Te Valkenberg ZH, Opragravingen 1962*, Groningen.

Goldsworthy, A., and I. Haynes (eds), 1999. 'The Roman Army as a community', *Journal of Roman Archaeology*, Supplementary Series **34**, Portsmouth, RI.

Gould, J., 1963–4. 'Excavations at Wall (Staffordshire), 1961–3, on the sites of the early Roman forts and the late Roman defences', *Transactions of the Lichfield and South Staffordshire Archaeological and Historical Society* **5**, 1–50.

Gould, J., 1966–7. 'Excavations at Wall (Staffordshire), 1964–6, on the site of the Roman forts', *Transactions of the Lichfield and South Staffordshire Archaeological and Historical Society* **8**, 1–38.

Gould, J., 1993. 'Further thoughts on *Letocetum*', *Transactions of the South Staffordshire Archaeological Historical Society* **33**, 1–6.

Green, H. J. M., 1975. 'Roman Godmanchester', in W. J. Rodwell and R. T. Rowley (eds), *The Small Towns of Roman Britain*, British Archaeological Reports British Series **15**, Oxford, BAR, 183–210.

Green, S., and C. J. Evans, 2001. 'Pottery discussion', in Green et al. (2001, 105–6).

Green, S., B. Dickinson, C. J. Evans, A. Hancocks, B. Hartley, K. Hartley, H. Pengelly, and D. Williams, 2001. 'Pottery (Areas 2–6)', in Jones (2001, 90–106).

Greene, K., 1993. 'The Fortress coarseware', in Manning (1993, 3–124).

Greig, J. R. A., 2002. 'When the Romans departed . . .: evidence of landscape change from Metchley Roman Fort, Edgbaston, Birmingham', *Acta Palaeobotanica* **42**(2), 177–84.

Greig, J. R. A., 2004. 'Pollen', in H. Wallis, 'Excavations at Mill Lane, Thetford, 1995', *East Anglian Archaeology* **108**, 105–11. https://archaeologydataservice.ac.uk/library/browse/issue.xhtml?recordi=1140606

Greig, J. R. A., 2005. 'Pollen and waterlogged seeds (Area 8 only)', in Jones (2005, 76–81).

Greig, J. R. A., 2012a. 'Pollen', in Jones (2012, 93–5).

Greig, J. R. A., 2012b. 'Charred plant remains', in Jones (2012, 89–93).

Greig, J. R. A., 2025a. 'Charred plant remains (Area M12A)', in Jones (2025, 39).

Greig, J. R. A., 2025b. 'Charred plant remains' (Area M20), in Jones (2025, 61–2).

Greig, J. R. A., in preparation. 'Pollen results from Cookley, Worcestershire'.

Grimm, E. C., 1991. *Tilia and Tilia* Graph*, Springfield, Illinois State Museum.

Hancocks, A., 2001. 'Area 6 pottery', in Green et al. (2001, 97–8).

Hancocks, A., 2005. 'Romano-British pottery (Areas 7–8)', in Jones (2005, 47–67).

Hanson, W. S., 2007. *Elginhaugh: A Flavian Fort and its Garrison*, Britannia Monograph Series **23**, London, Society for the Promotion of Roman Studies.

Harden, D. B., 1960. 'Glass', in Webster (1960, 95).

Harden, D. B., K. S. Painter, R. H. Pinder-Wilson, and H. Tait, 1968. *Masterpieces of Glass*, London: Trustees of the British Museum.

Hartley, B. R., 1987. 'The Samian', in Frere (1987a, 80–84).

Hartley, K. F., 2001. 'Mortaria (Areas 2–4)', in Jones (2001, 98–101).

Hartley, K. F., 2005a. 'Mortaria (Area 7)', in Jones (2005, 60).

Hartley, K. F., 2005b. 'Mortaria (Area M11)', in Jones (2005, 107).

Hartley, K. F., 2011a. 'Mortaria (Area M9)', in Jones (2011, 65–6).

Hartley, K. F., 2011b. 'Mortaria', in Jones (2011, 32–3).

Haselgrove, C., and T. Moore (eds), 2007. *The Later Iron Age in Britain and Beyond*, Oxford, Oxbow.

Hassell, M., 1998. 'Units doubled and divided and the planning of forts and fortresses', in Bird (1998, 31–9).

Hobley, B., 1969 'A Neronian–Vespasianic site at "The Lunt", Baginton, Warwickshire', *Transactions of the Birmingham Warwickshire Archaeological Society* **83** (1965), 65–129.

Hobley, B., 1973. 'Excavations at "The Lunt" Roman site, Baginton, Warwickshire: Second Interim Report, 1968–71', *Transactions of the Birmingham Warwickshire Archaeological Society* (1971–3) **85**, 7–92.

Hobley, B., 1975. 'The Lunt Roman fort and training school', *Transactions of the Birmingham Warwickshire Archaeological Society* **87**, 1–55.

Hodder, M. A., 2011. *Birmingham: The Hidden History*, Stroud, History Press.

Hodder, M. A., 2018. 'Forts, farms, fields and industries: the Roman period in west midlands county', in White and Hodder (eds) (2018, 158–73).

Hodgson, N., and P. T. Bidwell, 2004. 'Auxiliary barracks in a new light: recent discoveries from Hadrian's Wall', *Britannia* **35**, 121–57.

Hogg, A. H. A., 1968. 'Pen Llystyn: a Roman fort and other remains', *Archaeological Journal* **125**, 101–92.

Hopewell, D., 2005. 'Roman fort environs in north-west Wales', *Britannia* **36**, 225–69.

Hopewell, D., and N. Hodgson, 2012. 'Further work at Llanfor Roman military complex', *Britannia* **43**, 29–44.

Hopla, E., and R. McKenna, 2025. 'Summary of the pollen and plant remains' (Area M25), in Jones (2025, 79–84).

Hughes, H. V., 1959. 'A Romano-British kiln site at Perry Barr, Birmingham', *Transactions and Proceedings of the Birmingham Archaeological Society* **77**, 33–9.

Hurst, D. (ed.), 2006. *Roman Droitwich: Dodderhill Fort, Bays Meadow Villa, and Roadside Settlement*, Council for British Archaeology Research Report **146**, London.

Hurst, D., 2011. 'Middle Bronze Age to Iron Age: a research assessment overview and agenda', in Watt (2011, 101–26).

Hurst, H. R., 1985. *Kingsholm*. Gloucester Archaeological Reports **1**, Gloucester, Gloucester Archaeological Publications.

James, S., 1999. 'The community of the soldiers: a major identity and centre of power in the Roman Empire', in P. Baker, C. Forcey, S. Jundi, and R. Witcher (eds), *TRAC 98: Proceedings of the Eighth Annual Theoretical Roman Archaeology Conference* (University of Leicester, 1998), Oxford, Oxbow, 14–25.

James, S., 2001. 'Soldiers and civilians: identity and interaction in Roman Britain', in S. James and M. Millett, *Britons and Romans, Advancing an Archaeological Agenda*, Council for British Archaeology Research Reports **125**, York, Council for British Archaeology, 77–89.

Johnson, A., 1983. *Roman Forts*, London, Batsford.

Jones, A. E., 1988. 'Metchley, Birmingham: an archaeological evaluation', BUFAU Report **46**, unpublished.

Jones, A. E., 1999. 'Greensforge: investigations in the Romano-British civilian settlement', 1994, *Transactions of the Staffordshire Archaeological and Historical Society* **38**, 12–31.

Jones, A. E., 2001. Roman Birmingham, vol. 1: *Excavations at Metchley Roman Forts 1963–4, 1967–9 and 1997*, *Transactions of the Birmingham Warwickshire Archaeological Society* **105**.

Jones, A. E., 2005. Roman Birmingham, vol. 2: *Metchley Roman Forts, Excavations 1998–9 and 2002: The Annexes and Other Investigations*, *Transactions of the Birmingham Warwickshire Archaeological Society* **108**.

Jones, A. E., 2011. Roman Birmingham, vol. 3: *Excavations at Metchley Roman Fort 1999–2001 and 2004–2005: Western Settlement, the Livestock Complex and the Western Defences*, British Archaeological Reports British Series **534**, Oxford, BAR.

Jones, A. E., 2012. Roman Birmingham, vol. 4: *Excavations at Metchley Roman Fort 2004–2005: The Western Fort Interior, Defences and Post-Roman Activity*, British Archaeological Reports British Series **552**, Oxford, BAR.

Jones, A. E., 2025. Roman Birmingham, vol. 5: *Metchley Roman Fort, Birmingham: Excavations in the Fort Interior and Defences 2003–2004, 2010 and 2017–2019*, British Archaeological Reports British Series **694**, Oxford, BAR.

Jones, A. E., B. Burrows, C. J. Evans, A. Hancocks, and J. Williams, 2008. *A Romano-British Livestock Complex in Birmingham: Excavations 2002–2004 and 2006–2007 at Longdales Road, King's Norton, Birmingham*, British Archaeological Reports British Series **470**, Oxford, BAR.

Jones, B., and D. Mattingley, 1990. *An Atlas of Roman Britain*, Oxford, Oxbow.

Jones, G. D. B., and S. Grealey, 1974. *Roman Manchester*, Stockport, Talisman Books.

Jones, M. J., 1975. *Roman Fort Defences to AD 117*, British Archaeological Reports British Series **21**, Oxford, BAR.

Jones, R. H., 2012. *Roman Camps in Britain*, Stroud, Amberley.

Kelly, D. B., 1965. 'Excavations at Watergate House', *Journal Chester Archaeological Society*, n.s. **52**, 1–25.

Kenward, H. K., A. R. Hall, and A. K. G. Jones, 1980. 'A tested set of techniques for the extraction of plant and animal macrofossils from waterlogged archaeological deposits', *Science and Archaeology* **22**, 315.

King, A., 1999. 'Animals and the Roman army', in Goldsworthy and Haynes (1999, 139–49).

Koster, A., 1997. *Description of the Collections in the Provincial Museum G. M. Kam at Nijmegen, 13: The Bronze Vessels 2. Acquisitions 1954–1996 (Including Vessels of Pewter and Iron)*, Nijmegen.

Leary, R., 1996. 'Roman coarse pottery', in Esmonde-Cleary and Ferris (1996, 40–63).

Leary, R., 1998. 'Pottery', in A. E. Jones, 'Excavations at Wall (Staffordshire) by E. Greenfield 1962 and 1964 (Wall Excavation Report No. 15)', *Transactions of the Staffordshire Archaeological Historical Society* **37**, 26–39.

Leary, R, 2008a. 'Pre-Roman Iron Age and Romano-British pottery', in Powell et al. (2008, 250–70).

Leary, R., 2008b. 'Romano-British pottery, industry and trade', in Powell et al. (2008, 471–91).

Leather, P., 1994. 'The Birmingham Roman roads project', *West Midlands Archaeology* **37**, 9–11.

Lyon, F., and J. T. Gould, 1960. 'A section through the defences of the Roman forts at Wall, Staffordshire', *Transactions of the Birmingham Warwickshire Archaeological Society* **79** (1960–61), 11–23.

McAvoy, F., 2006. 'Dodderhill, Droitwich excavations 1977–85', in Hurst (2006, 3–19).

Macey-Bracken, E., 2011. 'Glass objects', in Jones (2011, 24–5).

Macey-Bracken, E., 2025. 'Glass objects' (Area M12 only), in Jones (2025, 23–4).

Macey-Bracken, E., with H. E. M. Cool, 2012. 'Glass objects', in Jones (2012, 71).

Macey-Bracken, E., and R. Ixer, unpublished. 'Stone objects', in Ellis et al. (unpublished).

McKenna, R., 2012. 'Further sampling of Phase 4A/ Phase 4C deposits for charred plant remains', in Jones (2012, 89–93).

Mackreth, D. F., 1996. *Orton Hall Farm: A Roman and Early Saxon Farmstead*, East Anglian Archaeology **76**.

Mackreth, D. F., 2001. 'Brooches (Areas 1–4)', in Jones (2001, 75–8).

Magilton, J., 2006. 'A Romano-Celtic temple and settlement at Grimstock Hill, Coleshill, Warwickshire', *Transactions Birmingham Warwickshire Archaeological Society* **110**.

Mahany, C. (ed.), 1994. *Roman Alcester*, vol. 1: *Southern Extra-Mural Area, 1964–66 Excavations. Part 1: Stratigraphy and Structures*, Council for British Archaeology Research Reports **96**, London, Council for British Archaeology.

Manning, W. H., 1981. *Report on the Excavations at Usk 1965–1976*, vol. 2: *The Fortress Excavations 1968–1971*, Cardiff, University of Wales.

Manning, W. H., 1993. *The Roman Pottery: Report on the Excavations at Usk 1965–1976*, Cardiff, University of Wales.

Manning, W. H., J. Price, and J. Webster, 1995. *Report on the Excavations at Usk 1965–1976: The Roman Small Finds*, Cardiff, University of Wales.

Margary, I. D., 1973. *Roman Roads in Britain*, London, J. Baker.

Marvell, A. G., and H. S. Owen-John, 1997. *Leucarum: Excavations at the Roman Auxiliary Fort at Loughor, West Glamorgan 1982–84 and 1987–88*, Britannia Monograph Series **12**, London, Society for the Promotion of Roman Studies.

Mattingley, H., 2006. *An Imperial Possession: Britain in the Roman Empire 54 BC to AD 409*, Penguin History of Britain, London, Allen Lane.

Mawer, A., and F. M. Stenton, 1936. *The Place-Names of Warwickshire*, Cambridge, English Place-Name Society **13**.

Maxfield, V. A., 1986. 'Pre-Flavian forts and their garrisons', *Britannia* **17**, 59–72.

Millett, M., 1990. *The Romanisation of Britain*, Cambridge, Cambridge University Press.

Moffett, L., 1996. 'Charred plant remains', in Esmonde Cleary and Ferris (1996, 206–18).

Monckton, A., 2001. 'Charred plant remains (Area 6)', in Jones (2001, 108–9).

Newstead, R., 1924. 'Report on the excavation on the site of the Roman camp at the Deanery Field, Chester', *Annals of Archaeology and Anthropology* **9**, 59–86.

Newstead, R., 1928. 'Records of archaeological finds at Chester', *Journal of the Chester Archaeological Society*, n.s. **27**, 59–199.

Newstead, R., and J. P. Droop, 1932. 'The Roman amphitheatre at Chester', *Journal of the Chester Archaeological Society*, n.s. **29**, 1–40.

Newstead, R., and J. P. Droop, 1940. 'Excavations at Chester, 1939: the Princess St clearance area', *Journal of the Chester Archaeological Society*, n.s. **34**, 1–47.

Peacock, D. P. S., 1977. 'Roman amphorae: typology, fabric and origins', *Collection de L'École Française de Rome* **32**, 261–78.

Peacock, D. P. S., 1978. 'The Rhine and the problem of Gaulish wine in Roman Britain', in J. Du Plat Taylor and H. Cleere (eds), *Roman Shipping and Trade: Britain and the Rhine Provinces*, Council for British Archaeology Research Report **24**, London, Council for British Archaeology, 49–51.

Pengelly, H., B. R. Hartley, and B. Dickinson, 2001. 'Samian (Areas 1–4)', in Jones (2001, 101–3).

Petch, D. F., and F. H. Thompson, 1959. 'Excavations in Commonhall St, Chester 1954–56: the granaries of the fortress', *Journal of the Chester Archaeological Society*, n.s. **46**, 33–60.

Powell, A. B., and K. Ritchie, 2008. 'Site 29, north of Langley Mill', in Powell et al. (2008, 306–18).

Powell, A. B., P. Booth, A. P. Fitzpatrick, and A. D. Crockett, 2008. *The Archaeology of the M6 Toll 2000–2003*, Oxford Wessex Archaeology Monograph **2**, Oxford, Oxford Wessex Archaeology.

Price, J., and H. E. M. Cool, 1985. 'Glass (including glass from 72 Dean's Way)', in Hurst (1985, 41–54).

Rackham, O., 1980. *Ancient Woodland: Its History, Vegetation and Uses in England*, London, Edward Arnold.

Rackham, O., 1999. *The History of the Countryside*, London, Phoenix Giant.

Reece, R., 2001. 'Coins (Areas 2–4)', in Jones (2001, 72).

Rees, H., 2006. 'Iron Age and Roman pottery', in Hurst (2006, 20–30).

Richmond, I. A., 1968. *Hod Hill*, vol. 2: *Excavations Carried Out Between 1951 and 1958 for the Trustees of the British Museum*, London, Trustees of the British Museum.

Richmond, I. A., and J. McIntyre, 1939. 'The Agricolan fort at Fendoch', *Proceedings of the Society of Antiquaries of Scotland* **73**, 110–54.

Richmond, I. A., and G. Webster, 1951. 'Excavations in Goss Street, Chester 1948–9', *Journal of the Chester Archaeological Society*, n.s. **38**, 1–38.

Riha, E., 1994. *Die Römischen Fibeln aus Augst und Kaiseraugst: Die Neufunde Seit 1975*, Augst, Forschungen in Augst **18**.

Round, A. A., 1983. 'Excavations at Wall (Staffordshire), 1968–1972 on the site of the Roman forts' (Wall Excavation Report No. 12), *Transactions of the South Staffordshire Archaeological Historical Society* **23**, 1–68.

Round, A. A., 1992. 'Excavations at the *Mansio* site at Wall (Staffordshire), 1972–78' (Wall Excavation Report No. 14), *Transactions of the South Staffordshire Archaeological and Historical Society* **32** (1990–91), 1–78.

St Joseph, J. K., and F. W. Shotton, 1937. 'The Roman camps at Metchley, Birmingham', *Transactions of the Birmingham Warwickshire Archaeological Society* **58**, 68–83.

Sauer, E., 2001. 'Alchester, a Claudian "vexillation fortress" near the western boundary of the Catuvellauni: new light on the Roman invasion of Britain', *Archaeological Journal* **157**, 1–78.

Sharpe, J., and M. Henig, 2001. 'Bone objects', in Jones (2001, 106).

Shepherd, J., 2001. 'Glass vessels', in Jones (2001, 89).

Sheratt, A., 2001. 'Flint', in Jones (2001, 85–6).

Shirley, E., 2001. *Building a Roman Legionary Fortress*, Stroud, Tempus.

Slater, T., 2002. *Edgbaston: A History*, Chichester, Phillimore.

Smith, D., 2005. 'Insect remains (Area 8 only)', in Jones (2005, 67–8).

Smith, W., 2011. 'Charred plant remains', in Jones (2011, 35–6).

Sommer, C. S., 1984. *The Military Vici in Roman Britain: Aspects of their Origins, their Location and Layout, Administration, Function, and End*, British Archaeological Reports British Series **129**, Oxford, British Archaeological Reports.

Sommer, C. S., 2006. 'Military *vici* in Britain revisited', in R. J. A. Wilson (ed.), *Romanitas: Essays on Roman Archaeology in Honour of Sheppard Frere on the Occasion of his Ninetieth Birthday*, Oxford, Oxbow, 95–146.

Stallibrass, S., and R. Thomas, 2008. *Feeding the Roman Army: The Archaeology of Production and Supply in NW Europe*, Oxford, Oxbow.

Strachan, I., 2001. 'Pollen (Area 3)', in Jones (2001, 107–8).

Swan, V. G., and P. Bidwell, 1998. 'Camelon and Flavian troop movements in southern Britain: some ceramic evidence', in J. Bird (ed.), *Form and Fabric: Studies in Rome's Material Past in Honour of B. R. Hartley*, Oxford, Oxbow Monograph **80**, 21–30.

Symonds, R. P., and S. Wade, 1999. *Roman Pottery from Excavations at Colchester, 1971–86*, in P. Bidwell and A. Croom (eds), Colchester Archaeological Report **10**.

Thomas, R., 2008. 'Supply-chain networks and the Roman invasion of Britain: a case study from Alchester, Oxfordshire', in Stallibrass and Thomas (2008, 31–51).

Thomas, R., and S. Stallibrass, 2008. 'For starters: producing and supplying food to the army in the Roman north-west provinces', in Stallibrass and Thomas (2008, 1–17).

Thompson, F. H., 1969. 'Excavations at Linenhall St., Chester 1961–2', *Journal of the Chester Archaeological Society*, n.s. **56**, 1–21.

Thompson, F. H., and F. W. Tobias, 1957. 'Excavations in Newgate St, Chester 1955', *Journal of the Chester Archaeological Society*, n.s. **44**, 29–40.

Timby, J., 2004. 'The pottery', in H. Brooks, *Archaeological Excavations at 29–39, Head Street, Colchester, Essex*, Colchester Archaeological Trust Archive Report **0268**.

Timby, J., 2011. 'Roman pottery (Areas M15–M16)', in Jones (2011, 76–81).

Timby, J., 2012. 'Romano-British pottery', in Jones (2012, 71–88).

Timby, J., 2025. 'Roman pottery' [Area M25], in Jones (2025, 75–9).

Timby, J., with A. Anderson, S. Anderson, G. Braithwaite, G. Dannell, M. Darling, B. Dickinson, C. J. Evans, J. Faiers, K. Hartley, G. Simpson, G. Webster, and D. Williams, 2000. 'The Roman pottery', in P. Ellis (ed.), *The Roman Baths and Macellum at Wroxeter: Excavations by Graham Webster 1955–85*, English Heritage Archaeological Report **9**, London, 193–313.

Todd, M., 2004. *The Claudian Conquest and Its Consequences*, in M. Todd (ed.), *A Companion to Roman Britain*, Malden, MA, Blackwell, 42–59.

Tomlin, R., 2011. 'Graffito', in Jones (2011, 57).

Tomlin, R., 2025. 'Intaglio' (Area M25), in Jones (2025, 74–5).

Turner, L., 2001. 'Quernstones', in Jones (2001, 86–8).

Ward, J., 1903. *The Roman Fort of Gelligaer in the County of Glamorgan*, Cardiff, Cardiff Naturalists Society.

Watt, S. (ed.), 2011. *The Archaeology of the West Midlands: A Framework for Research*, Oxford, Oxbow Books.

Webster, G., 1953. 'Excavation on the legionary defences at Chester 1949–52, part ii', *Journal of the Chester Archaeological Society*, n.s. **40**, 1–23.

Webster, G., 1954. 'Further excavations at the Roman forts at Metchley, Birmingham', *Transactions of the Birmingham Warwickshire Archaeological Society* **72**, 1–4.

Webster, G., 1960. 'The discovery of a Roman fort at Waddon Hill, Stoke Abbott, 1959', *Proceedings of the Dorset Natural History Archaeological Society* **82**, 88–108.

Webster, G., 1966. 'Fort and town in early Roman Britain', in J. Wacher (ed.), *The Civitas Capitals of Roman Britain*, Leicester, Leicester University Press, 31–45.

Webster, G., 1973. 'The pottery', in Hobley (1973, 55–63).

Webster, G., 1993. *Rome Against Caractacus: The Roman Campaigns in Britain AD 48–58*, London, B. T. Batsford.

Webster, G., 1998. *The Roman Imperial Army of the First and Second Centuries AD*, 3rd edn, Norman, University of Oklahoma Press.

Webster, G., 2001. 'Copper alloy objects', in Jones (2001, 75–81).

Webster, G., 2002. *The Legionary Fortress at Wroxeter: Excavations by Graham Webster, 1955–86* (ed. J. Chadderton), English Heritage Archaeological Report **19**, London.

Welfare, H., and V. Swan, 1995. *Roman Camps in England: The Field Archaeology*, Swindon, Royal Commission on the Historic Monuments of England.

Wheeler, H., 1986. 'Derby north-west sector excavations', *Derbyshire Archaeological Journal* **105**, 39–153.

White, R. H., 2007. *Britannia Prima: Britain's Last Roman Province*, Stroud, Tempus.

White, R. H., 2012. 'Copper alloy objects', in Jones (2012, 70).

White, R. H., 2015. 'Discussion', in Allen with Cane (2015, 142–6).

White, R. H., 2018. 'Fortresses, forts and the impact of the Roman army in the West Midlands', in White and Hodder (2018, 15–32).

White, R. H., 2025. 'Copper alloy object' (Area M20), in Jones (2025, 55–6).

White, R. H., and M. A. Hodder, 2018a. 'The archaeology of the Romano-British West Midlands: overview and research priorities', in White and Hodder (2018, 1–14).

White, R., and M. A. Hodder (eds) 2018b. *Clash of Cultures? The Romano-British Period in the West Midlands*, Oxford, Oxbow.

White, R. H., and A. Wigley, 2018. 'Shropshire in the Roman period', in White and Hodder (2018, 115–35).

Wigley, A., 2007. 'Rooted to the spot: the "smaller enclosures" of the later first millennium in the central Welsh Marches', in C. Haselgrove and T. Moore (eds), 172–89.

Wild, F., 2011. 'M14 Samian', in Jones (2011, 35).

Wild, F., 2012. 'Samian ware', in Jones (2012, 75–8).

Williams, D. F., 2001. 'Amphorae', in Jones (2001, 103–5).

Williams, D. F., 2005a. 'Amphorae', in Jones (2005, 64–5).

Williams, D. F., 2005b. 'Amphorae', in Jones (2005, 107–8).

Willis, S. H., 1998. 'Samian pottery in Britain: exploring its distribution and archaeological potential', *Archaeological Journal* **155**, 82–133.

Willis, S. H., 2005. 'The Samian pottery', in Jones (2005, 60–64).

Willis, S. H., 2011. 'Samian pottery (Area M9)', in Jones (2011, 66–70).

Wilson, D. R., 1984. 'Defensive outworks of Roman forts in Britain', *Britannia* **15**, 51–62.

Zant, J., 2009. *The Carlisle Millennium Project: Excavations in Carlisle 1998–2001*, vol. 1: *Stratigraphy*, Lancaster, Lancaster Imprints **14**.

Index

Page numbers in *italics* refer to maps and illustrations.

www.ingramcontent.com/pod-product-compliance
Lightning Source LLC
Chambersburg PA
CBHW051302270326
41926CB00030B/4698